Relationship Marketing

Creating Stakeholder Value

Martin Christopher
Adrian Payne
David Ballantyne

BUTTERWORTH
HEINEMANN

OXFORD   AMSTERDAM   BOSTON   LONDON   NEW YORK   PARIS
SAN DIEGO   SAN FRANCISCO   SINGAPORE   SYDNEY   TOKYO

Butterworth-Heinemann
An imprint of Elsevier Science
Linacre House, Jordan Hill, Oxford OX2 8DP
225 Wildwood Avenue, Woburn MA 01801-2041

First published 2002

British Library Cataloguing in Publication Data
A catalogue record for this book is available from the British Library

Library of Congress Cataloguing in Publication Data
A catalogue record for this book is available from the Library of Congress

ISBN 0 7506 4839 2

For more information on all Butterworth-Heinemann publications visit
our website at www.bh.com

Typeset by Keyword Typesetting Services Ltd, Wallington, Surrey
Printed and bound in Great Britain by Biddles Ltd. *www.biddles.co.uk*

Contents

Acknowledgements

In preparing this revised edition of *Relationship Marketing*, we have drawn on the work of many colleagues. Fellow academics such as Evert Gummesson, Christian Grönroos and Jag Sheth have shared ideas and frameworks at conferences and colloquia. We have gained much from the writings of others who have sought to extend our understanding of this subject. Particular acknowledgement must be given to past and present collaborators Moira Clark, Sue Holt, Uta Jüttner and Helen Peck, who have co-authored with us many previous works from which we have drawn in preparing this book.

Introduction

I t is over ten years since *Relationship Marketing: Bringing quality, customer service, and marketing together*, on which this book is based, was published. During that time there has been an astonishing growth of interest in the theory and practice of relationship marketing. It is hard to believe that ten years ago many people thought it was just another fashion and that the marketing world would soon forsake it and move on to something new.

It is now widely accepted that the real purpose of a business is to create and sustain mutually beneficial relationships, especially with selected customers. Equally widely accepted is the view that the cement that binds successful relationships is the two-way flow of value – that is, the customer derives real value from the relationship which converts into value for the organisation in the form of enhanced profitability.

Some people have argued that the emergence of relationship marketing in the 1990s was not so much a discovery but a rediscovery of an approach that had long been the cornerstone of many successful businesses. Relationship marketing has been described as a 'new-old concept',[1] and modern relationship marketing has many historical antecedents.

But while many of the ideas behind relationship marketing have already been addressed – although not under the modern title of relationship marketing – the topic of relationships was noticeably absent from pre-1980s' marketing literature. Berry[1] has described relationship marketing as moving to the forefront of marketing practice and academic marketing research after being 'on marketing's back burner for so many years'. Researchers and practitioners from all sectors are now embracing relationship marketing, but the modern concept has its origins in industrial and services marketing.

The use of the term 'relationship marketing' can be traced to the industrial and services marketing literature of the 1980s. In the industrial marketing literature, the early work of Levitt[2] focused on the notion that the real value of a relationship between a customer and a supplier occurs after the sale. He argued that the supplier's emphasis needed to shift from closing a sale to delivering superior customer satisfaction throughout the lifetime of the customer relationship. Further work by Jackson[3] was among the first literature to differentiate between transaction marketing and relationship marketing. Her work outlined the importance of relationships and how the context of the industrial sale sets the scene for the type of relationship that is possible. She argued that building and enhancing long-term customer relationships involves concentrating on a number of things that have to be executed over long periods and in a consistent manner. Her work was based on organisations operating in the shipping, communications and computer industries.

In the services area, it was researchers at Texas A & M University who started to research how relationship marketing could be applied to services. Berry's landmark paper[4] was one of the earliest to define relationship marketing as 'attracting, maintaining, and ... in multiservice organisations ... enhancing customer relationships'. His work drew attention to the importance of the role of internal marketing in creating an organisational climate that supports the external marketing activities. He also drew attention to a number of relationship-building strategies an organisation could use.

Within Europe, the research of Nordic academics, including Grönroos, Gummesson and a number of their colleagues at the Swedish School of Economics and Business Administration in Finland, Stockholm University in Sweden and other institutions, has gained a wide audience. Their work on relationship marketing draws strongly on their earlier work in services marketing and service quality (e.g. Grönroos[5,6] and Gummesson[7]).

In other parts of Europe the work of the Industrial Marketing and Purchasing (IMP) Group has been highly influential. This group, which originally consisted of twelve researchers from Germany, France, Italy, Sweden and the UK, is concerned with interactions and relationships among networks in industrial markets. Since the

1980s the IMP Group has made a considerable contribution to the literature on industrial markets. A number of books have summarised this work, including Turnbull and Cunningham,[8] Håkansson,[9] Ford,[10] Axelsson and Easton[11] and Ford *et al.*[12] The IMP work has attracted special attention because it places equal emphasis on the characteristics of both buyer and seller.

The research undertaken by those outlined above had a significant influence on a number of other groups within the UK, Europe and the United States. By the early 1990s further groups of researchers were starting to pursue separate but related work in relationship marketing.

In an effort to characterise some of these approaches Coote[13] identified three broad approaches to relationship marketing: the Anglo-Australian approach, the Nordic approach and the North American approach. The first approach, according to Coote, is based on the work of Christopher, Payne and Ballantyne[14] and emphasises the integration of quality management, services marketing concepts and customer relationship economics. The second approach derives from the work of Nordic academics such as Grönroos.[15] Coote suggests that the Nordic approach is founded on the interactive network theory of industrial marketing, services marketing concepts and customer relationship economics. The third approach, which emphasises the relationship between the buyer and seller within the organisation, is characterised by the work of Berry and Levitt. These approaches are shown in Figure 1.

During the past decade, there has been widespread and growing concern about the validity of the traditional marketing approach and a recognition that relationships are becoming ever more important in increasingly complex and mature markets. Many commentators within the UK and the rest of Europe have voiced these concerns, including Christopher, Payne and Ballantyne[14] and Grönroos.[16]

In the UK, these concerns led to a broader view of relationship marketing. Payne[17] summarised this view as:

■ a move from functionally-based marketing to cross-functionally-based marketing;

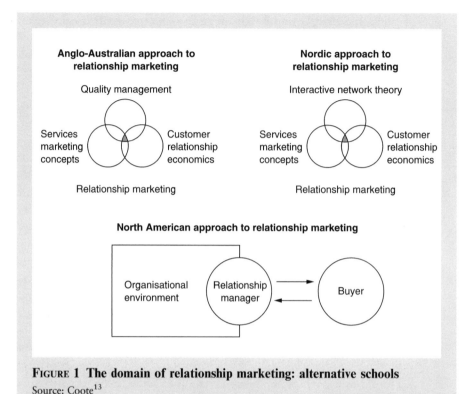

FIGURE 1 The domain of relationship marketing: alternative schools
Source: Coote[13]

- an approach which addresses six key market domains, not just the traditional customer market;
- a shift from marketing activities which emphasise customer acquisition to marketing activities which emphasise customer retention as well as acquisition.

This shift to cross-functional marketing reflects the difficulties traditional hierarchically-structured and functionally-oriented organisations encounter when they adopt a departmental or functional approach to marketing. The new view of relationship marketing emphasises the organisation of marketing activities around cross-functional processes rather than organisational functions.

This view is consistent with that of Ostroff and Smith,[18] who argue the need for a horizontal mode of organisation, in which cross-functional, end-to-end work flows link internal processes with the needs and capabilities of both suppliers and customers. This suggests organisations need to co-ordinate their approach to relationships with other 'markets', including suppliers and internal staff as well as customers, if they are to maximise relational value.

A number of authors have suggested the scope of marketing should be expanded. For example, Kotler[19] argues for a broader perspective to take into account the relationships between an organisation and its publics. Gummesson[20] went further to include thirty relational forms. Other models advocating multiple markets have been suggested in the United States[21] and the UK.[22] Sharma and Sheth[23] suggest a framework for value creation through supplier partnering, alliance partnering and customer partnering.

Since the first edition of this book was published, customer relationship management (CRM) has emerged as a massive area of interest around the world. The advent of computer-based information technology that allows companies to assemble and manipulate data on customers and consumers has transformed the way marketing is practised in many industries. But we view CRM as a platform on which to enable relationship marketing rather than as an end in itself.

Indeed, you could view CRM as another step in the journey from the birth of modern marketing in the 1950s as a largely consumer-focused concern, to the current pan-company orientation. Figure 2 suggests that our current understanding of relationship marketing has, in fact, been the result of a process of evolution as the basic tenets of the marketing concept spread across all aspects of commercial and non-commercial activity.

This book focuses on creating relationships with key stakeholders, including customers, through the exchange of value. Value has always been recognised as the key concept on which economic activity is based. But more recently, the idea of marketing as *value exchange* has emerged and this gives an added dimension to the role of marketing in today's business. Marketing can be the orchestrator of a pan-company value-exchange process. Our book builds on this idea and hopefully delivers actionable insights into how companies can plan for and implement the value-exchange process.

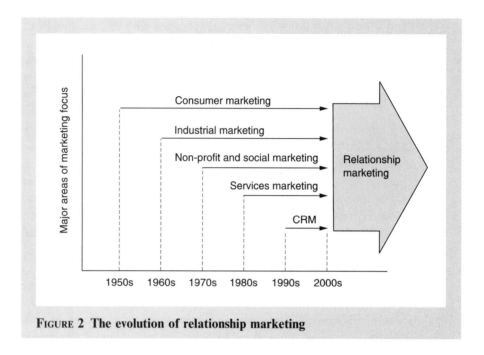

FIGURE 2 **The evolution of relationship marketing**

The structure of the book is outlined in Figure 3.

We begin by looking at how value for the customer is created and how, in turn, customers create value for the organisation. We then explore the ways in which organisations can develop relationship strategies for their multiple stakeholders, paying particular attention to the role of relationships across networks.

The book moves on to revisit the theme that provided the foundation for the first edition – the integration of quality, customer service and marketing. The concluding chapter examines the issues involved in developing and implementing a relationship marketing strategy.

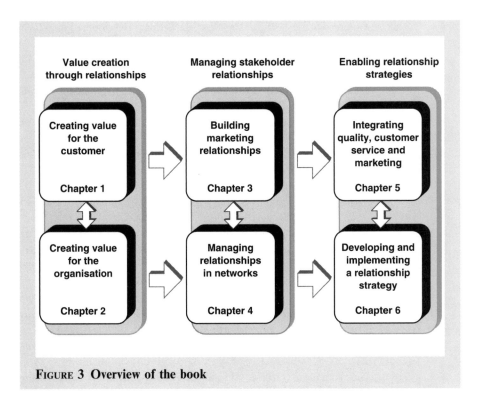

FIGURE 3 Overview of the book

References

1   Berry, L.L. (1995), 'Relationship Marketing of Services – Growing Interest, Emerging Perspectives', *Journal of the Academy of Marketing Science*, **23**, 4, 236–45.

2   Levitt, T. (1983), 'After the Sale is Over', *Harvard Business Review*, September, 87–93.

3   Jackson, B.B. (1985), *Winning and Keeping Industrial Customers: The Dynamics of Customer Relationships*, Lexington: D. C. Heath.

4   Berry, L.L. (1983), Relationship Marketing, in Berry, L.L., Shostack, G.L. and Upah, G. D. (eds), *Emerging Perspectives on Services Marketing*, Chicago, IL: American Marketing Association, pp. 25–8.

5   Grönroos, C. (1989), 'Defining Marketing: A Market-Oriented Approach', *European Journal of Marketing*, **23**, 1, 52–60.

6   Grönroos, C. (1991), 'The Marketing Strategy Continuum: A Marketing Concept for the 1990s', *Management Decision*, **29**, 1, 7–13.

7   Gummesson, E. (1987), 'The New Marketing – Developing Long-Term Interactive Relationships', *Long-Range Planning*, **20**, 4, 10–20.

8   Turnbull, P.W. and Cunningham, M.T., (1981), *International Marketing and Purchasing*, London: Macmillan.

9   Håkansson, H. (ed.) (1982), *International Marketing and Purchasing of Industrial Goods*, Chichester: Wiley.

10 Ford, D. (ed.) (1990), *Understanding Business Markets: Interaction, Relationships, Networks*, Academic Press.

11 Axelsson, B. and Easton, G. (eds) (1992), *Industrial Networks: A New View of Reality*, London: Routledge.

12 Ford, D., Gadde, L.-E., Håkansson, H., Lundgren, A., Snehota, I., Turnbull, P. and Wilson, D. (1997), *Managing Business Relationships*, Chichester: Wiley.

13 Coote, L. (1994), Implementation of Relationship Marketing in an Accounting Practice, in Sheth, J. N. and Parvatiyar, A. (eds), *Relationship Marketing: Theory, Methods and Applications*, 1994 Research Conference Proceedings, Emory University, Atlanta.

14 Christopher, M., Payne, A and Ballantyne, D. (1991), *Relationship Marketing: Bringing Quality, Customer Service and Marketing Together*, Oxford: Butterworth-Heinemann.

15 Grönroos, C. (1990), 'Marketing Redefined', *Management Decision*, **27**, 1, 5–9.

16 Grönroos, C. (1994), 'From Marketing Mix to Relationship Marketing: Towards a Paradigm Shift in Marketing', *Asia–Australia Marketing Journal*, **2**, 1, 9–29; also in *Management Decision*, **32**, 2, 4–20.

17 Payne, A. (ed.), (1995), *Advances in Relationship Marketing*, Kogan.

18 Ostroff, F. and Smith, D. (1992), 'The Horizontal Organization', *McKinsey Quarterly*, Winter, 148–167.

19 Kotler, P. (1992), 'It's Time for Total Marketing', *Business Week Advance Executive Brief*, 2.

20 Gummesson, E. (1999), *Total Relationship Marketing: From the 4Ps to the 30Rs*, Oxford: Butterworth-Heinemann.

21 Morgan, R.M. and Hunt, S.D. (1994), 'The Commitment-Trust Theory of Relationship Marketing', *Journal of Marketing*, **58**, July 20–38.

22 Doyle, P. (1995), 'Marketing in the New Millenium', *European Journal of Marketing*, **29**, 13, 23–41.

23 Sharma, A. and Sheth, J.N. (1997), 'Relationship Marketing: An Agenda for Enquiry', *Industrial Marketing Management*, **26**, 2, 87–90.

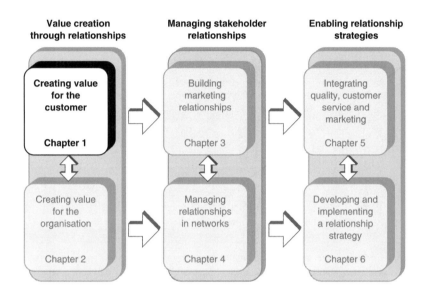

Value creation through relationships	Managing stakeholder relationships	Enabling relationship strategies
Creating value for the customer — Chapter 1	Building marketing relationships — Chapter 3	Integrating quality, customer service and marketing — Chapter 5
Creating value for the organisation — Chapter 2	Managing relationships in networks — Chapter 4	Developing and implementing a relationship strategy — Chapter 6

INTRODUCTION

The widespread adoption of the marketing concept by organisations is a relatively recent event. With one or two exceptions marketing literature is barely fifty years old. But during those fifty years the way we think about marketing and the way it is practised has changed significantly. Marketing has progressed from a simplistic focus on 'giving the customers what they want' to a pan-company orientation in which the specific capabilities of the business are focused around creating and delivering customer value to targeted market segments.

Philip Kotler, who has probably done more than any writer in the past fifty years to articulate the changes in marketing thinking, captured the essence of conventional marketing in the first edition of his groundbreaking book *Marketing Management*[1] in 1967:

> 💬 Marketing is the analysing, organising, planning and controlling of the firm's customer-impinging resources, policies, and activities with a view to satisfying the needs and wants of chosen customer groups at a profit.

In the growth markets of the 1960s and 1970s, the marketers' challenge was to capture as much of that growth in demand as early as possible. This led them to focus on volume and market share, or what we would now term a 'transactional' approach to marketing. As many markets matured in the closing decades of the twentieth century, the emphasis gradually switched from the corporate objective of maximising market share towards a concern with the 'quality of share' in recognition of the fact that not all customers are equally profitable. This has led to the notion that the purpose of marketing is to create profitable and enduring relationships with selected customers. A key role of marketing in this new framework is to determine what value propositions to create and deliver to which customers.

Today's marketing-oriented companies are actually 'market driven', in the sense that they are structured, organised and managed with the sole purpose of creating and delivering value to chosen markets. Ideas and phrases such as customer intimacy, customer-centric and customer focus summarise the new concept of the corporation as an entity that exists to deliver value to carefully selected market segments. This is not some altruistic or idealistic view of the firm as the provider of customer satisfaction at any cost. Rather it is a hard-edged business model that recognises that long-term profits are more likely to be maximised through satisfied customers who keep returning to spend more money.

This is the backdrop against which the recently emerged paradigm of 'relationship marketing' should be viewed.

The evolution of relationship marketing

Marketing literature provides a useful guide to the way marketing theory and practice have developed. In the 1950s frameworks were formulated to manipulate and exploit market demand. The most enduring of these was the idea of the 'marketing mix', particularly as enshrined in the shorthand of the '4Ps' of product, price, promotion and place. These were the levers that, if pulled appropriately, would lead to increased demand for the company's offer. Marketing management aimed to devise strategies that would optimise expenditure on the marketing mix to maximise sales.[2]

The fundamental concept of the marketing mix still applies today in the sense that organisations need to understand and manage the influences on demand. Yet we need to remember that these original frameworks for marketing action were devised in a unique environment. They emerged from the United States during a period of unprecedented growth and prosperity, and focused on fast-moving consumer goods.

But though the tools and techniques developed in a particular era and for particular products might not necessarily be successfully applied more universally, the basic ideas of '4Ps marketing' were rapidly extended into industrial markets,[3] then service markets[4] and even not-for-profit markets.[5]

During the closing years of the twentieth century some of these basic tenets of marketing were increasingly being questioned. The marketplace was vastly different from that of the 1950s. In many instances consumers and customers were more sophisticated and less responsive to the traditional marketing pressures – particularly advertising. There was greater choice, partly as a result of the globalisation of markets and new sources of competition. And many markets had matured, in the sense that growth was low or non-existent.

As a result of these and many other pressures, brand loyalty is weaker than it used to be[6] and simplistic 4Ps marketing is unlikely to win or retain customers either in consumer or industrial markets. The efficacy of conventional marketing has been repeatedly challenged in articles and conference papers along the lines of 'Is marketing dead?'[7,8]

It is against this background that the new wave of marketing thinking has become apparent, and the label 'relationship marketing' applied to describe the revised framework or paradigm.[9]

In the earlier edition of this book,[10] we developed a general model of relationship marketing. We have since refined it, but it still embodies the following elements. Relationship marketing:

- emphasises a relationship, rather than a transactional, approach to marketing;
- understands the economics of customer retention and thus ensures the right amount of money and other resources are appropriately allocated between the two tasks of retaining and attracting customers;
- highlights the critical role of internal marketing in achieving external marketing success;
- extends the principles of relationship marketing to a range of diverse market domains, not just customer markets;
- recognises that quality, customer service and marketing need to be much more closely integrated;
- illustrates how the traditional marketing mix concept of the 4Ps does not adequately capture all the key elements which must be addressed in building and sustaining relationships with markets;
- ensures that marketing is considered in a cross-functional context.

This broader concept of relationship marketing is depicted in Figure 1.1.

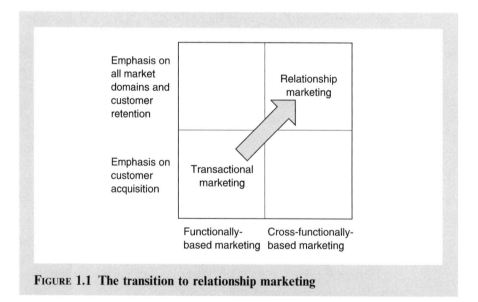

FIGURE 1.1 The transition to relationship marketing

The fundamental principles of relationship marketing

As Figure 1.1 suggests, a number of characteristics distinguish relationship marketing from earlier frameworks. The first is an emphasis on extending the 'lifetime value' of customers through strategies that focus on retaining targeted customers. The second is the recognition that companies need to forge relationships with a number of market domains or 'stakeholders' if they are to achieve long-term success in the final marketplace. And the third is that marketing has moved from being the sole responsibility of the marketing department to become 'pan-company' and cross-functional.

Maximising the lifetime value of a customer is a fundamental goal of relationship marketing. In this context, we define the lifetime value of a customer as the future flow of net profit, discounted back to the present, that can be attributed to a specific customer. Adopting the principle of maximising customer lifetime value forces the organisation to recognise that not all customers are equally profitable and that it must devise strategies to enhance the profitability of those customers it seeks to target. We go on to explore these ideas in more depth in Chapter 2. But, in essence, companies need to tailor and customise their relationship marketing strategies even to the extent of so called 'one-to-one' marketing.[11]

> Maximising the lifetime value of a customer is a fundamental goal of relationship marketing.

The second differentiating feature of relationship marketing is the concept of focusing marketing action on multiple markets. Conventionally, marketing strategy has been structured solely around the customer. Of course, the ultimate aim of relationship marketing strategies is to compete successfully for profitable customers. But to do this firms need to define more broadly the markets that need to be addressed. Relationship marketing recognises that multiple market domains can directly or indirectly affect a business's ability to win or retain profitable customers. These other markets include suppliers, employees, influencers, distributors and alliance partners. We have previously defined[10] this multiple market focus as the 'six markets model'. But there is nothing sacrosanct about the number six, and in any given circumstance firms may need to encompass fewer or more 'stakeholders' within their overall relationship marketing strategies. We explore the concept of the multiple market model in greater detail in Chapter 3.

The third key element of relationship marketing is that it must be cross-functional.

David Packard, a co-founder of Hewlett-Packard, is reported to have said that 'marketing is too important to be left to the marketing department'. You could interpret this in a number of ways (for example, the marketing department is not up to the task!) but we choose to understand it as a call to bring marketing out of its functional silo and inculcate the concept and the philosophy of marketing across the business.

In practice this needs to be accompanied by an organisational change that fosters cross-functional working and develops the mindset that everyone within the business serves a customer, be they internal or external customers.

In addition to these three key differentiators, the new paradigm of relationship marketing has a number of other characteristics that distinguish it from conventional marketing. For many years market share was the overriding goal of many organisations, which often followed the precepts particularly associated with the Boston Consulting Group.[12] The market share model held that growing market share relative to the competition enabled a company to move down 'the experience curve' more quickly, resulting in lower costs and greater profits. But while winning market share early in a growth market can indeed lead to long-term profitability, when markets mature and the growth rate declines, the cost of winning extra percentage points of market share can be prohibitive. This is the reason why many companies, such as Vodafone, have switched their strategic focus from volume towards establishing longer-term relationships with fewer but more profitable customers (see Case Study below). Such companies now talk about 'share of wallet' as much as they do about absolute market share.

CASE STUDY   **Retention – Vodafone rethinks loyalty policy**

Cell phone operator Vodafone UK is refocusing its business on customer retention, a move that, on paper at least, confirms a shift in thinking for a major European company.

The dramatic changes at Vodafone will focus on encouraging its distribution channel to provide long-term customers, rather than users enticed merely by introductory offers and associated 'freebies'. This means the distribution channel will get reduced bonuses and subsidies for winning 'Pay as you Talk' and pre-paid customers, and that 'All in One' mobile phone packages will be scrapped altogether. The reduction in bonuses will effectively bump up the high street starting price of a Pay as you Talk package to around £70, although Vodafone says that the distributors will ultimately set prices.

Peter Bamford, chief executive of the UK, Middle East and Africa region, explains: 'These changes in Vodafone UK's commercial policies reflect the move of the UK market into a phase of greater maturity and our recognition of the need to reduce the current levels of expenditure on customer acquisition. We aim to reward our distribution channel for quality customers, rather than the quantity of customers, thereby ensuring the increasing focus on customer retention and development across the business.'

The moves come as a result of Vodafone chiefs studying the effects of active and non-active (not using the phone for more than three months) customers and concluding that a greater number of non-active customers come from the non-subscription band. Consequently Vodafone intends to prise more funds from each customer and push customers towards contracts. Chris Gent, Vodafone Group chief executive, described the change in priority as being towards 'margin improvement and cash flow rather than growth and market share'.

Based on: *Customer Relationship Management* magazine (2001), Southampton: Wilson Publications.

Underpinning this idea of an ongoing relationship with individual customers is a greater emphasis on service and on tailoring the offer to meet their precise needs. The concept of customer service is wide-ranging and relates to the totality of encounters between suppliers and buyers. It extends from the pre-purchase stage of customer engagement, through to the transfer of the offer from the supplier to the customer, and continues through the life cycle of usage.

A prime objective of any customer service strategy should be to enhance customer retention. While customer service obviously plays a role in winning new customers, it is perhaps the most potent weapon in the marketing armoury for retaining customers. Researchers at management consultants Bain & Co have found that retained customers are more profitable then new customers for the following reasons:

- the cost of acquiring new customers can be substantial. A higher retention rate implies that fewer customers need be acquired more cheaply;
- established customers tend to buy more;
- regular customers place frequent, consistent orders and, therefore, usually cost less to serve;
- satisfied customers often refer new customers to the supplier at virtually no cost;
- satisfied customers are often willing to pay premium prices for a supplier they know and trust;
- retaining customers makes market entry or share gain difficult for competitors.

Customer service is critically important in cementing relationships. Marketing is concerned with 'exchange relationships' between the organisation and its customers, and quality and customer service are key linkages in these relationships. At its simplest, the exchange relationship is the customer paying for the benefits they receive. But the relationship marketing view is that the customer gives loyalty in exchange for their expectation that value will flow to them from the relationship. This flow of value includes not just product benefits but a number of less tangible benefits relating to the quality of the experience within a wider customer service context. So the challenge to the organisation is to align marketing, quality and customer service strategies more closely. In the past organisations have tended to treat these as separate and unrelated. Consequently, decisions affecting customer service may have been taken by diverse functions such as distribution, manufacturing or sales. Likewise, quality was seen as the preserve of a specific quality control or assurance

> Customer service is critically important in cementing relationships.

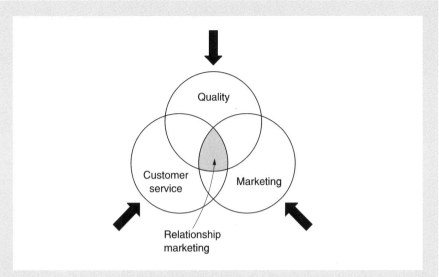

FIGURE 1.2 The relationship marketing orientation: bringing together customer service, quality and marketing

function. Under the relationship marketing paradigm these three areas are merged and given a sharper focus (Figure 1.2).

The expanded marketing mix

Traditionally, marketing has been seen as the process of perceiving, understanding and stimulating the needs of specially selected target markets, and channelling resources to satisfy those needs. Marketing is concerned with the dynamic relationships between a company's products and services, the customer's wants and needs and the activities of the competition.

Conventional marketing proposes that a company manages and co-ordinates a number of critical elements – commonly known as 'the marketing mix' – in order to achieve its objectives.

Marketing mix is the term traditionally used to describe the important ingredients of a marketing programme. The origins of the concept lie in work done by Borden at the Harvard Business School in the early

1960s.[13] He suggested that companies should consider twelve elements when formulating a marketing programme, namely:

- product planning
- pricing
- branding
- channels of distribution
- personal selling
- advertising
- promotions
- packaging
- display
- servicing
- physical handling
- fact finding and analysis

The marketing mix concept has become widely accepted, particularly since Borden's rather long list was condensed and simplified into a much shorter one, usually known as the '4Ps'. These four categories have now been enshrined in marketing theory and practice.

The 4Ps comprise:

- Product   the product or service being offered.
- Price   the price charged and the terms associated with the sale.
- Promotion   advertising, promotional and communication activities.
- Place   the distribution and logistics processes involved in fulfilling demand.

Each of the 4Ps is, of course, a collection of sub-activities (for example, promotion includes both advertising and personal selling). Even so, the 4Ps' model tends to oversimplify the complex process of winning and keeping customers, particularly in today's more complex and fast-moving climate, as we suggested earlier. This has led to suggestions that we need an expanded marketing mix.

This expanded marketing mix, as outlined in Figure 1.3, comprises seven broad elements – the traditional 4Ps of product, price,

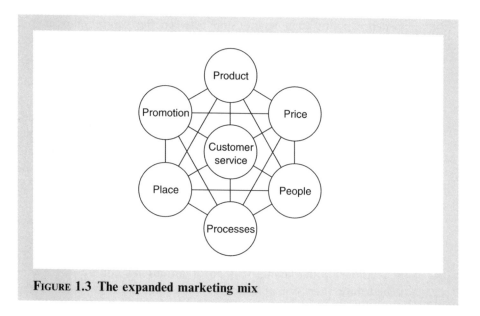

FIGURE 1.3 The expanded marketing mix

promotion, and place plus three additional elements of people, processes and customer service.

We alluded earlier to the central importance of customer service in relationship marketing, and will discuss it in greater detail in Chapter 5. But the two additional elements of 'people' and 'processes' have a critical role to play in this expanded marketing mix.

People

Most companies acknowledge the importance of their people in creating a successful business, but only a few go beyond lip-service. There is a strong argument for human resource management and marketing management to be much more closely integrated. In Chapter 3 we examine the vital stakeholder domain of 'internal markets' more closely. But it is worth exploring briefly here some of the key connections between the 'people' element of the expanded marketing mix and the creation of enduring relationships with customers.

We hear a lot these days about 'corporate culture' and 'shared values'. Essentially these ideas reflect the fact that organisations where everyone is pursuing the same goals are likely to be the most successful. The evidence points to a relationship between the way employees and managers feel about their company, the values they share, their job satisfaction and their approach to customer service. In short, satisfied employees make for satisfied customers.

Because employees are a key element in an organisation's success, some companies have introduced formal mechanisms to include them in their overall marketing strategy. These mechanisms are broadly described as 'internal marketing'. Internal marketing can be defined as the creation, development and maintenance of an internal service culture and orientation that will help the organisation achieve its goals.[14] The internal service culture directly affects just how service- and customer-oriented employees are. Developing and maintaining a customer-oriented culture is a critical determinant of long-term success in relationship marketing. It is an organisation's culture – its deep-seated, unwritten system of shared values and norms – that has the greatest impact on employees, their behaviour and attitudes. The culture of an organisation in turn dictates its 'climate' – the policies and practices that characterise it and reflect its cultural beliefs.

The structure of the organisation can prevent internal marketing strategies being effectively deployed. Classic, conventional organisations are built around 'vertical' departments that often become functional 'silos'.

If employees are to become more connected to the market, the organisations themselves need to become 'customer-centric'. In other words, they need to shed hierarchical, inward-facing structures in favour of cross-functional, team-based approaches and much greater integration between 'front-office' and 'back-office' activities.

Process

> Processes are the ways in which firms create value for their customers.

One of the biggest changes in the way in which we think about organisations has been our new understanding of the importance of 'processes'. Processes are the ways in which firms create value for their customers. They are fundamental and largely generic across the spectrum of businesses. Davenport[15] defines a process as:

> a specific ordering of work activities across time and place, with a beginning, an end, and clearly identified inputs and outputs: a structure for action.

Processes are 'horizontal', in that they cut across traditional 'vertical' functions (see Figure 1.4). They are inter-disciplinary and cross-functional.

The following 'high-level' business processes are critical:

- the market understanding process;
- the innovation management process;
- the supply chain management process;
- the customer relationship management process.

Within these generic processes there are 'sub-processes' that also need to be managed across functions.

We will examine each of these key business processes in turn.

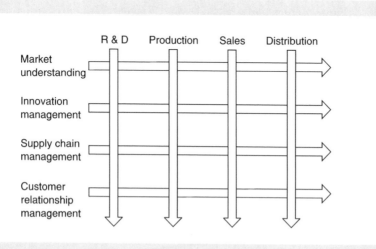

FIGURE **1.4 Processes cut across conventional functions**

The market understanding process

Successful marketing strategies are built around a deep understanding of the marketplace. In particular, the motivations of buyers and the things they value must be the building blocks of any marketing strategy. Being in close touch with customers is a prerequisite in fast-changing markets. It is not only the marketing department's responsibility to have this ongoing dialogue with customers; all parts of the business have to be informed by customers. It is just as critical for production management and procurement, for example, to be closely connected to needs of customers as it is for, say, marketing or sales people.

Being customer focused has always been, and always will be, a fundamental foundation of a market-oriented business, but it is no longer enough to identify customer needs purely through market research. Companies today need to be 'ideas driven' and 'customer informed'. In other words, they need to extend and leverage their knowledge in ways that create value for customers. In today's marketplace knowledge management is a critical component of market understanding. Successful companies are utilising superior knowledge proactively to create products and services rather than reacting to emerging market trends.

Ideas and knowledge are ubiquitous – they exist across the business and beyond it. Consequently, the business needs processes in place to capture ideas and knowledge and convert them into marketing opportunities. In a sense, the market understanding process underpins all the other business processes.

The innovation process

Every business faces the continuing challenge of maintaining a flow of successful new product/service introductions into the marketplace. As life cycles become ever shorter and demand more volatile, being able to respond to changes in customer requirements and to exploit new technology-based opportunities has become a key competitive capability.

Again, innovation has to be managed cross-functionally. It cannot be the sole preserve of any one particular department. Those companies that have adopted a cross-functional approach to innovation management have found it has paid significant dividends. Typically, such companies have formed inter-disciplinary teams that bring together a multitude of skills and knowledge bases. These teams are self-managed and autonomous, able to take decisions and to short-circuit the conventional and time-consuming procedures for taking new products to market.

Such teams benefit from the interplay of ideas from different disciplines and, by performing activities concurrently or in parallel, they can condense the time it takes to move an idea from the drawing board into the marketplace. In the car industry such teams are now the norm for new product development. Indeed, not only do these teams draw their membership from different functions across the business, they often exploit further opportunities for innovative thinking by including representatives from suppliers too.

The supply chain process

Once demand has been generated, how will it be fulfilled? This is the role of the demand chain process. In the past, fulfilling orders was not regarded as being strategically significant. While it was a necessary activity it was a cost, and therefore something to be managed as efficiently as possible. Today the emphasis has shifted. The way that a business satisfies demand and services its customers has become a fundamental basis for successful and enduring relationships.

This process is commonly termed the 'supply chain', but the label 'demand chain' more accurately describes its central role in satisfying demand. Whatever the terminology, the important principle is that it should be managed as a horizontal business process that connects customers with the organisation and extends upstream into the supplier base. Ideally, we should aim to manage the business as an 'extended enterprise' from the customer's customer back through the internal operations of the firm to the supplier's supplier. Figure 1.5 depicts this notion of an integrated supply chain.

The purpose of managing the supply chain as an integrated process is to enable the organisation to become more 'agile' in its response to demand. Agility is an increasingly important competitive capability.[16] As demand becomes more volatile and less predictable the ability to move quickly, to change direction and to meet changed requirements in shorter time-frames is critical. Agility is not a single company

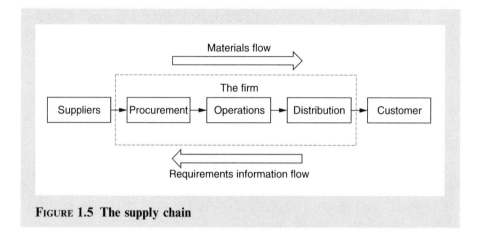

FIGURE 1.5 **The supply chain**

concept; it requires the closest connections upstream and downstream, particularly through sharing information on demand. A demand chain is, in effect, an 'information highway' where all the partners in the chain have access to the same information.

In a sense, these three critical business processes are all subsidiary to, and form the basis of, the fourth key process – the customer relationship management process.

The customer relationship management process

In a way, the whole of this book is devoted to developing an understanding of the customer relationship management (CRM) process. We define CRM as follows:-

CRM is a strategic approach to improving shareholder value through the development of appropriate relationships with key customers and customer segments. CRM unites the potential of IT and relationship marketing strategies to deliver profitable, long-term relationships. Importantly, CRM provides enhanced opportunities to use data and information both to understand customers and implement relationship marketing strategies better. This requires a cross-functional integration of people, operations and marketing capabilities enabled through information technology and applications.

Customer relationship management, we suggest, builds on the philosophy of relationship marketing by utilising information technology to enable a much closer 'fit' to be achieved between the needs and characteristics of the customer and the organisation's 'offer'. Figure 1.6 highlights the connection between relationship marketing, CRM and the more tactical management of specific customer relationships.

CRM allows a business to target customers more closely and implement 'one-to-one' marketing strategies where appropriate. As a concept and a set of tools it is equally appropriate for business-to-business (b2b) or business-to-consumer (b2c) marketing.

Business-to-business marketing – managing relationships with business customers rather than consumers – has attracted much attention over recent years. It has long been acknowledged that marketing to other organisations requires a deep understanding of those customers' business processes and value-creation processes. For a start, there will typically be a number of people involved in purchase decisions in a business customer. This group is usually referred to as the decision-making unit (DMU). It is conventional[17] to classify the members of a DMU as follows:

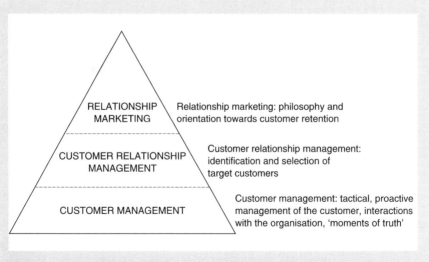

FIGURE 1.6 **Relationship marketing and CRM – a hierarchy**

Gatekeeper	Not involved in the final decision but can control access and the flow of information to others.
Influencer	May influence the opinions and the decisions of the buyer or decision-maker.
User	End user of the product who generally initiates the request.
Buyer	Identifies possible suppliers, negotiates terms of purchase.
Decision-maker	Has formal or informal power to select suppliers and approve purchase.

These roles may be separate or they may overlap. But organisations marketing to other organisations clearly need to understand the composition of the specific DMU and the types of issues that concern the various players. In a sense, a prime goal of CRM is to establish appropriate relationships with each of these players.

In b2c marketing, the same principles of understanding the DMU apply. Where there are multiple members of a household – typically families – many purchase decisions involve more than one person. So relationships need to be established at many levels. Marketing to children is a good example, in that the DMU possibly includes gatekeepers, influencers and decision-makers as well as the end user.

One particular b2b relationship management model that has gained widespread acceptance in recent years is the formation of cross-functional teams to manage specific customers. Thus for major accounts a business will often create a multi-disciplinary team that is capable of managing multi-level relationships with the client organisation. In this type of relationship traditional 'selling' has been replaced by 'customer management'.

From transactions to relationships: the role of customer value

Relationship marketing differs from transactional marketing in a number of important ways. These are summarised in the box:

Transactional marketing	Relationship marketing
• Focus on volume	• Focus on profitable retention
• Emphasises product features	• Emphasises customer value
• Short timescale	• Longer-term timescales
• Little emphasis on customer service	• High customer service emphasis
• Moderate customer contact	• High customer contact
• Primary concern with product quality	• Concern with relationship quality

As the old model is increasingly viewed as inadequate to cope with today's business environment, marketing is entering a new era. In an environment characterised by global competition, overcapacity and the inevitable trend towards 'commoditisation' of markets, the focus has to switch from volume growth to profit growth. The challenge that this changed environment poses to the organisation is to identify how to build enduring relationships with profitable customers.

It is now fairly widely accepted among marketing practitioners and academics that customers base purchasing decisions on the value they perceive they will derive from that purchase. This is not a new idea; in essence it has formed the basis for much economic theory since the time of the early economist Alfred Marshall, if not before.

Customers of every sort, from individual consumers to industrial corporations, seek to acquire value through their purchasing behaviour. Broadly defined, value represents an acceptable 'solution' to a buying 'problem'. In other words, given that buyers are goal oriented – there is a rationale for their purchasing behaviour – they will seek a solution that best achieves that goal.

One of the early marketing writers on the subject, Bradley Gale, defined customer value as 'market-perceived quality adjusted for the relative price of your product', where market-perceived quality is defined as 'the customer's opinion of your products (or services) compared to those of your competitors'.[18]

Gale adopted a concept of quality that is wider than the conventional product-based definition. He believed quality applies to every area that matters to the customer. His model of customer value is shown as

Figure 1.7 and it provides a useful starting point for our discussion on the role of customer value.

What is value from a customer perspective? At its simplest, customer value is the relationship between the customer's perception of the benefits they believe they will derive from a purchase compared to the price they will have to pay. However, the definition of 'price' needs to be elaborated in this context. Price is not simply the immediate out-of-pocket cost, but also includes all those preliminary and ongoing costs that may be involved – the so-called life-cycle costs – as well as 'risk' costs if things go wrong. Equally, the total benefit package includes not just the benefits that flow from the functional attributes of the product, but those that flow from the related service attributes as well.

Figure 1.7 suggests that customer value can be defined as the ratio of perceived benefits to the perceived 'sacrifice' that is involved. Clearly the word 'perceived' is critical here since both benefits and costs are, to a certain extent, subjective.

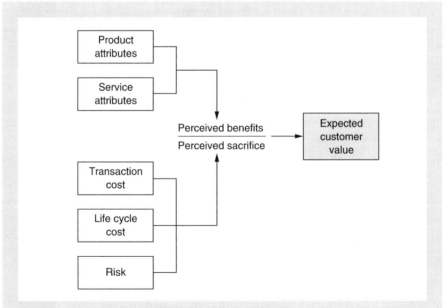

FIGURE 1.7 **Components of customer value**

Source[19]: From *Customer Value Toolkit, 1st Edition*, by E. Naumann and R. Kordupleski © 1995. Reprinted with permission of South-Western College Publishing a division of Thomson Learning. Fax 800 730-2215.

This framework could apply equally to consumer and industrial markets since ultimately all purchase behaviour in any context will be influenced by the customer's perception of total costs and benefits.

> Relationships are built on the creation and delivery of superior customer value on a sustained basis.

Customer value is a highly significant component of relationship marketing, as we mentioned earlier. Indeed, we argue throughout this book that relationships are built on the creation and delivery of superior customer value on a sustained basis. This is why a thorough understanding of what constitutes customer value in specific markets and segments is so important.

The overall value-creation process can be considered in terms of the three key elements shown in Figure 1.8. These are determining what value the company can provide to its customers (the 'value customer receives'); determining the value the organisation receives from its customers (the 'value organisation receives'); and, by managing this value exchange, maximising the lifetime value of desirable customer segments.

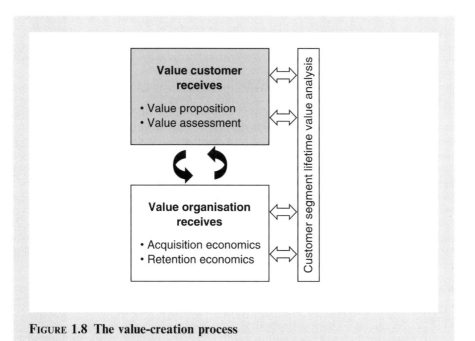

FIGURE 1.8 The value-creation process

In this chapter, we consider the first box in Figure 1.8 – the value the customer receives – focusing in particular on developing and assessing a value proposition. Chapter 2 goes on to examine how an organisation can create value for itself by managing both the value it gets from its customers and the value exchange between itself and its customers.

Understanding customer value

Today's successful companies tend to base their marketing strategy around a clearly defined and strongly communicated 'value proposition'. The value proposition is a summation of all the reasons why a customer should buy the company's product or services. The value proposition, if successful, will also provide the basis for differentiation and the foundation for an ongoing buyer–seller relationship.

Lanning and Michaels, originally at McKinsey & Co, have developed a framework called the value delivery sequence,[20] which reflects the shift from the traditional view of business as a series of functional activities to an externally-oriented view which sees the business as being concerned with value delivery. Figure 1.9 shows the value

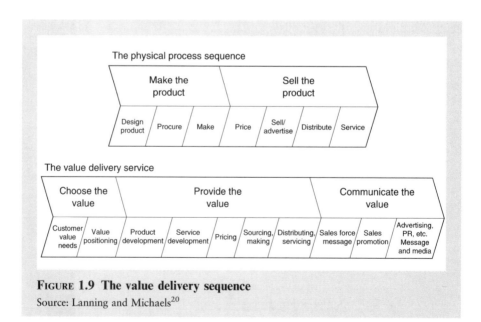

FIGURE **1.9 The value delivery sequence**
Source: Lanning and Michaels[20]

delivery sequence. This builds on the idea that customers buy promises of satisfaction and they only purchase products because they are of some value to them.

The McKinsey approach argues that focusing on the traditional physical process sequence of 'make the product and sell the product' can be ineffecient. The value delivery sequence, by contrast, depicts the business as viewed from the customer's perspective rather than as a series of internally-oriented functions.

The value delivery sequence consists of three key steps: choose the value, provide the value and communicate the value.

- **Choose the value.** Customers typically select products and services because they believe they offer superior value. In this context companies need to understand two things. They need to understand changing customer needs, in terms of the forces driving demand as well as customer economics and the buying process. They also need to understand how well the competition meets those needs, particularly in terms of the products themselves, the service and the price charged.
- **Provide the value.** The second stage, providing the value, is concerned with developing a product/service package that creates clear and superior value. This involves focusing on things such as product quality and performance, service cost and responsiveness, manufacturing cost and flexibility, channel structure and performance, and price structure.
- **Communicate the value.** This involves the various aspects of promotional activity needed to persuade customers that the values are better than those offered by competitors. It involves organising sales promotion, advertising and the sales force, as well as providing outstanding service in a way that is continually recognised by the target audience.

You can define superior value delivery as providing a product or service that the customer considers gives a net positive value greater than that offered by competitors. So, the current value proposition of Dell Computer Corporation is based on a promise to configure the equipment the way the customer wants and to have it up and running within a matter of days. In this case the value proposition is based not on technology, price or image, but on customisation and service.

Similarly, Volvo's value proposition of high levels of safety and reliability at a modest price has resulted in superior perceived value in the eyes of a significant customer segment.

McKinsey suggests that companies wishing to implement a value proposition approach should adopt a three-step sequence:

1 Analyse and segment markets by the values customers desire.
2 Vigorously assess the opportunities in each segment to deliver superior value.
3 Explicitly choose the value proposition that optimises these opportunities.

Lanning and Michaels[20] point out that success does not just come down to choosing the right value proposition, but is also based on how thoroughly and innovatively it is delivered and communicated. Creating a strategy and implementation plan that really provides and communicates value is challenging, but it can prove to be a source of differentiation that competitors find very difficult to replicate. The consultants also argue that creating and managing the value delivery sequence helps integrate the different functions within the business and that involving every employee in delivering the chosen value gives added meaning to teamwork.

The 'one-to-one' world

For many years a fundamental principle of marketing strategy has been identifying appropriate 'segments' around which to focus the firm's offer. In consumer markets these segments may be determined by factors such as age, sex or lifestyle, and in business-to-business markets by industrial sector, size of company and so on.

The concept of segmentation is still valid today, but we are seeing markets fragment into ever smaller segments. It has been suggested that we may have to address 'segments of one' in some markets. There are many possible explanations for this trend towards greater fragmentation, but it seems that customers – consumers and organisations – are increasingly seeking specific solutions to their buying 'problems'. Organisations cannot just offer a choice these days; they have to be able to meet their customers' precise requirements. Relationships

> **Relationships will increasingly be built on the platform of one-to-one marketing.**

will increasingly be built on the platform of one-to-one marketing,[11] where the customer and the supplier in effect create a unique and mutually satisfactory exchange process. The Internet now provides a powerful means of involving customers much more closely in the marketing process through enabling dialogue rather than one-way communication.

Companies need to determine the appropriate level of market segmentation 'granularity' – that is, macro-segmentation, micro-segmentation or a 'one-to-one' approach. The decision will be based on a number of factors, including the existing and potential profitability of different customer types; the available information on customers; and the opportunity to 'reach' customers in terms both of communication and physical delivery.

Despite its name, 'one-to-one' marketing does not imply adopting a 'one-to-one' approach with every single customer. Rather, it suggests understanding customers in terms of their economic importance, and then adjusting the marketing approach to reflect the existing and potential profitability of different customer groups.

Clearly segmenting the customer base and adopting the correct level of segment granularity is an important element of customer strategy.

But to survive in such a one-to-one world, suppliers must have a deep understanding of the requirements of these ever-smaller customer segments – even down to the level of individual customers – and the flexibility to tailor their offer to meet those specific needs.

We will consider each of these challenges in turn.

Customer understanding

Customer understanding needs to go beyond classic market research, which tends to be descriptive and aggregates results together, and drill down at a micro level into the characteristics of the customer/consumer value chain. In other words, we need to understand the processes that customers engage in – running an assembly line, retailing groceries, doing the laundry, cooking meals, and so on – and then recognise the opportunities to create value within those processes. We create value either by making those processes more effective (that is, doing them better) or more efficient (doing them more cheaply).

To help businesses identify such value-creating opportunities, Sandra Vandermerwe[21] has developed the concept of mapping what she terms the 'customer activity cycle'. Essentially the idea is to try to gain a deep understanding of what customers 'do' (including activities before and after the 'doing') through a detailed mapping of the stages in these customer processes. Once these activity cycles are mapped, the next step is to understand where the opportunities lie to enhance value. Which elements of that activity cycle are the most complex, uncertain, frustrating or time-consuming, for example? Which elements is the customer most dissatisfied with? Relationship-oriented market research should focus around these fundamental issues, but in our experience too little of this type of research is conducted either in business-to-business or business-to-consumer marketing. We examine the concept of the customer activity cycle in greater detail in Chapter 5.

Flexible response

To be able to exploit fully the opportunities presented by the myriad of potential individual customer activity cycles, suppliers need to be highly flexible and responsive. By definition, one-to-one marketing requires individual solutions for individual buying problems. Customers may not want the physical product to be differentiated (although many do), but require the accompanying service package to be tailored.

Today the search is on for cost-effective strategies to achieve what is now termed 'mass customisation'.[22] Mass customisation is the ability to take standard components, elements or modules and, through customer-specific combinations or configurations, produce a tailored solution. In a manufacturing environment the aim would be to produce generic semi-finished products in volume to achieve economies of scale, and then finish the product later to meet individual customer requirements.

An oft-quoted example of mass customisation is the Japanese National Bicycle Company, which offers customers the opportunity to configure their own bicycle from different style, colour, size and components options. Within two weeks the company delivers the tailored bike to the customer. The company has become the market leader in Japan as a result of this marketing and logistics innovation.

Value-creating relationships

A prime objective of relationship marketing is to create superior customer value at the one-to-one level. The premise is that while it is impossible to have a relationship with a market or even a segment, it may be possible to establish a relationship with an individual customer or consumer.

Though the general principles of relationship marketing apply across the entire spectrum of business-to-business (b2b) to business-to-consumer (b2c) companies, there are some specific issues associated with each of these two key areas.

B2b relationships

In b2b environments, there has been a noticeable trend towards customers seeking to do business with suppliers on an entirely different basis from in the past.

Historically, companies would have multiple suppliers so as not to keep all their eggs in one basket and to keep vendors at arms' length. Information sharing was minimal. Today there are signs that this almost adversarial approach to buyer/seller relations may be changing. The emphasis now is on reducing the supplier base, moving sometimes to single sourcing for any one item; and working much more collaboratively, supported by transparent information.

Companies have changed their approach because they have realised that they can greatly enhance the efficiency and effectiveness of their supply chain through collaborative working. Conventional supply chains are based upon each entity – whether buying or selling organisation – seeking to optimise their own operations. Such approaches have led to resources and assets being duplicated, and have even resulted in sub-optimisation across the chain as a whole. Conventional wisdom suggests that those companies with the greatest internal resources and capabilities will gain competitive advantage, but the new school of thought recognises the mutual dependencies between organisations and the importance of leveraging the combined capabilities of the supply chain as a whole.

The more firms outsource activities they used to do themselves, the greater these external dependencies are, and hence the greater the need to pay particular attention to the way in which they manage their relationships with supply chain partners.

This changed perspective gives suppliers the opportunity to develop a value-based relationship strategy. Such strategies are based on identifying opportunities to improve the customer's value-creation process, and help them do a better job of serving *their* customers at less cost. Value-based strategies seek to generate innovative solutions that will help customers achieve greater differentiation in their markets and improve their profitability. At one level suppliers might contribute to their customer's new product development process, at another they might help the customer respond to changing demand through integrating their logistics processes.

Suppliers have a powerful opportunity to create value-based relationship strategies by reducing the customer's 'costs of ownership'.[23] These costs of ownership extend beyond the actual purchase price and include the costs that the customer occurs in in-bound quality control, re-work, the costs of holding inventory, operating costs, maintenance, training and even the costs of disposal. But if they are to develop strategies that can lead to demonstrable improvements for the customer, suppliers need to understand these costs of ownership even better than their customers do. One example of such a strategy is vendor-managed inventory (VMI). With VMI, the supplier manages the flow of product into the customer's operations, removing the need for the customer to place orders (so reducing their transaction costs) and reducing or eliminating the need for the customer to carry safety stock (so reducing the cost of financing inventory). But for VMI to be possible, the customer has to tell the supplier the rate at which that product is being used or sold.

Many companies are now taking advantage of developments in information technology – including the Internet – to install such integrated processes, and are creating stronger, mutually beneficial partnerships as a consequence. Such arrangements are being extended into initiatives such as collaborative planning, forecasting and replenishment (CPFR) agreements. These initiatives involve buyers and sellers coming together jointly to agree strategies to develop a particular line of business, and to improve the efficiency of product flow, reducing inventories and improving sales through fewer stock-outs. In the retail market, a closely related concept is category management. Typically, category management involves customer and supplier working together to agree a marketing strategy for a product category, including promotions, pricing, shelf-positioning and possibly vendor-managed inventory too.

B2c relationships

Conventionally, most marketing effort has been expended on creating a strong franchise with consumers in the final marketplace. This franchise was effectively based on loyalty to the brand. The argument was that if a company could create strong brand 'values' then consumers seeking those values would be drawn to the brand and reject alternative offers. So marketing effort focused on creating a brand 'image'.

This approach worked well for many years, but as competition intensified and consumers became more experienced and sophisticated, these relatively crude approaches became less effective. The evidence today points to a gradual decline in brand loyalty and, in its place, an increased willingness by consumers to choose from a portfolio of brands.

While individual consumers may well have brand preferences, they are quite happy to select alternative brands if the first choice is not available. In fact, research has shown that up to two-thirds of all consumer buying decisions are made at the point of purchase.

In this new world, the need for strong b2c relationships is still as great as ever. However, the conventional means of creating this relationship – brand values – needs to be augmented through a much wider range of marketing activities.

One reason why traditional brand loyalty has declined is that consumers are tending to see their relationship as being more with the retailer than with the brand. Thus store loyalty rather than brand loyalty may be the emerging pattern of the future.

Though this trend may continue, it does not preclude the manufacturer of branded products from seeking alternative ways of developing a dialogue with consumers and through that creating a different type of relationship. Some companies, for instance, have sought to establish direct-to-consumer channels to complement existing indirect channels. In many cases the Internet has given brand owners easy access to consumers. For example, in the United States Procter & Gamble has established Reflect.com to offer customised cosmetics and related products to end users. Clearly there are potential problems of channel conflict if these new channels are seen to compete with existing channels. The growing use of database marketing (DBM) can help companies understand and communicate with customers who have specific characteristics and attributes. Using data from a number of sources and increasingly sophisticated software, it is possible to zero in on relatively small groups of customers with similar profiles. This direct marketing allows companies to develop a much more targeted approach.

Making use of computerised customer information files which are constructed on a 'relational' basis (that is, different elements of information can be brought together from separate files) enables the marketer to target more precisely the message to the individual customer or prospective customer.

But it is the rapid growth of detailed information on individual customers combined with computer technology that has made DBM a reality. A major spur to the use of DBM in consumer markets particularly has come through the fast developing field of 'geo-demographics'.

Geo-demographics is the generic term applied to the construction of relational databases which draw together data on demographic variables (such as age, sex and location), socio-economic variability (occupation and income, for example), purchase behaviour, lifestyle information and, indeed, any data that might usefully describe the characteristics of an individual customer.

DBM also allows companies to personalise customer communication much more precisely, making direct mail more specific and relevant to the recipient. Catalogues, newsletters and even magazines can be tailored to the known interests and preferences of the individual. The use of DBM is spreading, particularly in the service sector. Frequent-flyer programmes and hotel club schemes have been around for some time, but companies are now developing their potential more fully. So not only do companies know all about an individual's purchase behaviour, they can correlate it with background information they have already collected on that individual. They can enhance relationships with customers through customising the service they offer them – for example, seating and food preferences on an airline or room preferences in a hotel can easily be catered for.

Fast-moving consumer goods (FMCG) companies are increasingly able to pinpoint likely targets for their products through the use of DBM. But what is more important is that they can use it to strengthen relationships with key customers by designing promotions and incentives that will bind customers more closely to them. More and more consumer durables companies are using DBM to improve customer retention rates. Many car companies, for example, collect information on their customers when they buy a car and then use this information to manage the relationship with them afterwards.

Market segmentation

In both b2b and b2c marketing, market segmentation can be a powerful aid to successful relationship marketing. A market segment is a distinct sub-group within the overall marketplace. Once companies understand the distinctive characteristics of segments, they can adopt a much more targeted approach to developing and implementing marketing strategies.

Market segmentation essentially involves dividing a total market up into a series of sub-markets (or market segments). A market segmentation exercise involves considering the alternative bases for segmentation, choosing specific segments (or a single segment) within that base, and determining appropriate marketing strategies for these segments. Organisations typically use three criteria to select target segments. Market segments should be:

■ *accessible* – companies should be able to communicate with segment markets with a minimum of overlap with other segments, and distribution channels should be available to reach them;

- *measurable* – companies should be able to measure or estimate the size of the segment and quantify the impact of varying marketing mix strategies on that segment;
- *potentially profitable* – the segment should be potentially profitable enough to make it financially worthwhile to service.

Markets may be segmented in many ways, but the following categories are the most important.

B2b segmentation

Segmentation by service

This approach is concerned with how customers respond to service offerings. Companies can offer a range of different service options, and provide different service levels within those options, giving them considerable scope to design service packages appropriate to different market segments. If a supplier measures the perceived importance of different customer service elements across market segments, they can respond to that segment's identified needs and allocate an appropriate service offering to it.

Segmentation by value sought

As we pointed out earlier in our discussion about customer value, different customers may respond differently to the seller's 'value proposition'. Knowing what customers value and what weight they put on the different elements of a value proposition can help a company develop more targeted solutions. It is critical to have a deep understanding of the motivations behind the purchase decision.

Segmentation by industry type

The segmentation of markets on the basis of Standard Industrial Classification (SIC) is quite widespread, but of only limited use. Sometimes these segments are thought of as 'vertical' markets and defined around business sectors such as the construction industry, or the telecoms industry, for example. The problem with this type of segmentation is that it provides no guide as to how the behaviour of buyers might differ simply because they happen to be in different industries.

B2c segmentation

Geographic segmentation

This approach differentiates customers on the basis of where they live. So customers may be segmented into urban, suburban or rural groups, for example. Customers are commonly segmented by postcodes, which might also represent different groups in terms of relative wealth, and socio-economic and other factors.

Demographic and socio-economic segmentation

Demographic and socio-economic segmentation is based on a wide range of factors including age, sex, family size, income, education, social class and ethnic origins. So it is helpful in indicating the profile of people who buy a company's product or services.

Psychographic segmentation

Psychographic segmentation involves analysing lifestyle characteristics, attitudes and personality. Recent research in several countries suggests that the population can be divided into between ten and fifteen groups, each of which has an identifiable set of lifestyle, attitude and personality characteristics.

Benefit segmentation

Benefit segmentation groups customers together on the basis of the benefits they are seeking from a product. For example, car buyers seek widely varying benefits, from fuel economy, size and boot space, to performance, reliability or prestige.

Usage segmentation

Usage segmentation is a very important variable for many products. It usually divides consumers into heavy users, medium users, occasional users and non-users of the product or service in question. Marketers are often concerned with the heavy user segment.

Loyalty segmentation

Loyalty segmentation involves identifying customers' loyalty to a brand or product. Customers tend to be very loyal, moderately loyal or disloyal. These groups are then examined to try to identify any common characteristics so that the product can be targeted at prospectively loyal customers.

Occasion segmentation

Occasion segmentation recognises that customers may use a product or brand in different ways depending on the situation. For example, a beer drinker may drink light beer with his colleagues after work, a conventional beer in his home and a premium or imported beer at a special dinner in a licensed restaurant.

We would advise both b2c and b2b companies to categorise markets according to value preferences, at least initially, when developing a market segmentation strategy in the context of relationship marketing. If organisations understand what different customers value and how this influences their purchase decisions, then they can subsequently see if those value preferences correlate with other segmentation criteria.

Once a business has determined the relevant segmentation base (or bases), it can then identify the market segments or sub-groups within the buyer, intermediary and consumer levels in the distribution chain. After that it can examine the opportunities these segments afford, identify the most attractive segments and develop appropriate strategies for winning and retaining customers within them.

The relationship management chain

Organisations making the transition from classical, transactional-based marketing to closer relationship-focused marketing need to assemble carefully many different pieces of the jigsaw. We have briefly described some of these pieces, such as the value delivery process and market segmentation. We use the idea of the 'relationship management chain' to bring them together. We explain the relationship management chain in greater detail in Chapter 6, but the key activities within it are shown in Figure 1.10.

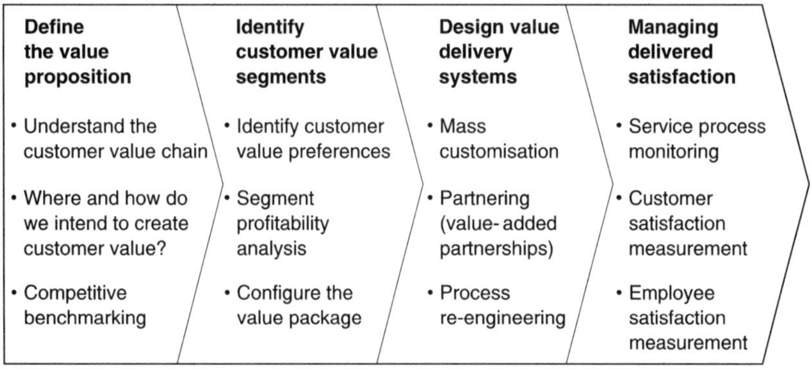

Define the value proposition	Identify customer value segments	Design value delivery systems	Managing delivered satisfaction
• Understand the customer value chain	• Identify customer value preferences	• Mass customisation	• Service process monitoring
• Where and how do we intend to create customer value?	• Segment profitability analysis	• Partnering (value-added partnerships)	• Customer satisfaction measurement
• Competitive benchmarking	• Configure the value package	• Process re-engineering	• Employee satisfaction measurement

FIGURE 1.10 Key activities in the relationship management chain

The idea behind the chain is that relationships are based on the exchange of value between customers and suppliers. The key activities in the chain follow a four-stage process:

1 Defining the value proposition.
2 Identifying appropriate customer value segments.
3 Designing value delivery systems.
4 Managing and maintaining delivered satisfaction.

These four stages should be seen as closely connected elements of a dynamic process, and companies will need to reassess and re-engineer relationship strategies continually as the nature of the market and customer requirements change.

Markets today are much more volatile and fluid than in the past, so both the definitions of value and the means of delivering that value will have to change.

SUMMARY

The change in orientation that we have described carries significant implications for the way marketing activity is organised. As the business becomes more focused around processes, marketing will be forced out of its functional silo to become a pan-company concern.[24] One of the biggest hurdles to becoming customer driven is the entrenched functional hierarchies that dominate much of industry. Customer value is created only through processes, so it makes sense that the process rather than the functional task should provide the foundation for the organisational structure.

A corporate culture that recognises that the delivery of customer and consumer value is the primary purpose of the business has to underpin any successful relationship marketing strategy. The structure of the organisation, its performance measurement system and its reward mechanisms must reflect this culture.

In Chapter 2 we explore in greater detail ways in which the business can leverage the delivery of value to customers to create greater value for itself through a deeper understanding of the customer acquisition and retention process.

Relationship marketing is more than a 'makeover' for conventional marketing. It is, in effect, a new model for how the organisation as a whole competes in the marketplace. This book is based on that fundamental notion.

References

1   Kotler, P. (1967), *Marketing Management: Analysis, Planning and Control*, 1st edn, Englewood Cliffs: Prentice Hall.

2   See, for example: Palda, K. (1969), *Economic Analysis for Marketing Decisions*, Englewood Cliffs: Prentice Hall.

3   See, for example: Robinson, P.J. (1967), *Industrial Buying and Creative Marketing*, Alwyn and Bacon.

4   See for example: Cowell, D. (1984), *The Marketing of Services*, Oxford: Butterworth-Heinemann.

5   See, for example: Lovelock, C.H. and Weinberg, C.B. (1984), *Marketing for Public and Non-Profit Managers*, John Wiley.

6   'Disloyalty becomes the norm', *Marketing*, 21st June 2001, pp 24–5.

7   Brady, J. and Davis, I. (1993), 'Marketing in Transition', *McKinsey Quarterly*, No. 2, pp 17–28.

8   *The Economist* (1994), 'Death of the Brand Manager', 9th April, 79–88.

9   Berry, L.L. (1983), 'Relationship marketing' in Berry, L.L., Shostack, G.C. and Upah, G.D. (eds), *Emerging Perspectives on Services Marketing*, Chicago, IL: American Management Association, pp 25–28.

10   Christopher, M., Payne, A. and Ballantyne, D. (1991), *Relationship Marketing*, Oxford: Butterworth-Heinemann.

11   Peppers, T. and Rogers, M. (1997), *Enterprise One-to-One*, New York: Doubleday.

12   The Boston Consulting Group (1968), *Perspectives on Experience*, Boston, MA.

13   Borden, N. (1965), The Concept of the Marketing Mix, in Schwartz, G. (ed.) *Science in Marketing*, New York: John Wiley.

14   Peck, H., Payne, A., Christopher, M. and Clark, M. (1999), *Relationship Marketing: Strategy and Implementation*, Oxford: Butterworth-Heinemann.

15   Davenport, T. (1993), *Process Innovation: Re-engineering Work Through Information Technology*, Harvard Business School Press.

16   Christopher, M.G. (1999), The Agile Supply Chain: Competing in Volatile Markets, *Industrial Marketing Management*, **29**.

17   Webster, F.E. and Wind, Y. (1972), *Organisational Buying Behaviour*, Prentice Hall.

18   Gale, B. (1994), *Managing Customer Value*, New York: Free Press, p.xiv.

19   Naumann, E. and Kordupleski, R. (1995), *Customer Value Toolkit*, first edition, South-Western College Publishing.

20   Lanning, M.J. and Michaels, E.G. (1998), 'A Business is a Value Delivery System', *McKinsey Staff Paper*, June.

21   Vandermerwe, S. (1996), *The Eleventh Commandment*, Chichester: John Wiley.

22   Pine, J. (1993), *Mass Customization*, Boston, MA: Harvard Business School Press.

23   Ellram, L.M. (1999), Framework for Total Cost of Ownership, *International Journal of Logistics Management*, **4**, No. 2, 49–60.

24   McDonald, M., Christopher, M., Knox, S. and Payne, A. (2001), *Creating a Company for Customers*, London: Pearson.

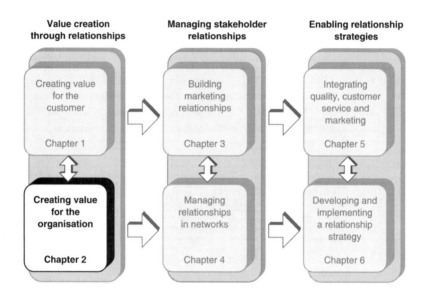

INTRODUCTION

The value-creation process consists of the three key elements shown in Figure 2.1 – determining what value the company can provide to its customers (the 'value customer receives'); determining the value the organisation receives from its customers (the 'value organisation receives'); and, by successfully managing this value exchange, maximising the lifetime value of desirable customer segments. Chapter 1 considered customer value from the perspective of how to create and deliver value to customers. This chapter examines the value-creation process in terms of creating value for the organisation. It then outlines an approach to identifying the customer needs and service strategies that both match service requirements and take into account the economic value of customer segments to the organisation.

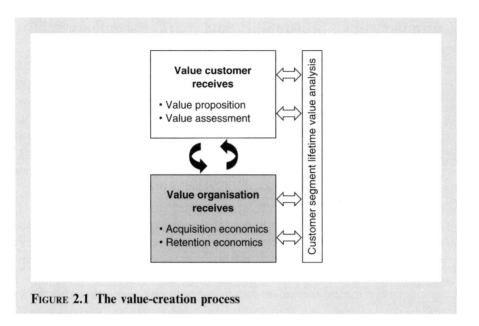

FIGURE 2.1 The value-creation process

The customer's value to the organisation is the *outcome* of providing and delivering superior value to the customer; deploying improved acquisition and retention strategies; and utilising effective channel management. Understanding the economics of customer acquisition and retention and their relationship with customer lifetime value is fundamental to the concept of customer value in this context, as is identifying opportunities for cross-selling, up-selling and building customer advocacy. It is particularly important to address value from a customer segment point of view rather than taking an aggregated approach.

This chapter explores the value the organisation receives from the customer. First, we review the importance of understanding customer value and profitability from a market segment and individual customer perspective. Second, we examine the relationship marketing ladder of customer loyalty. Third, we discuss the economics of customer acquisition. Fourth, we examine the economics of customer retention and customer lifetime value analysis. Finally, we outline a framework for developing a segmented service strategy that considers both the value the customer receives and the value the organisation receives.

Customer value, profitability and market segments

Segmentation is perhaps the most important aspect of value creation from a relationship marketing perspective, as it provides the opportunity to tailor the offer to the needs of specific segments. Carefully segmenting the market and developing an approach that maximises the value of your most desirable customer segments and the corresponding lifetime value that these customer groups produce for your company, lies at the heart of the value-creation process.

> Segmentation is perhaps the most important aspect of value creation.

Market segmentation is important from both the perspectives of value shown in Figure 2.1. First, as we explained in Chapter 1, market segmentation is essential in order for companies to target relevant offers and value propositions to specific groups. Second, it is critical to understand the existing profitability of customer segments (and, in certain businesses, the profitability of individual customers) and initiate action to realise the potential profitability of those segments and consequently improve customer lifetime value.

It is perhaps surprising that most companies focus on identifying the profitability of products rather than customers,[1] when it is customers who generate profits, not products. Products create costs but customers create profits. This distinction is more than mere semantics. We find that the difference between profit and loss is typically determined *after* the product is manufactured. The costs of storing, moving and supporting products are significant. Customers differ widely in their requirements for delivery service, in their ordering patterns and, indeed, in the products they purchase. Each product has its own unique profile of margin, value/density, volume and handling requirements. Similarly, customers will order different product mixes, will have their own unique requirements as to the number of delivery points and, of course, the number of times they order, and the complexity of their orders will differ. Putting all these factors together can produce widely differing cost implications for the supplier.

The so-called 'Pareto Law', or 80/20 rule, tells us not only that 80 per cent of the total sales volume of a business is generated by just 20 per cent of its customers, but also that 80 per cent of the total costs of servicing all the customers will probably be incurred by only 20 per cent of the customers (but probably not the same 20 per cent).

Figure 2.2 illustrates the shape of the profit distribution resulting from the uneven spread of revenues across the customer base. From this example you can see the 'tail' of customers who are actually unprofitable and who therefore reduce total profit contribution. It is essential to understand into which segment these customers fit.

One of the key tenets of relationship marketing is that ideally the firm should only seek intense relationships with customers in segments that are, or have the potential to become, very profitable. So being able to create customer segment profit and loss accounts is fundamental to a successful relationship marketing strategy. And suppliers need to create individual profit and loss accounts for their large corporate customers.

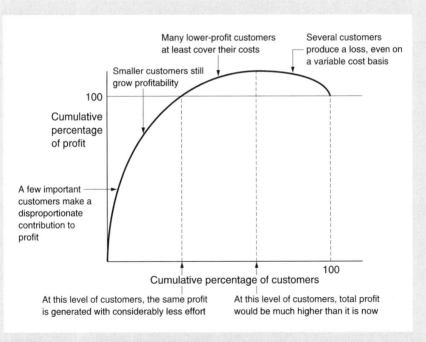

FIGURE 2.2 Customer profitability analysis
Source: Based on Christopher[1]

The problem is that traditional accounting systems make it difficult, if not impossible, to identify the true costs of serving individual customers. Companies often assume that there is an 'average' cost of serving a customer, thus forgoing the opportunity to target those customers or segments that have real potential for transforming their own bottom line.

Why should customers differ in their real profitability?

The first reason why customers' profitability differs is that different customers will often buy a different mix of products. Because individual products have different gross margins, the mix of products customers buy will affect those customers' particular profitability.

But there are also substantial differences in the costs of servicing individual customers. As we have already noted, profitability is largely determined by what happens *after* the point of production.

The costs of service begin with the order itself: how much time does the sales person spend with the customer? is there a key account manager who spends their time wholly or in part working with that customer? what commissions do we pay on these sales? and so forth.

Then there are the order processing costs which themselves differ according to the number of lines on the order, the number of orders and their complexity. Beyond this there are transport costs, materials handling costs and often – particularly if goods are held on a dedicated basis for a customer, such as own-label products – inventory and warehousing costs.

With large corporate customers, suppliers often allocate specific funds for customer promotions, advertising support, additional discounts and the like. Promotions – a special pack for a particular retailer, for instance – will often carry additional hidden costs to the supplier. For example, the disruption to production schedules and the additional inventory holding cost is rarely accounted for or assigned to customers.

The basic principle of customer profitability analysis is that the supplier should seek to assign all costs that are specific to individual accounts. A useful test to apply when looking at these costs is to ask: What costs would I *avoid* if I didn't do business with this customer? The benefit of using the principle of 'avoidability' is that many costs of servicing customers are actually shared among several or many customers. The warehouse is a good example: unless the supplier could release warehousing space for other purposes then it would be incorrect to allocate a proportion of the total warehousing costs to a particular customer.

A checklist of costs a manufacturing company might include when drawing up the 'profit and loss account' for specific customers is given in Figure 2.3.

Although it may be impractical to undertake such analysis for individual accounts, organisations should be able to select a sample of representative customers in order to gain a view of the relative costs

Revenues   Net sales value
Less
Costs
(attributable costs only)

- Cost of sales (actual product mix)
- Commissions
- Sales calls
- Key account management time
- Trade bonuses and special discount
- Order processing costs
- Promotional costs (visible and hidden)
- Merchandising costs
- Non-standard packaging/unitisation
- Dedicated inventory holding costs
- Dedicated warehouse space
- Materials handling costs
- Transport costs
- Documentation/communications costs
- Returns/refusals
- Trade credit (actual payment period)

FIGURE 2.3 The customer profit and loss account
Source: Based on Christopher[1]

associated with different types of accounts, distribution channels and market segments.

The recommended procedure for implementing customer profitability analysis is highlighted in the flow chart shown as Figure 2.4.

What often emerges from customer profitability studies is that the largest customers in terms of volume, or even revenue, may not be the most profitable because they cost so much to service. Although these larger customers may gain bigger volume-based discounts, they require more frequent deliveries to more dispersed locations and they may insist on non-standard pallets, for example.

What ultimately should be the purpose of this analysis? Ideally we require all our customers to be profitable in the medium to long term and where customers currently are profitable we should seek to build and extend that profitability further.

The customer profitability matrix illustrated in Figure 2.5 provides some generalised guidance for strategic direction.

Briefly, the appropriate strategies for each quadrant of the matrix are:

- **Build:** These customers are relatively cheap to service but their net sales value is low. Can you increase volume without proportionately increasing the costs of service? Can you direct the sales team to seek to influence these customers' purchases towards a more profitable sales mix?
- **Danger zone:** You should look at these customers very carefully. Is there any medium- to long-term prospect of a strategic reason for keeping them? Do you need them for their volume even if their profit contribution is low?
- **Cost engineer:** These customers could be more profitable if the costs of servicing them could be reduced. Is there any scope for increasing drop sizes? Can deliveries be consolidated? Would developing new accounts in the same geographic area make delivery more economic? Is there a cheaper way of gathering orders from these customers, such as via telesales?
- **Protect:** High net-sales-value customers who are relatively cheap to service are worth their weight in gold. You should seek relationships with these customers which will make them less likely to turn

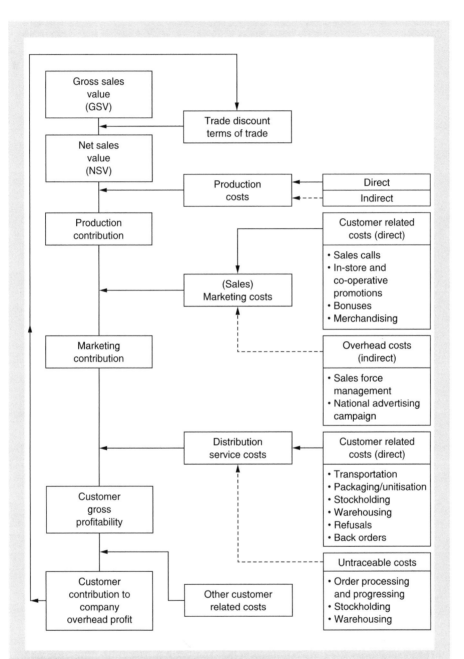

FIGURE 2.4 Customer profitability flow chart
Source: Based on Christopher[1]

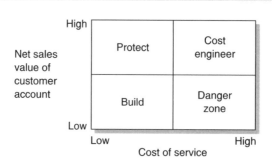

FIGURE 2.5 The customer profitability matrix
Source: Based on Christopher[1]

to alternative suppliers. At the same time you should constantly seek opportunities to develop the volume of business that you do with these customers, while keeping strict control of costs.

Ideally the organisation should seek to develop an accounting system that routinely collects and analyses customer profitability data. Unfortunately most accounting systems are product rather than customer focused. Likewise, costs are traditionally reported on a functional rather than a transactional basis. So, for example, we know the costs of the transport function as a whole or of making a particular product. But we do not know the costs of delivering a specific mix of product to a particular customer.

Businesses have to define more clearly the value they want to provide for their chosen customer segments and then focus on ways to deliver that value most cost-effectively.

Why relationship development adds value

> Existing customers are easier to sell to and are frequently more profitable.

In mature markets, and as competition intensifies, it becomes imperative for organisations to recognise that existing customers are easier to sell to and are frequently more profitable. But though managers may agree intellectually with this view, the practices within their organisations often tell a different story. They take existing customers for granted, while focusing their attention and resources on attracting new customers. Only when there is a breakdown in service quality and the customer leaves or is on the point of leaving does the company turn its attention to existing customers.

There are a number of examples of organisations that have invested too heavily in unselective customer acquisition only to find they have attracted a customer base that may be unprofitable and is not appropriate for further development. For example, some suppliers in the competitive mobile telephony market have gained many low-usage customers through undiscriminating advertising and poor customer targeting. As a consequence, customers have left in droves (up to 50 per cent a year in some segments) and profitability has plummeted.

Companies need to apply different strategies to new and existing customers and allocate differing portions of the marketing budget to them. The way funds are divided between new and existing customers will depend on a number of industry and company-specific factors. A start-up company, or one in a growing market or fledgling industry, will need to spend considerable resources on developing new customers, for example, while a well-established company in a mature market will need to focus primarily on retaining existing customers and intermediaries. But though the markets in most developed economies are mature, many companies still spend too much of their time and money on acquiring customers and too little on keeping them.

The relationship marketing ladder of loyalty

Experience suggests that most companies direct the greater part of their marketing activity at winning new customers. But while businesses need new customers, they must also ensure that they are directing enough of their marketing effort at existing customers. Those companies that focus too much on marketing to new customers often experience the 'leaking bucket' effect, where they lose customers because they are directing insufficient marketing activity generally, and customer service specifically, at them. Davidow has highlighted this problem: 'It has always been incredible to me how insensitive companies can be to their customers. Most of them don't seem to understand that their future business depends on having the same customer come back again and again'.[2] Too many companies, having secured a customer's order, then turn their attention to seeking new customers without understanding the importance of maintaining and enhancing the relationships with their existing customers.

The relationship marketing ladder of loyalty, illustrated in Figure 2.6, identifies the different stages of relationship development. Sales management and charity marketing have used such ladders for many years.[3] The ladder is relevant for all groups within a company's distribution chain – buyers, intermediaries and consumers. We go on to discuss these groups in more detail in Chapter 3, where we refer to them collectively as 'the customer market domain'.

The first task is to move a 'prospect' up to the first rung to a 'purchaser'. The next objective is to turn the new purchaser into a 'client' who purchases regularly, and then a 'supporter' of the company and its products. The next step is to create 'advocates' who provide powerful

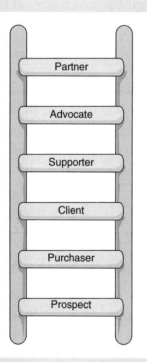

Partner: someone who has the relationship of a partner with you

Advocate: someone who actively recommends you to others, who does your marketing for you

Supporter: someone who likes your organisation, but only supports you passively

Client: someone who has done business with you on a repeat basis but may be negative, or at best neutral, towards your organisation

Purchaser: someone who has done business just once with your organisation

Prospect: someone whom you believe may be persuaded to do business with you

FIGURE 2.6 **The relationship marketing ladder of loyalty**

word-of-mouth endorsement for a company. In a business-to-business context an advocate may ultimately develop into a 'partner' who is closely linked in a trusting and sharing relationship with the supplier.

But it is not necessarily desirable to progress a relationship with every customer. Some customers or customer segments may not justify the investment needed to develop a 'supporter' or 'advocate' relationship, as it may prove too costly to do so. Frequently an organisation may need to change its marketing activities and increase marketing expenditure on the relationship building elements of the marketing mix. Managers therefore need to consider the existing and potential lifetime value of customers and determine whether it is appropriate to make this commitment.

The role of advocacy

The 'advocate' level on the relationship marketing ladder of customer loyalty is worthy of special emphasis. Referrals from customers are among the most relevant, effective and believable sources of information for other customers. A number of researchers have argued that word-of-mouth is the most effective source of information for consumers. While commercial sources normally inform the buyer, personal sources legitimise or evaluate products for them. Ligitimisation makes the step of converting prospects into customers on the ladder of loyalty that much easier.

Research by Jones and Sasser has found that, except in rare cases, total or complete customer satisfaction is key to securing customer loyalty, and that there is a tremendous difference between the loyalty of merely satisfied and completely satisfied customers. They cite Xerox research that found totally satisfied customers were six times more likely than satisfied customers to repurchase Xerox products and services over the following eighteen months. In discussing the measurement of loyalty, they point out that:[4]

> Customer referrals, endorsements, and spreading the word are extremely important forms of consumer behaviour for a company. In many product and service categories, word of mouth is one of the most important factors in acquiring new customers. Frequently, it is easier for a customer to respond honestly to a question about whether he or she would recommend the product or service to others than to a

question about whether he or she intended to repurchase the product or service. Such indications of loyalty, obtained through customer surveys, are frequently ignored because they are soft measures of behaviour that are difficult to link to eventual purchasing behaviour.

Which companies have a high proportion of customers who make such referrals and endorsement and exhibit advocacy? Discussions with many consumers and marketing executives suggest the following as examples:

- Airlines: Virgin Atlantic, Southwest (a US airline)
- Banking: First Direct
- Computers: Dell Computer
- Healthcare: Shouldice (a Canadian hospital)
- Industrial services: Service Master (a US cleaning services company)
- Motor cars: Lexus, Mercedes
- Retailing: Nordstroms (a US retailer)
- Trucks: Scania, Volvo
- Watches: Rolex

But neither company practice nor academic research pay sufficient attention to the important area of advocacy and referral marketing. Few organisations have any formal processes that utilise referrals from existing customers. Though many organisations recognise that customers can be the most legitimate source of referrals to their prospective customers, most tend simply to let referrals happen rather than proactively developing marketing activities to leverage the power of advocacy.

Virgin Atlantic is an interesting example of this. In a recent executive seminar in the UK, 120 managers were asked to indicate whether they were advocates of various commercial organisations. Around 20 per cent claimed to be advocates of Virgin Atlantic, including five people who had never flown with the airline. Subsequently, one of the authors asked Sir Richard Branson to what extent he sought to leverage this advocacy. 'It just happens and we enjoy the benefits of it,' Sir Richard replied. We believe companies should adopt a more proactive approach to leveraging the power of advocates and try to reap benefits beyond ad hoc recommendations. We shall return to the role of advocacy as an important element of referral marketing in Chapter 3.

Customer acquisition and its economics

As noted above, the economics of customer acquisition and retention play a major role in creating value for the organisation and ultimately in the lifetime value of major customer segments. In this and the following sections we examine the economics of both acquisition and retention.

The importance of customer acquisition varies considerably according to a company's specific situation. For example, a new market entrant to the fast-paced world of e-business will focus primarily on acquiring customers, while an established manufacturing company operating in a mature market may be more concerned with retaining them.

Improving the customer acquisition process is typically concerned with:

- acquiring customers at a lower cost;
- acquiring more customers for the same (or less cost);
- acquiring more attractive customers;
- acquiring customers utilising new channels.

The first step towards understanding customer value from the perspective of the supplier organisation is to determine how much the organisation currently spends acquiring customers within its existing channels, and how these costs vary across different segments or micro-segments.

Customer acquisition at Electro plc

To illustrate the economics of both customer acquisition and retention we will use an example from Electro plc, a fictional company based on a large UK electricity supplier.[5] From the late 1990s the residential sector of the market changed substantially as a result of electricity companies being able for the first time to sell electricity outside their traditional geographic boundaries. Electro faced competition within its own territory from other electricity providers, but now could also market its services outside its traditional geography.

Electro segmented its customer base and identified four key market segments. Each of these displayed different characteristics in terms of socio-economic grouping, expected switching behaviour and customer profiles.

Electro collected the data it needed to analyse its customer acquisition and retention economics at the segment level. The data included: the number of existing customers within each segment; annual customer acquisition targets with reference to the total UK customer base; the cost of acquisition (per customer); and estimates of profit per customer per annum for each segment. It also considered the likely annual retention rates in the new competitive environment. It estimated different levels of retention for each segment, and one scenario of the broad characteristics of these segments is shown in Figure 2.7. Some of the figures stated have been adjusted to protect proprietary information.

As shown in Figure 2.7, Electro estimated the acquisition costs per customer at the segment level to be:

Segment 1 – 'struggling empty nest super-loyals' – £110;
Segment 2 – 'older settled marrieds' – £70;

Segment number	Segment name	No. existing customers	Acquisition target for year	Cost of acquisition	Annual retention rate (%)	Profit per customer per year
Segment 1	Struggling empty nest super-loyals	421 300	500	£110	96	£6
Segment 2	Older settled marrieds	618 000	66 000	£70	94	£9
Segment 3	Switchable middles	497 900	110 000	£55	90	£18
Segment 4	Promiscuous averages	459 600	220 000	£30	80	£22

FIGURE 2.7 Customer segment data template for Electro plc

Segment 3 – 'switchable middles' – £55;
Segment 4 – 'promiscuous averages' – £30.

But to make the comparison of acquisition costs meaningful, you also have to consider the expected profitability of the average customer in each segment along with the overall profit potential of each segment.

The profit per customer per annum in Segment 1 (the 'struggling empty nest super-loyals') was £6, making a break-even of 18.3 years. As this segment comprises elderly people, many of the customers will die before they break even. In the case of Segment 4 (the 'promiscuous averages') the profit per customer per annum was £22, making a break-even of 1.36 years. This segment is highly attractive in terms of acquisition economics, especially if a company puts in place relationship marketing strategies to retain customers successfully.

Unfortunately, many organisations operating in consumer markets still do not differentiate their customer profitability analysis activities at the segment level. As Electro used to, they contact each prospect the same number of times, rather than applying a level of effort consistent with each prospect's cost of acquisition and profit potential. This is not only a wasted investment, it can also annoy customers who are getting either too much or too little attention.

Acquisition across different channels

> Electronic communication channels enable companies to acquire customers at a fraction of the cost of using more traditional channels.

Once they have determined the acquisition costs for different segments, companies then need to consider how acquisition costs may vary across different channels. The advent of websites and electronic communication channels has enabled companies to acquire customers at a fraction of the cost of using more traditional channels such as direct mail.

In the business-to-business sector, RS Components – a leading international supplier of electrical components and other products – understands extremely well the cost and customer service benefits of using the Internet alongside its more conventional channels. The company deals with its customers through physical branches, a call centre and, more recently, a highly sophisticated and personalised website. It has acquired a significant number of new customers and improved its profitability as a result of its Internet-based sales channel.

In the business-to-consumer sector, frozen food retailer Iceland also supplemented its traditional sales channels with a website. The initiative has proved highly successful, helping Iceland acquire customers from the more affluent segment that was not well represented in its existing customer base. What is more, the average order size of these online customers was higher and more profitable than that of the company's more traditional customers who shopped in its retail branches.

Improving customer acquisition

Equipped with a sound understanding of how acquisition costs vary at both the segment and channel levels, companies can then seek to acquire more, and more attractive, customers more cheaply. Companies can often improve their customer acquisition by acting on insights drawn from developing a customer value proposition. More refined promotional campaigns and encouraging customer referrals can also attract customers who meet its target criteria. First Direct, the leading UK bank, boasts the highest levels of advocacy in the retail banking sector. Approximately one-third of all its customers join as a direct result of customer referral – which carries the added bonus of reducing First Direct's average customer acquisition cost.

Customer retention and its economics

Writers and researchers have suggested that it costs around five times more to win a new customer than it does to keep an existing one. Yet, as we have pointed out, many companies have traditionally focused their marketing activity on acquiring new customers, rather than retaining existing customers. This may be due to the historical convention in many companies that rewards customer acquisition to a much greater extent than customer retention, or it may be caused by a lack of understanding of why customer retention can be such a boon to commercial profitability.

The profit impact of customer retention improvement

While most companies recognise that customer retention is important, relatively few understand the economics of customer retention within their own firm. Until fairly recently, there was little research that critically evaluated the relative financial benefits of customer acquisition versus customer retention. In 1990 Fred Reichheld and Earl Sasser, respectively a partner at consulting firm Bain & Co and a professor at Harvard Business School, published some revealing research demonstrating the financial impact of customer retention.[6] They found even a small increase in customer retention produced a dramatic and positive effect on profitability: a five percentage points increase in customer retention yielded a disproportionate improvement in profitability in net present value (NPV) terms. Increasing the customer retention rate from, say, 85 per cent to 90 per cent resulted in NPV profits rising from 35 per cent to 95 per cent among the businesses they examined. Later research showed this figure could be as high as 125 per cent, as shown in Figure 2.8.

These findings have been very influential in drawing attention to the critical role customer retention plays in developing a relationship marketing strategy.

The impact of retention on profitability

Why should retention have such a great effect on profitability? Reichheld and Sasser[6] suggested a number of reasons to explain their findings:

- Acquiring new customers involves costs that can be significant and it may take some years to turn a new customer into a profitable customer.
- As customers become more satisfied and confident in their relationship with a supplier, they are more likely to give the supplier a larger proportion of their business, or 'share of wallet'.
- As the relationship with a customer develops, there is greater mutual understanding and collaboration, which produces efficiencies that lower operating costs. Sometimes customers are willing to integrate their IT systems, including planning, ordering and scheduling, with those of their suppliers, and this further reduces costs.

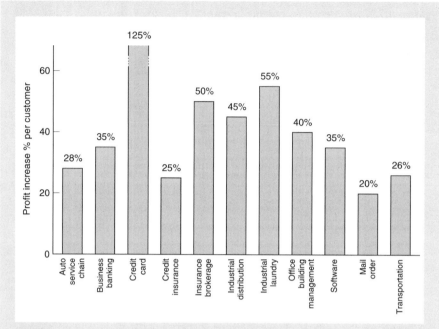

FIGURE 2.8 Profit impact of a 5 percentage points increase in customer retention for selected businesses
Source: based on Bain & Co

- Satisfied customers are more likely to refer others, which promotes profit generation as the cost of acquisition of these new customers is dramatically reduced. In some industries customer advocacy can play a very important role in acquiring new customers, particularly when there is a high risk involved in choosing a supplier.
- Loyal customers can be less price-sensitive and may be less likely to defect due to price increases. This is especially true in business-to-business markets where the relationship with the supplier becomes more valued and switching costs increase.

But companies need to treat measurement systems that provide aggregated measures with caution, as these may overlook individual differences. Companies need measurement systems that allow them to analyse their customer base, identify the profit potential within each segment and then to develop plans, including customer service strategies, to retain the most profitable segments. An important part of this process is establishing the potential profitability. Companies can do this by comparing segment profit increases during the period of time that interests them – five or ten years, say – or by comparing the net present value of the segments.

Relationship marketing – what managers measure

> Management needs to understand the economics of customer acquisition and retention.

We have suggested that management needs to understand the economics of customer acquisition and retention in order to determine both present and future profitability prospects. In particular, they need to be aware of the dramatic impact that customer retention can have on profitability. We now examine the extent to which managers are actually using such measures and focusing on improving customer retention in their businesses.

Research by one of the authors among 200 large UK organisations indicates that many organisations are not allocating their marketing budget appropriately between acquisition and retention activities. The review identified three categories of organisation: 'acquirers', 'retainers' and 'profit maximisers', as shown in Figure 2.9.

'Acquirers' spent too much on customer acquisition activities at the expense of customer retention activities. The majority of firms – 80 per cent – fell into this category. 'Retainers', by contrast, spent too much on customer retention activities at the expense of customer acquisition. This group represented 10 per cent of firms. The 'profit maximisers' represented only 10 per cent of firms in the survey. Only the companies in this last category considered that they had identified and allocated expenditure appropriately between acquisition and retention activities.

Related research examined the extent to which UK managers measure the impact of their relationship marketing strategies. A study of marketing directors and senior marketing managers in large UK organisations suggests that managers have been slow to switch their marketing activities towards customer retention.[7] It surveyed the marketing practices of 225 large UK organisations and revealed that while 41 per cent of marketing budget was spent acquiring customers, just 23 per cent went on retaining them. Some 35 per cent of respondents spent more than 40 per cent of their total marketing budget on acquiring

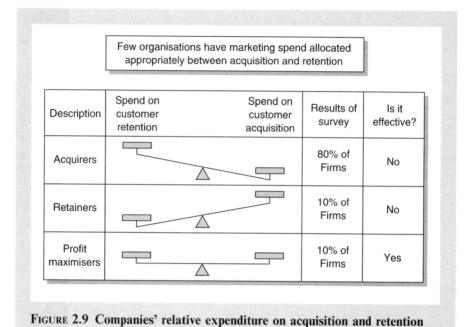

Few organisations have marketing spend allocated appropriately between acquisition and retention

Description	Spend on customer retention	Spend on customer acquisition	Results of survey	Is it effective?
Acquirers			80% of Firms	No
Retainers			10% of Firms	No
Profit maximisers			10% of Firms	Yes

FIGURE 2.9 Companies' relative expenditure on acquisition and retention

customers, while only 7 per cent spent more than 40 per cent on retaining them.

The study also investigated which measures managers considered important and which they used to evaluate their marketing activities. Measures included customer acquisition, customer retention, customer satisfaction, profit per customer and employee satisfaction. Customer acquisition (68.4 per cent) and customer satisfaction (64.4 per cent) were the most frequently measured. Customer retention was measured by 54.2 per cent. Profit per customer was measured by 52 per cent of organisations and 41.3 per cent measured employee satisfaction. It is interesting how few of the organisations surveyed measure *all* the important variables, given the importance of customer retention, the fact that customer and segment profitability vary greatly, and the findings, discussed later in this chapter, of the service profit chain research on the impact of employee satisfaction.[8]

Overall, the study showed that although many organisations understand the importance of customer retention, very few measure the economic value of their customer retention strategies. The study also showed that many organisations are neglecting to develop and use marketing metrics to help direct their relationship marketing strategy. Given that the sample probably represents some of the more sophisticated organisations, the overall picture in industry is probably worse than these findings suggest.

Improving customer retention

Because of the dramatic impact that improved customer retention can have on business profitability and the fact that many organisations continue to place too much emphasis on acquiring customers at the expense of keeping them, organisations clearly need to adopt a structured approach to enhancing their customer retention and profitability levels. There are three major steps in such an approach: measuring customer retention, identifying root causes of defection and key service issues, and developing corrective action to improve retention.

Step 1: Measuring customer retention

> Organisations clearly need to adopt a structured approach to enhancing their customer retention and profitability levels.

Measuring retention rates for existing customers is the first step towards improving customer loyalty and profitability. It involves two major tasks: measuring customer retention rates and analysing profitability by segment.

To measure customer retention, organisations need to analyse a number of dimensions in detail. These include measuring customer retention rates over time, by market segment, and in terms of the product or service offered. If customers buy from a number of suppliers, share of wallet should also be identified.

As a result of this first step, companies should be able to define customer retention clearly, measure present customer retention rates and understand the existing and future profit potential for each market segment.

Step 2: Identifying causes of defection and key service issues

This step involves identifying the underlying reasons why consumers leave the company. Traditional marketing research into customer satisfaction does not always provide accurate answers as to *why* customers abandon one supplier for another. All too often customer satisfaction questionnaires are poorly designed, superficial and fail to address the key issues, forcing respondents to tick pre-determined response choices.

Companies need to identify clearly and understand the root causes of customer defection before they can begin to implement a successful customer retention programme. Highly experienced market researchers are often required to undertake this task.

Step 3: Corrective action to improve retention

The final step in the process of enhancing customer retention involves taking remedial action. At this point, plans to improve retention become highly specific to the organisation concerned and any actions taken will be particular to the given context. Some key elements include: marshalling top management commitment; ensuring employees are satisfied and dedicated to building long-term customer relationships; utilising best practice techniques to improve performance; and developing a plan to implement a customer retention strategy.

Increasingly, organisations recognise that enhanced customer satisfaction leads to better customer retention and profitability. Many organisations are now reviewing their customer service strategies to find ways to boost retention rates as a means of improving their business performance. This often entails a fundamental shift in business emphasis from customer acquisition to customer retention. Achieving the benefits of long-term customer relationships requires a firm commitment from everyone in the organisation to understanding and serving the needs of customers.

Customer retention at Electro plc

Returning to the Electro plc example above we now review the economics of customer retention. Electro reviewed how it could potentially and realistically improve customer retention through a relationship marketing strategy based on improved service and the relative attractiveness of the four segments it had identified. It used the views of several executives who were experienced in this area to identify the following achievable improvement targets:

Segment 1 ('struggling empty nest super-loyals') – 1 per cent,
Segment 2 ('older settled marrieds') – 2 per cent,
Segment 3 ('switchable middles') – 5 per cent, and
Segment 4 ('promiscuous averages') – 9 per cent.

The company used these planned increases in retention rates to model the increase that an improved service strategy would have on 'gross' profit in five and ten years. It then compared this with the base case, as shown in Figure 2.10.

Segment	Existing retention rate		Retention rate with improved service	
	Profit in 5 years (£m)	Profit in 10 years (£m)	Profit in 5 years (£m)	Profit in 10 years (£m)
1	2.697	2.089	2.848	2.331
2	4.477	5.112	5.347	6.692
3	6.377	7.586	9.343	12.704
4	8.167	8.989	14.663	18.828
Total	21.718	23.776	32.201	40.555

FIGURE 2.10 Profit projections with and without improved service

This modelling showed an increase in overall gross profit, before costs of improved service, of 48 per cent at year 5 (from £21.7 million to £32.2 million) and 71 per cent at year 10 (from £23.8 million to £40.6 million). The results within each of the four different segments varied significantly because of differences in planned retention rates and other inputs to the modelling.

Although few organisations evaluate segment profitability in anything other than basic terms, the broad approach is straightforward. It involves understanding the profit potential (gross profit less costs) of a segmented service approach in each segment, and selectively managing the segments to maximise profits.

Improving customer retention does not need to be expensive. The most attractive relationship marketing initiatives are those that the customer values a lot, but cost the supplier little to implement. The first thing organisations should do is consider reallocating existing expenditure to put greater emphasis on those segments with the greatest potential for increasing net present value profitability. This involves no significant increase in costs. The organisation can then identify market segments for additional incremental expenditure, with the objective being to ensure that the overall cost-benefit is significantly enhanced lifetime profitability.

Customer segment lifetime value analysis

The balance between the marketing efforts directed towards new and existing customers will vary greatly depending on whether the business is a start-up such as a 'dot.com', or a mature 'bricks and mortar' company. But in general, as we have seen, marketing expenditure is unbalanced with too much attention being directed at acquiring customers and too little at retaining them.

> A company must look at the projected profit over the life of the account.

Companies need to understand acquisition and retention economics at the segment level in order to make decisions on how much marketing emphasis to place on them. To calculate a customer's real value a company must look at the projected profit over the life of the account. This represents the expected profit flow over a customer's lifetime. The key metric used here is customer lifetime value (CLV), which is defined as the net present value of the future profit flow over a customer's lifetime.

Companies will not want to retain all their customers. Some customers may cost too much to service, or so much to acquire, that they will never prove to be worthwhile and profitable. Clearly, it would be inadvisable to invest further in such customer segments. It is likely that within a given portfolio of customers, there may be some segments that are profitable, some that are at break-even point and some that are unprofitable. So increasing customer retention does not always lead to increases in customer profitability; indeed, in some instances, increasing the retention of unprofitable customers will reduce the company's profits. However, unprofitable customers may be valuable in their contribution towards fixed costs, and businesses need to exercise considerable caution when allocating fixed and variable costs to ensure that customers who make a contribution are not simply discarded.

The minimum data needed for retention modelling are shown in the headings in Figure 2.7. To recap, for each segment or micro-segment, you need to estimate: the number of existing customers; annual customer acquisition targets; the cost of acquisition per customer; and the profit per customer per annum. Changes in these variables over the time period chosen also need to be considered.

We suggest modelling profit on both an annual basis and on a CLV basis, as some managers still find year-on-year profit projections more concrete than discounted cash flows and net present values. Such modelling is important in helping organisations determine customer value in terms of potential profits and CLV. However, few organisations have reached the stage of understanding their *existing* acquisition economics and retention economics, let alone gone beyond it. Those that have can move on to modelling potential future profit improvement for each market segment.

Achieving increased profitability

When organisations model their potential future profit they need to take into account the fact that individual consumers may be persuaded to buy other products – cross-selling – or more of an existing product over time – 'up-selling'. Also, corporate customers tend to buy from a range of suppliers. By improving its service a supplier may be able to increase 'share of wallet' as well as market share, especially through exploiting alternative channel structures such as the Internet.

So far, we have emphasised how companies can manage customer acquisition and retention to improve their profitability. But to become even more profitable they need to develop integrated programmes that address not only acquisition and retention, but also other related activities – such as cross-selling and up-selling – that can improve customer lifetime value.

One approach for reviewing such profit opportunities is the ACURA model shown in Figure 2.11.

ACURA is an acronym for 'acquisition, cross-sell, up-sell, retention and advocacy'.[9] Rarely do companies systematically build strategies that focus on all elements in the ACURA model. While companies seek

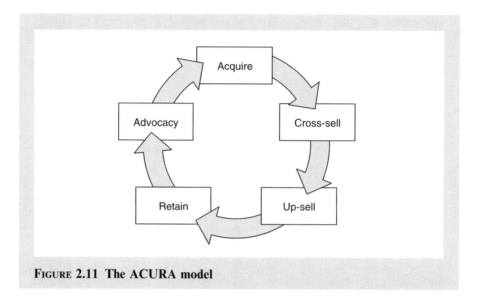

FIGURE **2.11 The ACURA model**

to improve customer acquisition and retention, they also need to exploit cross-selling and up-selling and advocacy opportunities. Companies such as American Express are excellent at cross-selling, McDonald's excels at up-selling; and Virgin Atlantic and First Direct excel at creating advocacy within their customer bases.

For each element of ACURA, companies can usefully review potential strategies to improve profitability by market segment and then identify their potential profit impact. An overview of an exercise for strategies to cross-sell in a supermarket is shown in Figure 2.12.

This approach first identifies generic strategies to improve each element in the ACURA model. It then considers the profit potential of applying these strategies for each different element to different customer segments. Finally, it assesses each relevant strategy in more detail and implements it where appropriate.

Putting it all together: a framework for segmented service strategy

Companies need to take an integrated approach to identifying different customer needs and developing service strategies that both match

Cross-sell	Segment			
	1	2	3	4
Wider product range		£££		
Linked offers				
Special offers		££		£
Loyalty cards		£		
Train staff to link products	£			
Shelf design	£		££	
In-store promotions			£	£
Buy in bulk			£££	£
Oven ready convenience foods				£

FIGURE 2.12 ACURA model cross-selling template for a supermarket

the service requirements and take into account the economic value of customer segments.

We now outline a framework for developing a segmented service strategy, as shown in Figure 2.13. This framework utilises the customer segment and profit potential approaches discussed above as well as some frameworks from the customer service literature. It integrates these elements into a structured approach to relationship marketing that aims to deliver both increased value to the customer and increased value to the organisation.

Step 1: Define the market structure

In order to segment the market properly you need to define the market structure clearly. 'Market mapping' is a technique that can help clarify the market structure and relationships between suppliers, intermediaries and customers. A market map defines the distribution and value-added chain between the suppliers and final users.[10] An example of a market map for an insurance company is shown in Figure 2.14.

Market maps can be used to show the percentage of turnover and the percentage of profit made through each distribution channel and to

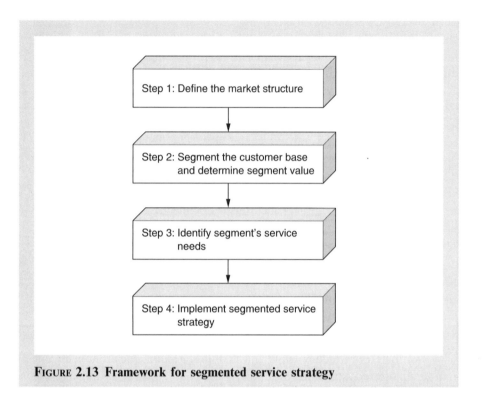

FIGURE 2.13 Framework for segmented service strategy

illustrate the current and future importance of that channel. In the example in Figure 2.14 the insurance brokers and high street branches provide relatively low profit returns because of large commissions and expensive overheads, so the company might decide to try to migrate these customers to direct call centre sales. And those customers who use computers for other forms of shopping might find the e-commerce channel using the Internet appropriate for their needs.

Customers may also interact with more than one channel. For example, Dell Computers has successfully used the Internet to enable customers to identify what model and configuration of computer they want. Although many customers still need to contact the call centre for further information and to purchase the computer, the overall customer acquisition costs for Dell have fallen significantly.

Once the company understands the market structure it can then take the appropriate steps for each channel and make strategic decisions

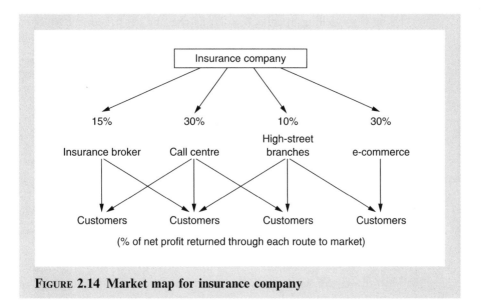

FIGURE 2.14 **Market map for insurance company**

about channel mix, re-channelling and the potential role of disinter-mediation. It needs to develop detailed metrics of market share, sales volume and profitability throughout the market map.

Step 2: Segment the customer base and determine segment value

Step 2 involves segmenting the customer base using appropriate seg-mentation criteria and estimating the value of the customer segments. In the electricity company example above, we described four segments. These segments were identified using criteria such as beha-vioural, usage and lifestyle characteristics. Where the seg-ments identified contain large numbers of customers, it may be appropriate to segment them further into micro-segments. Companies also need to consider channel impli-cations for each segment, derived from the market map.

> Companies also need to consider channel implications for each segment.

For example, a pharmaceuticals distributor we have worked with segmented its customer base by product usage, strength of relationship, and complexity of decision-making unit. Its analysis of the potential value of segments led to it placing new emphasis on its emerging web sales channel and de-emphasising its traditional catalo-gue sales channel.

Using a modelling approach, such as the one described above, companies should then consider customer segments on the basis of their projected lifetime profitability. Each segment (or micro-segment) is analysed using profitability modelling over an appropriate time period. This process involves:

■ Determining the profit projections in each segment.
■ Determining the realistic opportunity for increasing customer retention in each segment and how this may vary across the time period under consideration. (An example of this is shown in the electricity company example above.)
■ Identifying the potential increase in projected 'gross' profits for each period and in lifetime profitability, as a result of improved customer retention.

This allows the segments to be prioritised initially according to their existing and potential expected lifetime value. Finally, the company needs to determine how much it will cost to make the changes in service needed to achieve the improved retention levels, in order to identify net profits for each segment. It may need to re-evaluate the segment priorities at this point.

Step 3: Identify segments' service needs

Step 3 is concerned with investigating the service needs, expectations and performance levels within each customer segment. Companies need to identify performance levels for both themselves and their competitors. Service needs and performance can be determined by a range of market research techniques such as focus groups and in-depth interviews with customers. Tools such as conjoint or trade-off analysis can be used to analyse the results. Using this research, companies can then identify segments with similar service priorities.

The pharmaceuticals company mentioned above used this approach. It found that in its potentially most profitable segments price was relatively unimportant to its customers, compared with speed of delivery and complete orders. Using this information, the company instigated next day delivery and a system of automatic product substitution. Its order fulfilment performance increased dramatically and it significantly cut its inventory replacement time.

Often, research will identify gaps between the customer's requirements and the actual offers available. Companies can use tools such as gap analysis, which we go on to discuss in Chapter 5, to help them understand unfulfilled needs.

Service performance charts[11] can be used to depict comparisons visually. These comparison charts appear to be much more widely used in logistics and customer service than in general marketing, but have considerable potential for helping companies develop a segmented service strategy. An example of such a chart is shown in the segment competitor profile in Figure 2.15. This uses data from the insurance company discussed above.

The segment competitor profile can be used to show customers' perceptions of the performance of the company and its competitors. It also shows the relative importance of each attribute to the customer. The segment performance chart, derived from this segment data and shown in Figure 2.16, provides a simple but visually powerful means of illustrating the customer's perception of the importance of each service attribute or need and how well the company performs against

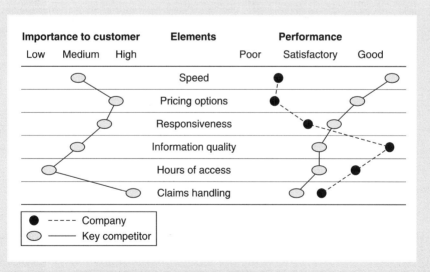

FIGURE **2.15 The segment competitor profile**

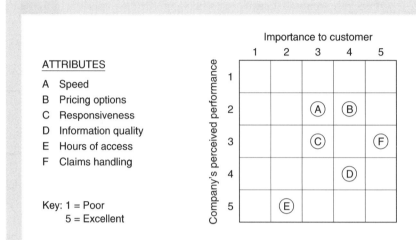

FIGURE **2.16 The segment performance chart**

them. This analysis needs to be undertaken for the company overall and for each market segment.

The attributes depicted in Figures 2.15 and 2.16 are those that are important for the insurance company discussed above. They enable the organisation to identify, overall and by segment, how it measures up against both customers' key performance criteria and customers' perception of their relative importance. Clearly, the organisation must seek to perform well in the areas that are most important to customers.

At this point the organisation should know, overall and for each segment, which are the most important customer criteria and how it is performing relative to its competitors. It can now start to consider to which customer segments its service capabilities and strengths are most suited.

Step 4: Implement segmented service strategy

The final step involves implementing a segmented service strategy based on the existing and potential value of the different customer segments and the organisation's service capabilities and strengths, relative to its competitors. This step involves three stages:

1. Reviewing existing segment performance to identify areas of over-performance and under-performance

If the company does not know which dimensions the customer values, it runs the risk of wasting resources through 'service over-performance' – that is, placing too much emphasis on a service dimension that the customer regards as relatively unimportant. Equally, the company needs to know where there is 'service under-performance' – dimensions where it places little emphasis, but which are important to the customer. These positions and the 'service target corridor' are shown in the service management matrix in Figure 2.17. The company needs to obtain competitive performance data and relative performance data[12] in order to identify areas of weakness (key areas for improvement) and areas of strength (where the company has competitive advantage).

Clearly the company needs to pay most attention to those areas that are most important to the customer and where the company's own performance is weak compared to the competition.

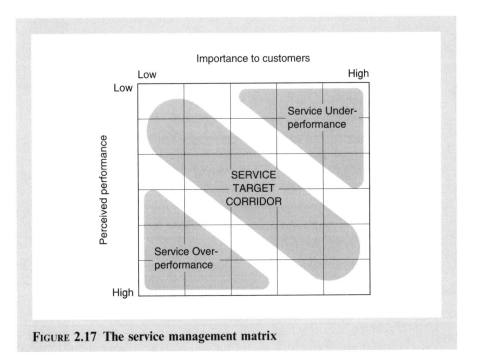

FIGURE 2.17 The service management matrix

2. Identifying costs of selectively improving service levels and fit with the company's capabilities

Based on the segment data the company has identified, it will need to consider five broad strategies:

1. For the most attractive existing segments, where there is a strong fit with the company's capabilities and overall good performance, the decision on where to invest should be clear.
2. Investment should be directed at segments which are not very profitable at present but where there is potential to increase their value.
3. Some segments are of secondary importance, so while strategies may be developed for maintaining the relationship there may be little reason to invest in customer service.
4. In segments where there is low or negative profitability and a poor match with the organisation's capabilities the company may elect to divest or deter customers.
5. For potentially high profit segments, which do not match existing capabilities of the firm, the strategy may not be clear. Should the company invest to improve performance or should it allow these groups to defect if they are dissatisfied with the service on offer?

A company should base decisions regarding these five groups on a review of the following:

- relating current segment performance to the company's capabilities;
- identifying all segments where costs can be saved through service reduction in over-performance areas;
- reallocating these funds to service improvement in under-performance areas based on customer importance and segment priorities;
- estimating additional costs required to reach the customer retention improvement targets, identified in Step 2;
- identifying the potential lifetime profits of segments in 'net' terms (that is, by reducing the potential increase in 'gross' profit calculated in Step 2 by the costs involved in improving retention);
- finalising segment priorities based on the above analysis.

For the potentially high profit segments, which do not match existing capabilities of the firm, each firm will need to make a decision based on its own circumstances. However, several businesses we have worked with have chosen not to pursue such segments. For example, a large telecom network provider has a policy of introducing competitors if its products represent a better solution for the customer.

3. Finalise segmented service strategy plan

> The outcome of the process should be a detailed segmented service strategy plan.

The outcome of the process outlined in this framework should be a detailed segmented service strategy plan that identifies:

- the choice of strategic position in terms of the organisation's 'offer' and the rationale for it;
- which segments are to be emphasised within each channel;
- the overall lifetime profit improvement opportunity based on selective improvement of service and resulting customer retention;
- clear and detailed metrics so that future performance of the relationship marketing strategy is continually monitored and reviewed.

A key element is calculation of the net lifetime value profit potential from implementing a segmented service strategy for each segment.

SUMMARY

Understanding the value-creation process is crucial in turning the outputs of a company's strategy into programmes that both extract and deliver value. If companies place insufficient emphasis on the value they provide to key customers, as opposed to the income they derive from them, they can seriously diminish the impact of the offer in terms of its perceived value to customers. Achieving the ideal equilibrium between giving value to customers and getting value from them is a critical component of relationship marketing and requires the company to manage the perception and projection of value within the reality of acquisition and retention economics.

Relationship marketing, with its focus on building long-term relationships, makes new demands on the measurement systems in organisations. Many organisations are not using appropriate metrics to guide their relationship marketing strategy. In particular, the retention of customers is now recognised as being critical to the profitability of organisations, yet our results show that organisations typically spend less than one quarter of their marketing budget on retaining customers.

> Marketing activity directed at retaining customers can be expensive and needs to be closely evaluated against measured results.

However, marketing activity directed at retaining customers can be expensive and needs to be closely evaluated against measured results. The most successful retention programmes segment customers according to their existing and potential lifetime profitability and identify the type and frequency of marketing activity that should be directed at each segment. More refined segmentation strategies, based on service requirements and relative performance, represent a great opportunity to build greater long-term customer value.

We have emphasised the importance of customers in the process of value creation. But for relationship marketing to be successful, organisations need systematically to consider additional stakeholders – including employees, shareholders, suppliers, alliance partners, the media and others. In Chapter 3 we examine how the organisation can analyse and build stronger relationships with all its key stakeholders.

References

1   This section draws on Christopher, M. (1997), *Marketing Logistics*, Oxford: Butterworth-Heinemann.

2   Davidow, H. (1986), *Marketing High Technology*, Free Press, p. 172.

3   Raphel, M. and Raphel, N. (1995), *Up the Loyalty Ladder – How to Make Your Customer Your Best Promoter*, Dublin: The O'Brien Press.

4   Jones, T. and Sasser W.E. (1995), 'Why Customers Defect', *Harvard Business Review*, November–December, 88–99.

5   This example draws on: Payne, A.F.T. and Frow, P. (1999), 'Developing a Segmented Service Strategy: Improving Measurement in Relationship Marketing', *Journal of Marketing Management*, **15**, 8, 797–818. and Payne, A. and Frow, P. (1997), 'Relationship Marketing: Key Issues for the Utilities Market', *Journal of Marketing Management*, **13**, 463–47.

6   Reichheld, F. F. and Sasser, W.E. Jr. (1990), 'Zero Defections: Quality Comes to Services', *Harvard Business Review*, September–October, 105–11.

7   Payne, A.F.T. and Frow, P. (1999), *op. cit.*

8   Heskett, J.L., Jones, T.O., Loveman G.W., Sasser, E.W., Jr and Schlesinger, L.A. (1994), 'Putting the Service-Profit Chain to Work', *Harvard Business Review*, March-April, 164–174.

9   Payne, A.F.T. (2001), The Value Creation Process in Customer Relationship Management, draft working paper, Cranfield School of Management.

10 McDonald, M. and Dunbar, I. (1998), *Market Segmentation: How to Do It, How to Profit From It*, 2nd edn, Macmillan Business.

11 Christopher, M. (1992), *The Customer Service Planner*, Oxford: Butterworth-Heinemann.

12 Smith, D. and Prescott, J. (1987), 'Couple Competitive Analysis to Sales Force Decisions', *Industrial Marketing Management*, **16**, 55–61.

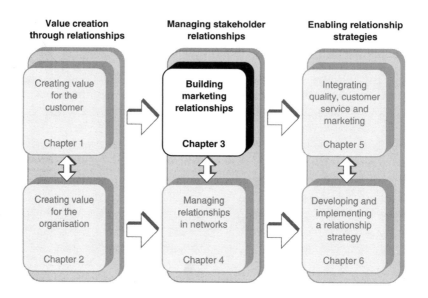

INTRODUCTION

I n the last two chapters we examined the role of value from the perspective of both the customer and the organisation. Value is a dynamic concept that is created and changed over time as a result of an ongoing series of interactions and relationships with key stakeholders. In this chapter we consider the role of multiple stakeholders in relationship marketing.

The mainstream marketing literature has neglected the important issue of understanding and building long-term relationships with both customers and other stakeholder groups. But managing the organisation's internal and external relationships with key stakeholders is now acknowledged as critical to economic profitability and, as such, needs to become a more central activity. Traditional

> Traditional marketing approaches have not placed sufficient emphasis on careful stakeholder management.

marketing approaches have not placed sufficient emphasis on careful stakeholder management. An exception is the approach to stakeholder management advocated within public relations (PR), and referred to as 'publics' by PR practitioners. However, some have argued that this approach is often insufficiently rigorous and lacks relational emphasis.[1]

Considerable work has been done in the business strategy field on stakeholder management, and insights from the strategy literature have influenced the development of multiple stakeholder approaches in relationship marketing. But relationship marketing literature on stakeholders has developed categorisation schemes to help companies consider value specifically in the marketing context.

The role of multiple stakeholders

All organisations have a large and diverse range of stakeholders. These include suppliers, the financial community, employees, customers, the government, trade unions, environmentalists, alliance partners and so on. The top managers of the organisation play a key role in managing these relationships in order to maximise customer and shareholder value. But all too often top management do not manage these stakeholders in an integrated manner.

Stakeholder management is frequently not integrated because, in practice, stakeholders are typically managed on a day-to-day basis within different parts of the organisation. For example, the marketing department is responsible for managing relationships with customers, the purchasing department with suppliers and the finance department with the financial community. The human resources department, together with line management, manages relationships with internal staff, potential recruits, unions and so on, and it falls to the public relations and corporate affairs departments to manage many of the other external stakeholders. As so many different parts of the organisation are involved, the various stakeholder groups are frequently managed in an unco-ordinated, disparate manner.

Over the past decade companies have used multiple stakeholder approaches in relationship marketing towards managing these stakeholder relationships. Two key concepts underpin the use of relationship marketing in this context. First, you can only optimise relationships with customers if you understand and manage relationships with other relevant stakeholders. Most businesses appreciate the critical role their employees play in delivering superior customer value, but other stakeholders also play an important role. Second, the tools and techniques used in marketing to customers, such as marketing planning and market segmentation, can also be used effectively to manage non-customer relationships.

Implementing relationship marketing strategies requires managers to go beyond their traditional functional roles. They need to take a broader perspective of the role of stakeholders in order to develop much closer relationships between suppliers, internal staff, customers and other relevant markets. Reorienting thinking and actions towards building a more customer-focused organisation through addressing multiple stakeholders represents a significant challenge for senior managers.

Some companies adopt a strong integrated relationship approach to managing their stakeholders, but they are in the minority. However, a growing number of companies are beginning to apply relationship marketing principles to non-customer markets.

Philip Kotler has proposed a new view of organisational performance and success, based on relationships, whereby the traditional marketing approach – based on the marketing mix – is not replaced, but repositioned as the toolbox for understanding and responding to all the significant stakeholders in the company's environment. He outlines the importance of the relationship approach to stakeholders:[2]

> if... companies are to compete successfully in domestic and global markets, they must engineer stronger bonds with their stakeholders, including customers, distributors, suppliers, employees, unions, governments, and other critical players in the environment. Common practices such as whipsawing suppliers for better prices, dictating terms to distributors, and treating employees as a cost rather than an asset, must end. Companies must move from a short-term *transaction-orientated* goal to a long-term *relationship-building* goal.

Kotler's comments emphasise the need for an integrated framework for understanding the key stakeholder relationships. In many large industrial organisations, marketing is still viewed as a set of related but compartmentalised activities that are separate from the rest of the company. Relationship marketing seeks to change this perspective by managing the competing interests of customers, staff, shareholders and other stakeholders. It redefines the concept of 'a market' more broadly as being one in which the competing interests are made visible and therefore more likely to be managed.

A number of researchers working in the relationship marketing field have developed models which propose the broadening of marketing to include relationships with a number of stakeholders or *market domains*.

The six markets relationship marketing framework is a useful and well-tested tool for reviewing the role of an extended set of stakeholders in creating total organisational value in both business-to-consumer (b2c) and business-to-business (b2b) markets. This framework proposes six key market domains, representing groups that can contribute to an organisation's marketplace effectiveness.[3] While customers are viewed in this framework as a major stakeholder, five other stakeholder groups, or market domains, are also identified: influence (including shareholder) markets, recruitment markets, referral markets, internal markets and supplier/alliance markets. The six markets framework is shown in Figure 3.1.

This framework was developed in 1991. With some minor terminology changes, it has proved to be a robust analytical framework and has been used in relationship marketing projects with more than 200 organisations. Similar approaches were advocated by Kotler in 1992 and by Morgan and Hunt in 1994.[4] Gummesson has provided a comparison of four of the approaches to classifying multiple stakeholders, including his own '30R approach'.[5] Gummesson's 30R approach goes considerably beyond the scope of our work in that it identifies relationships (such as the criminal network relationship) that go beyond the stakeholder relationships that are of central interest to us here.

Relationship marketing emphasises building stronger relationships between the organisation and all its stakeholder markets. In this new millennium, organisations need to place greater emphasis on

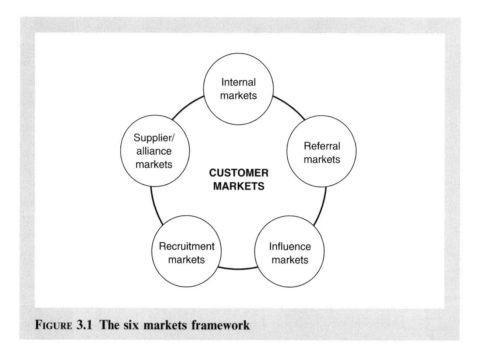

FIGURE 3.1 The six markets framework

fundamental issues such as understanding the dynamics of these markets and identifying the critical features which not only influence and drive a company's strategy but also affect its competitive position.

The six markets framework, shown in Figure 3.1, illustrates the key stakeholder 'markets' or market domains where business leaders need to review their companies' performance. While these market domains are interdependent, they vary in importance. For most organisations three groups – customers, employees (internal markets) and shareholders (the dominant group within the influence market) – are especially critical. As a result of this review, companies need to determine which market domains are most relevant to them. We will address the importance of and interrelationships between these three groups later in this chapter.

Any one group may be involved in a number of these markets. For example, customers may play a role within the customer market (where the interaction is between a firm and its customers) and in the referral market (where the interaction is between an existing customer and a prospective customer).

Many organisations have used this framework to consider the multiple markets they must address. Coutts Bank is one example (see Case Study).

Relationship marketing at Coutts Bank: It's not just about clients

Relationship management is not just about clients. Coutts is looking long and hard at the way it services five distinct markets, in addition to its traditional client market, to make sure it maintains consistent, high quality relationships with them.

Coutts Group's additional relationship markets

Internal markets: Coutts involves and communicates with all staff – relationship managers, product managers and support staff – in and about its relationship management priorities. As such it is seeking to ensure there is no weak link in the chain that makes up the whole Coutts service offering.

Referral markets: Referral markets are a critical area of focus for Coutts. Lawyers, consultants and financial advisers are a significant source of new business for the bank. These people meet prospective clients every day and advise them on how best to invest their wealth, be it the gains from selling a company recently or a newly-acquired inheritance. Coutts calls these sources of referral regularly and delivers regular tailored information to them so that Coutts is at the front of their minds when they are advising their clients with whom to place their wealth.

Suppliers: Suppliers are equally important to Coutts. Although the bank is a service provider, it needs to ensure that every tangible offering – from brochures to events to its premises to its lapel badges – matches the quality image it tries to portray through its staff. It works very closely with just a few suppliers who, over time, get to know its ways and the standards it sets.

Potential employees: Coutts knows how important it is that employees and prospective employees perceive the organisation as one they can relate to and want to work for. In banking, a new client relationship manager can often bring a new portfolio of business with them so Coutts is at pains to sustain its quality image among its peers in order to attract the best recruits.

Influencers: Influence markets are important to Coutts in the broad review of relationship management and marketing. One of its key influence markets is the governments and financial authorities of the jurisdictions in which it works. These authorities actively seek the bank's views on legislative changes to safeguard their jurisdiction's status, and on the kind of new product opportunities that might attract investment to their countries in the future.

Source: Based on Shaw[6]

The six markets model enables any business to undertake a diagnostic review of the key market domains that may be important to them. As a result of this diagnosis, they will be able to identify a number of key groups within the market domains that are particularly important. But the number of domains a business will need to focus on will vary from organisation to organisation. Let us now consider each of these market domains in turn.

The customer market

The customer market domain is the central market within the six markets model. While customers are the prime focus of marketing activity, companies should direct their marketing activities less at transactional marketing, with its emphasis on the single sale, and more at building long-term customer relationships. The customer market domain addresses three broad groups: direct buyers, intermediaries, and final consumers. These groups are shown in Figure 3.2.

> The customer market domain is the central market within the six markets model.

To illustrate these groups, we will use the example of a manufacturer of domestic appliances such as dishwashers. This manufacturer sells to a number of approved wholesalers, who in turn sell the products to retail outlets, who in turn sell the appliances to individual consumers.

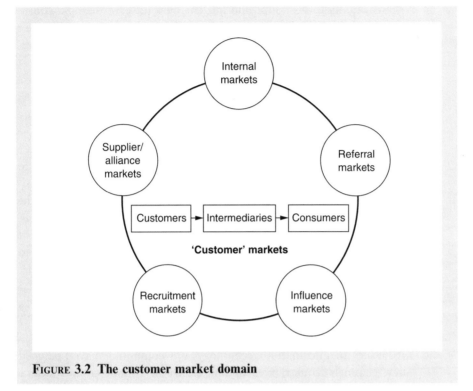

FIGURE 3.2 The customer market domain

In this example, the wholesaler is the buyer, the retailer the intermediary and the individual who purchases the appliance from the retailer is the consumer. We will use the term 'customer' generally to apply to all these groups.

In this example, the three groups in the customer market domain are:

■ **buyer** – the direct customer of the manufacturer, that is, the wholesaler;
■ **intermediary** – the retailer to whom the wholesaler sells the appliances;
■ **consumer** – the individual at the end of the channel who purchases the appliance from the retailer.

However, in some industries there may be further intermediaries, which create additional steps within the distribution channel shown in this figure.

Many organisations adopt multiple channels to serve the final consumer, while others use only one channel. For example, some insurance companies, such as Direct Line, market directly to the final consumer. Other insurance companies sell both through the traditional broker channel as well as direct. For example, Zurich Financial Services, a large insurance company, markets indirectly to final consumers through a large network of insurance brokers. It also has a separate division, Zurich Direct, which markets directly to final consumers.

A company may choose from a wide range of distribution options to serve its final consumer. It should base its choice on the value proposition it has identified as being relevant to the final consumers in the segments it wishes to serve. It should regularly scrutinise its distribution options as circumstances change and new opportunities present themselves. It is increasingly being acknowledged that a firm needs to create a supply chain that is more effective than that of its competitors if it is to be successful. So it is supply chains or market networks that compete, rather than just companies. We will discuss market networks in more detail in Chapter 4.

Advances in information technology and computing have spawned new channels to market, including electronic commerce and mobile commerce. These channels will grow dramatically over the next decade. Ultimately it will be the desire of companies to build channel relationships with selected customers to maximise their lifetime value that will drive the use of both new and existing channels.

Companies considering a relationship marketing programme must undertake a detailed market analysis at each level in their value delivery network and identify the type of marketing activity they need to direct at each of the various channel members including direct buyers, intermediaries and final consumers. They then need to do further analysis, in terms of segmenting and understanding the decision-making units of different levels, before determining what level of marketing expenditure and effort to direct at each level. Constructing a market map, as we outlined in Chapter 2, will help the company analyse its value delivery network.

A company needs to evaluate regularly and change, when appropriate, the amount of marketing effort it directs at different channel members. In some industries, for example, intermediaries may be a valuable channel member, while in others the value of intermediaries is being challenged. Unless the intermediary is adding value to the customer relationship, it may prove to be an unnecessary cost and may be bypassed. Many organisations are now finding that in order to build stronger relationships with final consumers they need to change the emphasis and expenditure at different channel levels or, alternatively, refocus the existing expenditure in ways that build deeper and more sustained relationships. We will illustrate this point with some examples.

A manufacturer of domestic dishwashing machines may have traditionally spent a large proportion of its marketing efforts and marketing budget on trade marketing aimed at getting the dishwashers into large retail outlets such as department stores. It may have directed much of its marketing expenditure at developing strong key account management; providing appropriate promotional activity; undertaking in-store point-of-sale merchandising; creating a discount structure based on volume; and establishing training programmes for sales staff in the retailers. It may have supplemented this with a considerable amount of trade advertising and trade promotion, aiming only a limited amount of advertising at final individual consumers. The manufacturer may, however, decide to review its marketing approach and implement an alternative marketing strategy that focuses more closely on the needs of the consumer. It may seek to identify the needs of final consumers through warranty cards or some form of direct promotional activity; send them a questionnaire to help identify their interest in a range of products and services; set up a major telephone call centre; create a customer club, and so on. It could consider these and other options as a means of building relationships with the final consumers.

Building relationships with final consumers

General Electric's (GE) Appliance Division in the United States is a good example of an organisation that has built a closer relationship with its final consumers through establishing a major call centre. GE's Answer Centre is widely regarded as one of the best in the world. In setting up its call centre GE sought to 'personalise GE to the consumer and to personalise the consumer to GE'. Unlike most manufacturers, who avoided any contact with the final consumer, GE took the unusual step of giving its phone number to customers. The Answer Centre has evolved over sixteen years into an increasingly important relationship marketing capability, and the current network of five call centres receives several million calls each year. Wayland and Cole have outlined how GE's Answer Centre has contributed to increased customer relationship value in three key areas:[7]

First, resolving immediate problems results in a probability-of-repurchase rate of 80 per cent for the previously dissatisfied customer, as compared to ten per cent for the dissatisfied but uncomplaining customer and 27 per cent for an average customer. In other words, by making it easier to reach the company and by responding effectively, GE gets more opportunities to convert dissatisfied customers and to strengthen relationships. Second, contact with the centre significantly increases customers' awareness of the GE appliance line and their consideration level. Finally, the knowledge that is generated through customer interactions provides valuable input to the sales, marketing, and new product development processes.

Many manufacturers fail to develop relationships with their final consumers. Most readers will no doubt have had disappointing experiences when purchasing a range of consumer durable products, including motor cars. They might have been motivated to buy a car as a result of promotional activity by the car manufacturer, only to be highly disappointed by the subsequent lack of interest by the dealer in maintaining the car and satisfactorily rectifying faults that occurred within the warranty period. The consumer may be further upset when they seek to obtain redress directly from the manufacturer and find the manufacturer is totally uninterested in having any dialogue with them. But within the motor car sector radical changes in both distribution and other marketing practices – not least the approach being adopted by Daewoo – are prompting other car manufacturers to find ways of developing closer relationships with their final consumers.

Other companies are also rethinking their marketing strategy and are developing direct relationships with consumers. Procter & Gamble, for instance, is now focusing on developing direct relationships with consumers through direct response promotion. For example, it is offering people who buy its Pampers brand of nappies the opportunity to obtain discounts by completing a coupon which provides valuable data including name, address, telephone number, and number and ages of children. This data allows P & G to track consumer needs more closely and make appropriate and timely offers to them. Many other manufacturers within the retail sector are looking at these activities with enormous interest.

Customer markets – a summary

Marketing has traditionally focused on winning customers and emphasised the value of the individual sale. But this transactional approach is gradually being replaced by a relationship marketing approach that emphasises the value of long-term relationships and repeat purchases. In Chapter 2 we outlined the benefits of customer retention, but noted that despite managers' growing awareness of the need to strike the right balance between acquiring and retaining customers, few companies have achieved that in practice. Focusing too heavily on marketing activities directed at new customers is dangerous. A company may spend too much on acquiring them, only to lose them later because it puts too little effort into keeping them. If customer service does not meet customer expectations, customers are likely to defect and damage the company's reputation by adverse word-of-mouth publicity.

Strategies aimed at retaining customers can be expensive as they often involve increasing customer service levels and tailoring the product or service to suit individual customers or customer groups. Successful retention programmes segment customers according to their potential lifetime profitability and then determine the type and frequency of marketing activity relevant for each group in order to exploit and increase this potential.

The referral market

> An organisation's existing customers are often its best marketers.

There are two main categories within the referral market domain – customer and non-customer referral sources. An organisation's existing customers are often its best marketers, which is why creating positive word-of-mouth referral, through delivering outstanding service quality, is so important. A variety of non-customers recommend organisations to prospective customers, including networks, multipliers, connectors, third party introducers and agencies.

The first category, existing (and former) customers, is usually very important for most organisations. The importance of the second category depends on the organisation concerned. The role of the different constituent groups varies both between companies in different industry sectors, and within different business units, divisions or product/service areas of a single company. Organisations can significantly increase their revenue and profits by using the principles of relationship marketing to manage relationships systematically with both these broad groups.

The main categories of the referral market domain are shown in Figure 3.3.

Customer referrals

There are two sub-categories in the existing and former customers' category of the referral market domain: advocacy referrals (or

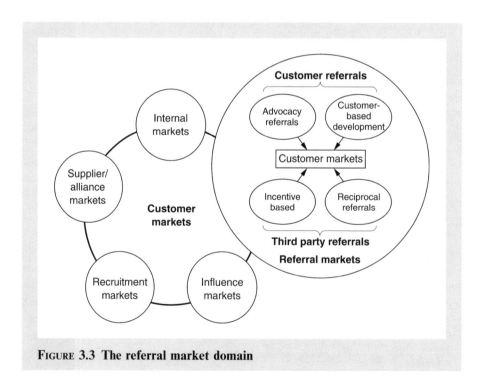

FIGURE 3.3 **The referral market domain**

advocate-initiated customer referrals) and customer-base development (or company-initiated customer referrals). We discussed the first sub-category in Chapter 2 when explaining the relationship marketing ladder of customer loyalty and briefly described the role of advocates in assisting a company's marketing efforts. The second sub-category of customer-base development relates to an organisation's explicit attempts to use its existing customers, as part of its marketing activities, to gain new customers.

1. Advocacy referrals (advocate-initiated customer referrals)

Customers become advocates when they are totally satisfied with a company's products or services. A relatively small number of organisations benefit greatly from their proactive efforts to turn their customers into advocates and getting them to refer other customers to them.

Advocacy referrals have contributed greatly to the success of UK bank First Direct, which became the world's first all-telephone bank. By 2000, it had attracted around 1 million high-net-worth individuals. A significant part of First Direct's growth has been through referral from its very satisfied customers. Research conducted by First Direct shows that around 85 per cent of its customers have referred new customers to the bank, compared to an average of 15 per cent for the other five major banks.

CASE STUDY   **Creating advocacy at Nordstrom**

One of the best examples of advocacy referrals is Nordstrom, a US chain of superior quality fashion department stores. Many people regard Nordstrom as the best retailer in the US. Despite the fact that most of its stores are on the West Coast of America, it has a strong following right across the US. Many people living overseas are also advocates of Nordstrom and travel to the US specifically to visit one of its stores. Nordstrom has a high degree of advocacy amongst its customers and uses formal organisational processes to leverage referrals. It is also renowned for its excellent recruitment process and internal marketing, and these contribute to the outstanding customer satisfaction and advocacy it enjoys.

Nordstrom reimburses customers unconditionally for any merchandise, whether they have used it or not, and with or without a sales receipt. This practice demonstrates how Nordstrom views referrals and the emphasis it puts on word-of-mouth referral marketing as opposed to advertising. Richard Pascale[8] quotes an executive vice-president who explains: 'Nordstrom literally grinds up truckloads of shoes each year. These are returned shoes that have been worn and cannot be sent back to vendors. At face value, it seems nuts to have a policy like this. But if we run one full page promotional ad in the Seattle newspaper, it costs us the equivalent of 500 pairs of shoes. And we do not know if the ad works. But give a customer a new pair of shoes with no hassle and it is a story that gets told and retold at parties and at the bridge table. Word-of-mouth endorsement really works. We know it.'

Heskett and his colleagues at Harvard Business School[9] argue that such stories have become more important to Nordstrom than the relatively low advertising that the company undertakes. 'It does not take many of these "service encounters" to encourage the development of a relationship either with Nordstrom or with the individual salesperson. Nordstrom does whatever it can to encourage these relationships,' they write.

2. Customer-base development (company-initiated customer referrals)

Advocacy referrals involve the customers initiating the referral. But for company-initiated customer referrals the company directs a set of activities or a programme at existing customers that are designed to lead to customer referrals. They may simply ask customers to refer other potential customers to them, or offer them some form of inducement to do so. Advocates on the relationship marketing ladder often actively initiate referrals, but 'supporters' – the next rung down the ladder – though positive about the organisation tend to be more passive. Asking supporters for a referral can be a very good way of generating business from them. For example, a study into referrals by lawyers' clients,[10] found that only 49 per cent of the clients said that law firms had asked them for a referral. But of those who were asked

95 per cent provided at least one referral, compared with just 8 per cent of those who were not asked. Few organisations with whom we have discussed this issue have any formal process for requesting refer-rals.

Membership organisations are one sector that is putting considerable effort into using the membership base to reach further members. American Express, the Institute of Directors, wine clubs and many similar organisations run regular promotions aimed at generating new customers through their existing customer base. These 'member get a member' marketing efforts are frequently accompanied by some form of incentive, inducement or reward.

Non-customer referrals (third party and staff referrals)

In addition to an organisation's customers, many other parties can be a great source of referrals for a business. Referrals may be made infor-mally when an individual's experiences of an organisation and its general reputation cause them to recommend that organisation to others. But some companies have more formal systems of referrals.

The wide range of non-customer referrals can be divided into a number of groups:

1 general referrals
2 reciprocal referrals
3 incentive-based referrals
4 staff referrals

1. General referrals

General referrals cover a broad range of referrals that result in business being generated for an organisation. These can be further divided into four sub-groups:

■ *Professional referrals* are those where one professional recom-mends the services of another. For example, a GP may refer a patient to a specialist consultant, or a solicitor may refer a client to a barrister.

- Customers may seek *expertise referrals* because of the referrer's specialist expertise or knowledge. These referrals are typically made on an irregular or ad hoc basis.
- *Specification referrals* are those where an organisation or person specifies or strongly recommends that a particular product or service is used. For example, architects building upmarket homes may mandate, within their specification, that a specific brand of electrical appliances such as washing machines and ovens are used within every kitchen.
- *Substitute and complementary referrals* occur in circumstances where organisations which are at over-capacity, have long lead times to undertake work, or cannot fulfil a specific need, may refer a customer to one of their competitors.

2. Reciprocal referrals

Historically, ethics in professions such as law and accounting have precluded advertising and aggressive competition. Up until the 1980s most of the professions' marketing activities were highly restricted by their professional bodies and they had to rely extensively on referrals from third parties. As a consequence, referrals have often been the main source of work for professional services firms.

Some referrals, especially those between professional firms, are interdependent and under this system referrals may be made backwards and forwards between those in different professions. For example, an accounting firm may recommend a law firm or bank, and vice versa.

3. Incentive-based referrals

Incentive-based referrals are appropriate in a number of circumstances. First, where members of the referral channel are mutually dependent it may be to their advantage to create a formal arrangement that helps reinforce this dependence. Second, if a business is receiving many referrals but giving back relatively few, and there is little potential to change this, it may seek to redress the balance by providing some incentive-based method of compensating its source of referrals.

The potential for using incentives varies considerably across industries. A company that incorporates financial incentives in its referral system must ensure it is managed ethically. Indeed, in some industry sectors incentives are considered unethical or may even be prohibited under the rules of a professional or regulatory body.

4. Staff referrals (from existing and former staff)

Staff are an important source of referrals within a number of industry sectors. Staff referrals are most common within service businesses, but there are many other examples of organisations where referrals can be generated between a number of different divisions or products aimed at similar customer segments.

Former staff may be a useful source of business referral in certain types of organisation. Again, professional service firms provide a good example. Consultants like McKinsey & Co and the large accounting firms place considerable emphasis on these 'alumni' and run a number of regular activities to keep them involved with their old firm.

Referral markets – a summary

Most organisations fail to exploit the opportunity to maximise referrals from their own customers, from third parties, and, where appropriate, from their own staff. What is more, many organisations still do not realise the power of customer delight and the benefits that accrue from significantly exceeding customer expectations.

However, there is a small, but increasing, number of companies that do significantly exceed customer expectations. These organisations have been able to grow through word-of-mouth referrals from highly satisfied customers (and other groups) and include First Direct and Nordstrom. Nordstrom has achieved its market position with relatively low levels of advertising while First Direct has achieved a strong market position despite television advertising that was not considered to be particularly effective.

Most organisations need to consider both existing customers and intermediaries as sources of future business. Therefore, they should identify both present and prospective referral sources and develop a plan for allocating marketing resources to them. They also need to make efforts to monitor the cost–benefit, while recognising that the benefits of increased referral marketing may take some time to come to fruition.

The supplier and alliance market

In the original version of this book, we used the term 'supplier market' to describe this market domain. In the past, when we have used the six markets framework and an alliance was considered important, we grouped it within the supplier market, on the grounds that alliances potentially provide new management skills, access to capital, market position, global coverage, technological skills and so forth. So the term 'supplier market' reflects a broader spectrum of supply. But because the number of strategic alliances has grown, we have now explicitly included 'alliances' within the supplier and alliance market domain.

> Supplier and alliance relationships both need to be viewed as partnerships.

Supplier and alliance relationships both need to be viewed as partnerships, but there is a subtle distinction between the contribution each can make to a successful relationship marketing strategy. We define them as follows:-

- **Supplier markets** – Suppliers (or vendors) provide physical resources to the business. Sometimes these resources are augmented by services, but typically suppliers are characterised as the upstream source of raw materials, components, products or other tangible items that flow on a continuing basis into and through the customer's business.
- **Alliance markets**– In a real sense alliance partners are suppliers too. The difference is that typically they supply competencies and capabilities that are knowledge based rather than product based. Alliance partners may well provide services too, and alliances are often created in response to the company's perceived need to outsource an activity within its value chain.

In the mid-1980s, the British Leyland car manufacturing company had well over 1000 suppliers with which it had arm's-length, often adversarial, relationships. The company – now called the Rover Group – has been transformed and enjoys close relationships with fewer than 500 preferred suppliers. Similarly, the UK high street retailer Bhs used to buy clothing products from 1000 suppliers at the beginning of the 1990s. By the end of the decade it was working closely with only 50 strategic suppliers. These two examples reflect a significant change in the way companies view their supplier base. Other organisations have engaged in alliances to import resources, capabilities and expertise into the business instead of trying to keep everything 'in-house' as they used to.

These new style relationships are a radical departure from companies' traditional focus on vertical integration, whereby they sought to bring as much of the value-added in the final product as possible under the same legal ownership. In its early days in North America, Ford used to own the steel mills that made the steel for its cars, as well as most of the factories that made the components. Courtaulds established a vast, vertically-integrated business in textiles with the capability to control the value chain from synthetic fibres to finished garments. Now, the emphasis is on 'virtual' integration – that is, a confederation of organisations combining their capabilities and competencies in a closely integrated network with shared goals and objectives.

Figure 3.4 brings together the concept of vertical supply relationships and horizontal alliance partnerships as a closely coupled network within the six markets model.

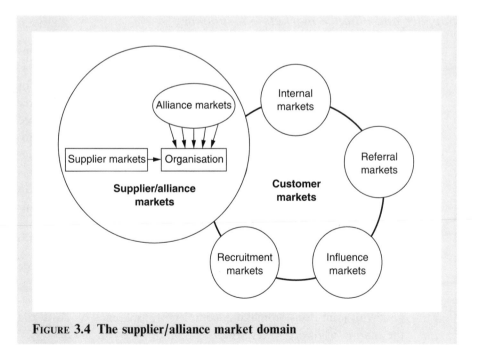

FIGURE 3.4 The supplier/alliance market domain

It is perhaps helpful to think of alliances as 'horizontal' partnerships – in the sense that an alliance partner plays a value-creating role within the firm's value chain – and suppliers as 'vertical' partnerships – in the sense that suppliers are an extension of the firm. In this approach, sometimes termed 'the extended enterprise', suppliers and alliance partners link with the core organisation to help present more cost-effective, timely and innovative offers to customers. Virtual integration seeks to reap the benefits that accrue to companies which focus on core competencies, while at the same time delivering the advantages of co-ordination and integration that can flow from vertical integration.

It is beginning to be recognised that managing these interlocking networks of organisations – and, in particular, the relationships between them – is vital to competitive success. We argue that the way supplier and alliance 'markets' are proactively managed is one of the central elements of a relationship marketing strategy. We go on to examine the topic of alliances and managing relationships in networks in much greater detail in Chapter 4.

Supplier and alliance markets – a summary

As we have suggested, it is useful to think of supply chain partnerships as 'vertical' relationships and alliances as 'horizontal' relationships. Alliances bring new skills or competencies into the business or strengthen existing skills and competencies. The move to outsource activities that are judged 'non-core' to the business has gathered pace in recent years, giving further impetus to the search for appropriate alliance partners. Increasingly, value creation is no longer confined to a single firm, but instead is rooted in a confederation of firms that contribute specialist skill and capabilities. The value chain, in effect, now spans several organisations that work as partners in creating and bringing products to market.

Such relationships need to be managed quite differently from more traditional 'subcontract' relationships. Top management in these 'network' or 'virtual' organisations needs to create a 'boundary-less' business with joint decision-making, complete transparency on costs and the sharing of risks and rewards.

The influence market

> The influence market domain usually has the most diverse range of constituent groups.

The influence market domain usually has the most diverse range of constituent groups. Among these are shareholders, financial analysts, stockbrokers, the business press and other media, user and consumer groups, environmentalists and unions. Each of these constituent groups can potentially exert significant influence over the organisation. The organisation can manage its relationships with them through applying a strategic marketing approach.

The relative importance of specific groups within the influence market will vary considerably according to industry sector. For example, companies selling infrastructure services such as telecommunications or utilities will place governments and regulatory bodies high on their list of important constituents within their influence market domain. Highly visible public listed companies may focus much of their attention on shareholders, financial analysts and the financial and business press. Manufacturing companies and the petrochemical sector may be especially concerned with environmentalists and government. Figure 3.5 illustrates several of the major groups within the influence market domain.

The relative importance of different groups within the influence market domain will also vary at different points in time. For example, a bank faced with fraud or insider trading may suddenly find the press, regulatory bodies and the central bank at the top of its influence market agenda. Similarly, actions by Greenpeace and other environmentalists over Shell's Brent Spar platform brought environmentalist to the top of Shell's agenda.

Understanding influence markets

While the influence market domain may comprise a considerable number of potential groups, a firm may need to address only a relatively few important ones at any given point. Several categories are of special interest because they are common to many organisations. These include:

1 financial and investor influence markets;
2 environmental influence markets;

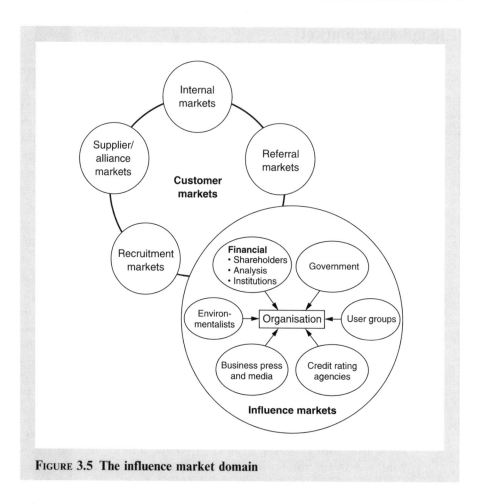

FIGURE 3.5 **The influence market domain**

> 3 competitor influence markets;
> 4 political and regulatory influence markets.

1. Financial and investor influence markets

Many organisations need to win the support and loyalty of a wide range of financial markets. Financial and investor influence markets are especially critical for organisations listed or planning to list on a stock market. But they are important to other organisations too, such as 'mutuals' – organisations owned by subscribers, depositors or customers – including non-listed insurance companies and building societies.

Investor loyalty is critically important in the financial and investor influence market. Reichheld[11] highlighted this in recent work that showed that investor churn in the average public company in the United States is more than 50 per cent a year. He concludes that managers find it nearly impossible to pursue long-term value-creating strategies without the support of loyal, knowledgeable investors. Reichheld's work is among a body of research that has begun to focus on financial and investor influence markets in recognition of their importance in relationship marketing.

2. Environmental influence markets

Environmental influence markets are a key group for organisations involved in industries such as petrochemicals, mining and manufacturing. Environmental bodies and pressure groups are becoming increasingly active and even militant, and can wreak serious damage on organisations that they target as being environmentally unfriendly.

The events following Shell's decision to dispose of its Brent Spar platform in the North Sea provide a stark illustration of the importance of this market domain. Greenpeace occupied the Brent Spar platform, activists in Germany and other countries fire-bombed petrol stations, and these and other events – including probable behind-the-scenes involvement by the British Government – led Shell to reverse its decision regarding the disposal of the Brent Spar platform. Shell clearly failed both to develop appropriate relational strategies and to communicate effectively with these key environmental groups.

By contrast, The Body Shop is an excellent example of an organisation that has managed its relationships with environmentalists and other influence market groups very well. For example, it has formed alliances with Greenpeace and Friends of the Earth and developed close relationships with other influence market groups, such as local communities, by ensuring that every one of its shops develops local community projects.

3. Competitor influence markets

Large organisations, especially those that are high profile or dominate their industry sector, need to consider carefully the relationships they have with their competitors. Adopting the stance of industry statesman can be a good strategy.

British Airways' industry statesmanship was eroded for a period during the mid-1990s amid fierce competition between BA and Virgin Atlantic. BA attracted negative publicity over its so-called 'dirty tricks' campaign and Virgin Atlantic's position in the marketplace was enhanced as a consequence. Virgin got lots of free positive publicity and its popularity and familiarity grew among the public at large.

4. Political and regulatory influence markets

The political category within the influence market domain covers a number of groups including members of parliament, government ministers, central and local government departments and other government and quasi-government bodies. These groups may affect organisations within a given country, within an economic region such as the European Union, or on a global basis.

Companies may need to direct marketing activity at government and regulatory bodies. Gummesson[12] has pointed out that these two groups are particularly relevant for companies that sell infrastructure equipment such as nuclear reactors, telephone systems and defence products. Such products may affect the country's economic performance, employment levels or financial status, or may be politically important.

Influence markets – a summary

The penalties of failing to manage influence markets properly is illustrated by the jewellery retailer Ratners. In 1992, chief executive Gerald Ratner made a speech at the Institute of Directors in which he described his jewellery products as 'total crap'. The general press picked up the story, which was reported widely. Ratners failed to manage strategic credibility during and after this event, which, together with an inappropriate and incomplete recovery programme, caused the group's fortunes to nosedive.

Companies involved with influence groups may not have formulated detailed and coherent relationship marketing strategies and plans to gain maximum advantage from managing these relationships. By adopting a marketing approach based on a closely defined set of specific objectives with a detailed marketing plan and an appropriate monitoring system to measure results, they can improve their chances of forging a constructive relationship with any given influence market.

The recruitment market

Increasingly, organisations are recognising that people are the most important resource in business. To attract and retain the highest quality recruits – those who share the organisation's values and will contribute significantly to its future success – firms have to market themselves to potential employees, or the recruitment market. This involves creating an appropriate organisational climate, and then communicating the benefits of that organisation to potential employees. Marketing to recruitment markets is particularly important for companies where staff are a key element of competitive advantage – service businesses for example – in order to secure a constant supply of high quality recruits.

The scarcest resource for most organisations is no longer capital or raw materials, but skilled people. A trained and experienced workforce is perhaps the most vital element in delivering customer service. Global economics and the changing nature of employment have not helped to enlarge the recruitment pool, even when unemployment is climbing to historic levels. In times of higher employment, demographic trends explain the lack of many skilled workers, but in the United States and many Western countries the number of people entering the workforce has dropped. If attracting the best quality recruits is important to business success then the recruitment market will become a priority for most companies.

> The scarcest resource for most organisations is no longer capital or raw materials, but skilled people.

The recruitment market comprises all potential employees together with the third parties that serve as access channels. Figure 3.6 shows the main access channels for the recruitment market domain.

Potential employees may join a business through a number of these third parties. They may respond to advertisements placed by the employer or their recruitment agency. For senior appointments, they

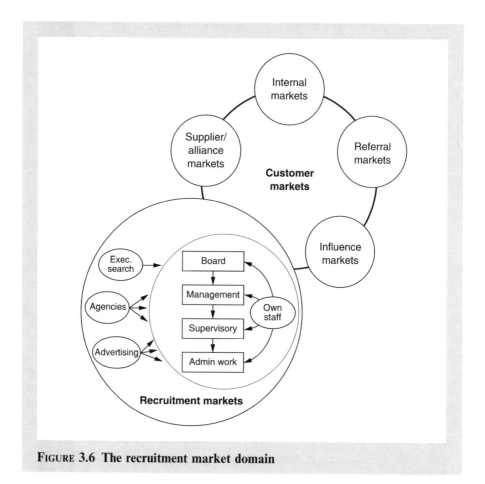

FIGURE 3.6 **The recruitment market domain**

may be approached by executive search consultants. Where there is a dearth of high calibre recruits, some firms are turning to their own staff to suggest potential applicants, offering substantial payments as inducements. Accenture, the consulting firm, and Cisco, for example, have both successfully used staff recommendations as part of their recruitment process. Companies may also recruit staff via placement departments in universities and colleges, direct approaches and, increasingly, through the Internet.

Large companies competing in a competitive job market need to manage a wide range of recruitment market channels. A department in human resources (HR) frequently manages this complex marketing task, but HR does not always have the marketing skills and competencies to manage this complex set of relationships in a sophisticated way. The following example demonstrates how companies could improve their recruitment.

A large and well-known accountancy practice was having difficulty attracting newly qualified recruits. It was not difficult to find out why. The firm's recruitment literature was old-fashioned and lacked visual impact. On visits to university campuses – a traditional source of recruits – the firm was represented by an old and uninspiring partner and disinterested administrative staff. The firm then instituted a marketing plan to try to improve the situation. This involved redesigning recruitment literature (with the help of recent graduates), sending the brightest partners on university visits accompanied by managers who had interesting experiences to recount, and sponsoring awards and prizes at target universities. As a result of the recruitment marketing campaign, the firm dramatically increased its 'offers to acceptances' ratio.

A number of studies have highlighted the impact of recruitment practices on company performance. Organisations need to market themselves in a way that attracts the calibre of person that matches the image of the firm they want to project to customers. More companies are now identifying a psychometric profile of the type of employee most likely to be successful in achieving customer-driven goals. The recruitment process itself is also an opportunity for the company to build a positive image with new recruits.

The value employees add to business success is tied closely to the way they are selected, trained, motivated and led. Examples abound of businesses failing or succeeding as a consequence of the way they manage their people. The expression 'our employees are our greatest asset' is increasingly common – but more often than not it is a platitude. If CEOs and their boards were more proactive in recognising the contribution of employees in winning and keeping customers, they would substantially enhance their firms' competitive performance. We will devote the rest of this section to discussing issues relating to recruiting and selecting employees within the recruitment market

Recruiting the best employees

Annual employee turnover is as high as 150 per cent in some service businesses. This represents a significant cost to the company in terms of advertising, interviewing time, administration, interview – and possibly relocation – expenses and training. There are also opportunity costs because of reduced productivity during the handover from an experienced employee to a new recruit or when a situation is vacant for a period of time. Estimates suggest that the cost of replacing an employee may be around 50 per cent of their annual salary.

With the costs of recruitment so high, it is becoming increasingly important to find employees who not only have the necessary skills and competencies and match the profile that the company wants to portray to its customers, but who are keen and likely to stay.

Potential employees need to be given realistic expectations of the job from the outset. Unless press advertisements, brochures and information supplied by third parties accurately reflect the job requirements and the company environment, the result will be disillusioned employees, low employee retention and poor word-of-mouth referrals.

McKinsey & Co argues that there is a 'war for talent' and that demographic and social changes are playing a growing role in this trend. In the United States and in most other developed countries the supply of workers in the 35 to 44 year-old age group is shrinking. Further, many of the best-trained people entering the workforce do not join traditional companies. A recent study found 30 per cent of MBAs in the United States preferred to work for a small business or start-up company.[13]

McKinsey found that 14 per cent of the managers in its 2000 survey (compared with 23 per cent in its 1997 survey) strongly agreed that their companies attract highly talented people. And only 3 per cent of the respondents to both surveys strongly agreed that their companies develop talent quickly and effectively.[14] The study also found that companies doing the best job of managing their talent deliver far better results for shareholders. Companies scoring in the top quintile of talent-management practices outperform their industry's mean return to shareholders by a remarkable 22 percentage points. McKinsey concluded that while talent management is not the only driver of such performance it is clearly a powerful one.

Selecting employees

Companies must choose their recruits carefully if they are to be successful and gain competitive advantage. The values and motivations of potential employees must be in keeping with the organisation's service ethic, so companies should not necessarily base candidates' suitability on their technical skills, which can be taught later, but on their psychological characteristics.

Selection techniques range from the traditional interview, through self-assessment, group methods and assessment centres, to the increasingly popular psychometric tests. Psychometric testing is an effective way of identifying the personality profile of people who are likely to be successful in delivering service quality and developing relationships with customers. Traditionally used more for management and graduate jobs, organisations are now using these techniques for a wider range of positions, including administrative, secretarial and manual. This reflects the importance that companies are now placing on the 'emotional content' of front-line positions.

Southwest Airlines in the United States is a good example of an organisation that understands the importance of emotional content among front-line employees. Southwest's selection strategy is based on finding individuals with a sense of humour and who genuinely enjoy serving people.[15] Southwest's hiring process is unconventional. The process they use to screen prospective flight attendants is similar to a Hollywood casting call. Candidates are evaluated by a panel that includes flight attendants, ground personnel, managers and customers. Among other things, they are asked to recount the most embarrassing experience in their life in front of other potential staff. Southwest's customers hold the airline in such high regard that they willingly give up their time to help the airline select the best flight attendants. Following the interview, the panel compares notes on each of the candidates. The process is also competitive and highly selective. In one year the company received some 85,000 job applications and hired only 3 per cent of the applicants. Southwest uses a psychometric profile that it has developed as a result of studying its most successful and least successful job roles, to help it recruit, for example, flight attendants. It uses this to supplement the panel interviews and help find the people who best fit the profile for each job within Southwest.

Recruitment markets – a summary

Research has shown that employees who are unclear about the role they are supposed to perform become demotivated, which in turn can lead to customer dissatisfaction and defection. So new employees must be carefully prepared for the work ahead of them, as their early days in a company colour their attitudes and perceptions towards it.

The best service companies place considerable emphasis on both selection and development. First Direct, for example, selects front-line employees with good communications capabilities and excellent listening skills, in the belief that these skills are more important than banking experience.[16] The recruiters seek confident people with a positive attitude who can project themselves well and convey a sense of energy. Successful applicants receive at least six weeks' intensive training. This training includes technical training as well as personal skills to help them develop effective telephone techniques. Further, they learn customer development skills such as identifying opportunities to up-sell and cross-sell the bank's products. First Direct's employees are probably the best in the UK banking environment as a result of their careful selection and intensive ongoing employee development and training.

Those organisations lacking a strong service ethos may need to implement a major change management programme aimed at all employees. Development programmes aimed at instilling a customer consciousness and service orientation in employees are increasingly being referred to as internal marketing.

The internal market

Many organisations underestimate the important collaborative role marketing can play, in conjunction with operations and HR managers, in getting the internal market exchange processes working better. Internal marketing encompasses many management issues, but has two main aspects.

First, every employee and every department in an organisation is both an internal customer and/or an internal supplier. So organisations need to work as effectively as possible to ensure that every department and individual provides and receives high standards of internal service.

> Internal marketing should ensure that all staff 'live the brand'.

Second, all staff must work together in a way that is aligned to the organisation's mission, strategy and goals. Here internal marketing should ensure that all staff 'live the brand' by representing the organisation as well as possible, whether face to face, over the phone, by mail, or electronically.

The structure of the organisation can severely impede the development of customer relationships. Traditional vertical organisations with a hierarchical structure and functional orientation often favour individual functions at the expense of the whole business and the customer. Relationship marketing, with its emphasis on cross-functional marketing, focuses on the processes that deliver value for the customer. Building an organisation that is focused on the customer requires a strong emphasis on internal marketing.

The fundamental aims of internal marketing are to develop awareness among employees of both internal and external customers, and to remove functional barriers to organisational effectiveness. Figure 3.7 illustrates the structure of the internal market based on the organisational chart. However, this particular version of the organisational chart is inverted, following one used by Jan Carlzon, the former CEO of SAS (Scandinavian Airline System).

Segmenting the internal market on the basis of organisation levels is obvious. However, not so obvious is inverting the organisational chart to reflect the critical role of front-line employees. This inverted chart reflects Carlzon's view that the primary purpose of the whole organisation is to support all front-line employees and ensure all their interactions with customers, or 'moments of truth', result in a superior experience for the customer.

In the 1980s and 1990s, SAS Airlines used internal marketing to create competitive advantage. It recognised the importance of treating employees in a caring way that customers would, in turn, appreciate. It encouraged employees to get involved in decision-making to achieve the greatest level of customer satisfaction. Thus staff were empowered to make decisions appropriate to particular customer requirements. SAS employees were trained to develop a responsibility towards the customer that was apparent in the relationship between the company and its employees.

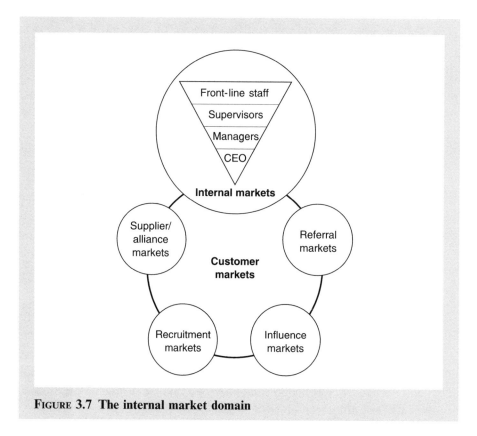

FIGURE 3.7 The internal market domain

Other leading organisations have adopted a similar approach in their internal marketing activities. For example, Nordstrom, the leading US retailer that we referred to earlier in this chapter, adheres to the philosophy that the staff on the sales floor are the major contributors in the organisation. In Nordstrom's version of the 'upside down' organisational chart, the customer is included at the top of the chart and salespeople occupy the highest internal rung on the chart. Next are buyers, merchandisers and department and store managers. At the very bottom of the organisation chart are the joint presidents of the organisation.

Richard Pascale,[8] a leading US consultant and academic, considers that Nordstrom 'has a particular genius at defining a unique relationship with its internal customer – the salesperson'. Anyone wanting to join the organisation and progress to a managerial position must start in the sales role on the floor regardless of the seniority of the position they may have occupied in another organisation. Nordstrom believes everybody must demonstrate the ability to respond to customers and to sell effectively and it has developed a unique culture where everybody is promoted from within. Pascale quotes a senior executive as saying that it is 'almost impossible' to overstate the importance of this common career track to Nordstrom's ability to communicate within the company. 'It's like we all speak a common language from top to bottom. It helps us avoid the we versus them mentality.'

If an organisation is to segment its internal market based on hierarchy, it must understand the most important levels of hierarchy and the type of staff at which internal marketing effort needs to be directed. For most organisations this will be front-line employees. In the case of SAS Airlines it was all staff that had any sort of interaction with the customer. That meant everyone from telephone sales, to check-in staff, to cabin crew and even baggage handlers. Nordstrom placed its internal marketing emphasis on the sales staff.

But in other organisations the main target for internal marketing activities may be different. In a large telecommunications company in Australia, for example, the principal focus of an internal marketing programme was middle management. Top management had decided the company must become more customer focused, but middle managers had become very technically oriented and were inhibiting the company's progress towards a customer orientation.

Segmentation of the internal market based on job role

Just as there are different ways of segmenting the customer market, there are alternative ways of segmenting the internal market. An essential aspect of internal market segmentation is to recognise the different marketing and customer contact roles within the business. Judd has developed a categorisation scheme based on the frequency of customer contact and the extent to which staff are involved with conventional marketing activities. This categorisation results in four groups: contactors, modifiers, influencers and isolates.[17]

Contactors have frequent or regular customer contact and are typically heavily involved with conventional marketing activities. They hold a range of positions in service firms including selling and customer service roles. Whether or not they are involved in planning or executing marketing strategy, they need to be well versed in the firm's marketing strategies. They should be well trained, prepared and motivated to serve customers on a day-to-day basis in a responsive manner. They should be recruited, evaluated and rewarded based on their potential and actual responsiveness to customer needs.

Modifiers are people such as receptionists, the credit department and switchboard personnel, who, though not directly involved with conventional marketing activities, nevertheless have frequent contact with customers. These people need a clear view of the organisation's marketing strategy and the role they can play in being responsive to customers' needs. They play a vital role particularly, but not exclusively, in service businesses. Modifiers need to develop high levels of customer relationship skills, and it is important to train them and monitor their performance.

Influencers are involved with the traditional elements of the marketing mix but have little or no customer contact. (Judd uses the word 'influencer' in a different context from the term 'influence market', which we described in the six markets framework above.) But these people play a big part in implementing the organisation's marketing strategy. Influencers work in roles such as product development, market research and so on. Companies recruiting influencers should seek people with the potential to develop a sense of customer responsiveness. They should evaluate and reward influencers according to customer-oriented performance standards, and programme opportunities to enhance the level of customer contact into their activities.

Isolateds are the various support functions that have neither frequent customer contact nor a great deal to do with conventional marketing activities. However, as support staff, their activities critically affect the organisation's performance. Staff falling within this category include the purchasing department, personnel and data processing. Such staff need to be sensitive to the fact that internal customers as well as external customers have needs which must be satisfied. They need to understand the company's overall marketing strategy and how their functions contribute to the quality of delivered value to the customer.

The adoption of internal marketing approaches by companies

Virgin Atlantic has long recognised the critical role internal marketing plays in its success. One of the secrets of the airline's success has been enthusiastic, empowered, motivated employees. Sir Richard Branson has said: 'I want employees in the airline to feel that it is *they* who can make the difference, and influence what passengers get.' Sir Richard explained:

> We aren't interested in having just happy employees. We want employees who feel involved and prepared to express dissatisfaction when necessary. In fact, we think that the constructively dissatisfied employee is an asset we should encourage and we need an organisation that allows us to do this – and that encourages employees to take responsibility, since I don't believe it is enough for us simply to give it.

Virgin Atlantic's philosophy has been to stimulate the individual, to encourage staff to take initiatives and to empower them to do so.

The Walt Disney Company has practised sophisticated internal marketing since its inception. Employees are rigorously trained to understand that their job is to satisfy customers. Employees are part of the 'cast' at Disney and must at all times ensure that all visitors ('guests') to their theme parks have a highly enjoyable experience. Strict dress and conduct rules are maintained in order that employees conform to standards.

Many retailers give a high priority to internal marketing. High street retailer Woolworths has recognised the importance of engaging its employees and has invested in a number of internal marketing programmes over the past five years. These include a communications cascade, involving all UK employees, to promote the organisation's mission and core values, and a brand development programme which, together with customer research, used many of the company's front-line employees to formulate the new brand proposition. Woolworths recently embarked on a 'brand engagement' programme to communicate the new brand proposition and promote a deeper understanding of customer needs among key members of staff.

Internal markets – a summary

The current interest in internal marketing has been prompted by the renewed acknowledgement by organisations of the importance of their people. Internal marketing strategies involve recognising the importance of attracting, motivating, training and retaining quality employees through developing jobs to satisfy individual needs. Internal marketing aims to encourage staff to behave in a way that will attract customers to the firm. Further, the most talented people will want to work in those companies they regard as good employers.

People now recognise internal marketing as an important component of a customer-focused organisation, and it is starting to be treated as an important management topic. Many companies are taking a serious approach to internal marketing and Lewis and Varey[18] have published a much-needed commentary on the current state of research and conceptual development in internal marketing.

Assessing performance in the six markets

> All businesses should aim to build a strong position in each of the six markets.

All businesses should aim to build a strong position in each of the six markets described above, but the precise emphasis they give to each needs to reflect their relative importance to any given firm. Companies can determine the appropriate level of attention and resources that should be directed at each through the following steps:

- identify key participants, or 'market' segments, in each of the markets;
- undertake research to identify the expectations and requirements of key participants;
- review the current and proposed level of emphasis in each market overall and for major participants in each market;
- formulate a desired relationship strategy and determine whether a formal market plan is necessary.

Identifying key groups or segments in each market domain is the first step in applying a multiple markets framework to an organisation. For example, Figure 3.8 lists the key markets and market segments for the property division of BAA (formerly British Airports Authority).

FOR CARDS
OUTSIDE
THE UK,
PLEASE
AFFIX A
POSTAGE STAMP

Jo Coleman
Information Update Service
Butterworth-Heinemann
FREEPOST SCE 5435
Oxford
Oxon
OX2 8BR
UK

Keep up-to-date with the latest books in your field.

Visit our website and register now for our FREE e-mail update service, or join our mailing list and enter our monthly prize draw to win £100 worth of books. Just complete the form below and return it to us now! (FREEPOST if you are based in the UK)

www.bh.com

Please Complete In Block Capitals

Title of book you have purchased:..

....

Subject area of interest:..

Name:...

Job title:..

Business sector (if relevant):...

Street:...

Town:..   County:......................................

Country:....................................   Postcode:..

Email:..

Telephone:..

How would you prefer to be contacted: Post ☐   e-mail ☐   Both ☐

Signature:..   Date:.......................................

☐ Please arrange for me to be kept informed of other books and information services on this and related subjects (✔ box if not required). This information is being collected on behalf of Reed Elsevier plc group and may be used to supply information about products by companies within the group.

FOR OFFICE USE ONLY

Butterworth-Heinemann,
a division of Reed Educational
& Professional Publishing Limited.
Registered office: 25 Victoria Street,
London SW1H 0EX.
Registered in England 3099304.
VAT number GB: 663 3472 30.

BUTTERWORTH HEINEMANN

A member of the Reed Elsevier plc group

Customer markets
Existing
- airlines
- utility services
- freight forwarders
- cargo handlers
- hotels

New
- off market airlines
- new airlines
- international airports
- logistics/integrators
- development around airports

Internal markets
- marketing 'property' to BAA group

Referral markets
- existing satisfied BAA customers
- other airport people
- business advisers/surveyors
- property consultants/surveyors

Supplier markets
- framework suppliers
- consultants
- contractors
- international suppliers

Recruitment markets
- employment agencies
- headhunters/search firms
- graduates
- internal transfers

Influence markets
- shareholders
- city analysts/stockbrokers
- business press
- general press and media
- regulator
- government
- local authorities

FIGURE 3.8 BAA – a review of key market participants in six markets

The next step is to identify the expectations and requirements of the key participants in each market. In some cases there will be sufficient information within the company; in others market research will be needed to gather information from outside.

Identifying emphasis on the six markets

Once the company has identified the broad groups and the segments within them for each market domain, it can assess what level of marketing emphasis it gives to each market domain currently, and what level it needs to give. It can use a relationship marketing network diagram (also known as a 'spidergram'), shown in Figure 3.9, to help it decide on the right level of emphasis.

This diagram has seven axes – two for customers (existing and new) and one for each of the other five relationship markets discussed earlier. The scale of 1 (low) to 10 (high) reflects the degree of emphasis (cost

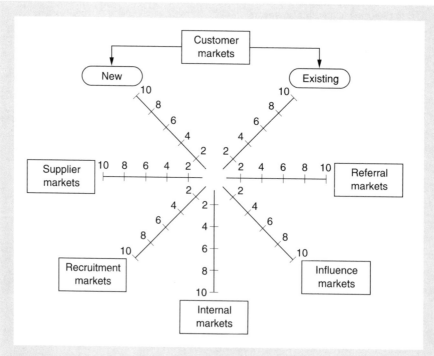

FIGURE 3.9 The six markets network diagram

and effect) placed on each relationship market. Dividing customers into 'new' and 'existing' reflects the two critical tasks within the customer domain, customer attraction and retention. A group of managers within a firm can assess their current and desired levels of emphasis on each market domain by means of a jury of executive opinion and plot the results on the relationship marketing network diagram.

We illustrate this approach to reviewing the six markets by reference to the relationship marketing network diagram for the Royal Society for the Protection of Birds (RSPB), a leading conservation charity, shown in Figure 3.10. This diagram is based on the views of a number of people, including former executives at RSPB, and represents an external assessment of developments in that organisation some years ago.

The RSPB might have considered a number of issues regarding the six markets, as shown in this figure, including:

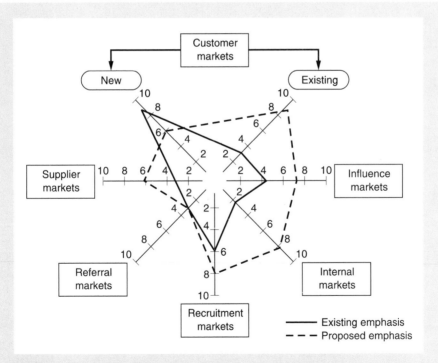

FIGURE 3.10 **RSPB relationship marketing network diagram**

- reducing its emphasis on acquiring members and increasing emphasis on retaining existing members;
- focusing more strongly on influence markets;
- reinforcing customer care and service quality issues with internal staff.

This analysis represents the first stage of the diagnostic process. The second stage examines the groups or segments within each market domain in terms of present and desired marketing emphasis. Further network diagrams can then be developed for each market domain. For example, Figure 3.11 shows a network diagram for the referral markets of an accounting firm.

The diagram illustrates five key referral markets identified by the firm: existing satisfied clients, the firm's audit practice, banks, joint venture candidates and offices of its international practice. The firm concluded that though it was doing a satisfactory job for its audit practice and

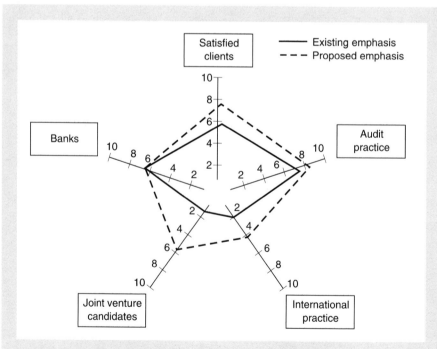

FIGURE 3.11 **Referral market audit for an accounting firm**

banks, it could improve referrals by putting more emphasis on the other three areas.

Planning for the six markets

The two levels of analysis described above identify the key groups or segments in each market domain and provide an initial view of the existing and potential levels of marketing emphasis directed at them. The final step involves determining the appropriate relationship strategies for each market including which of them require a detailed marketing plan to be developed. We will examine these relationship strategies in more detail in Chapter 6.

SUMMARY

This chapter has stressed that marketing activities directed at customers are necessary, but do not in themselves constitute relationship marketing. Organisations must also address the other relevant market domains and the segments within them. Successful relationship marketing involves an informed and integrated approach to all these market domains in order to achieve competitive advantage.

This stakeholder approach to relationship marketing recognises a diversity of key markets or market domains that organisations need to consider. It identifies where organisations should direct their marketing activity and where they may need to develop detailed marketing strategies.

The six markets framework has been successfully applied in a range of organisations including those in the business-to-business, business-to-consumer and non-profit sectors. Since it was developed in 1991, more than 200 organisations have used the six markets model to develop plans for each of their market domains (and market segments within them) and to demonstrate the benefits of adopting a relationship marketing perspective. The approach has proved a robust tool to help organisations recognise and respond to their network of markets.

This chapter has focused on the stakeholder relationships a company must develop with its markets. Companies' growing emphasis on developing relationships, partnerships and alliances with other companies is particularly important, and has given rise to the concept of the network organisation. We go on to explore this concept in Chapter 4.

References

1   Payne, A. (2000), Relationship Marketing: The UK Perspective, in Sheth, J.N. and Parvatiyar, A. (eds) *Handbook of Relationship Marketing*, Thousand Oaks, CA: Sage, 39–68.

2   Kotler, P. (1992), 'It's Time for Total Marketing', *Business Week* Advance Executive Brief, 2.

3   Parts of the discussion in this chapter draw on: Peck, H., Payne, A. F., Christopher, M. G. and Clark, M. K. (1999), *Relationship Marketing: Strategy and Implementation, Text and Cases*, Oxford: Butterworth-Heinemann.

4   See: Kotler, P. (1992), *op. cit.*, and Morgan, R.M and S.D. Hunt, (1994), 'The Commitment-Trust Theory of Relationship Marketing', *Journal of Marketing*, 58 (July), 20–38.

5   Gummesson, E. (1999), *Total Relationship Marketing*, Oxford: Butterworth-Heinemann.

6   Shaw, N. (1997), 'Unification Theory', *Customer Service Management*, June, 26–29.

7   Wayland, R. E. and Cole, P. M. (1997), *Customer Connections: New Strategies for Growth*, Boston, MA: Harvard Business School Press.

8   Pascale, R. (1993), *Nordstrom*. (This case study is reproduced in Peck, H., Payne, A. F., Christopher, M. G. and Clark, M. K. (1999), *Relationship Marketing: Strategy and Implementation, Text and Cases*, Oxford: Butterworth-Heinemann.)

9   Heskett, J. L., Sasser, Jr, W. E. and Schlesinger, L. A. (1997), *The Service Profit Chain*, New York: Free Press.

10 File, H. M., Judd, B. B. and Prince, C. A. (1992), 'Interactive Marketing: The Influence of Participation on Positive Word-of-Mouth and Referrals', *The Journal of Services Marketing*, 6, 4, 5–14.

11 Reichheld, F. F. (1990), *The Loyalty Effect*, Boston: Harvard Business School Press.

12 Gummesson, E. (1987), 'The New Marketing–Developing Long-Term Interactive Relationships', *Long-Range Planning*, 20, 4, 10–20.

13 *The Universum Graduate Survey 2000*, American Edition, Stockholm: Universum.

14 Axelrod, E.L., Handfield-Jones, H. and Welsh, T.A. (2000), 'War for Talent: Part Two', *McKinsey Quarterly*, No. 2.

15 This brief discussion is based in part on an interview on a video made by Harvard Business School.

16 Lovelock, C. (1994), *Product Plus*, McGraw Hill.

17 Judd, V.C. (1987): 'Differentiate with the 5th P: People', *Industrial Marketing Management*, 16, 241–7.

18 Lewis, B. and Varey, R.J. (2000), *Internal Marketing*, Taylor and Francis Book Ltd.

Managing relationships in networks

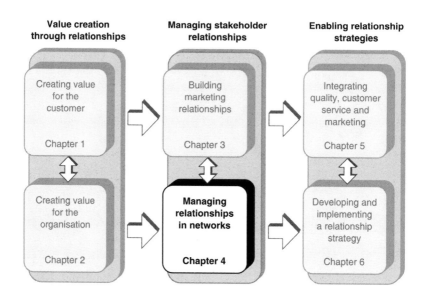

Creating value for the customer

Chapter 1

Building marketing relationships

Chapter 3

Integrating quality, customer service and marketing

Chapter 5

Creating value for the organisation

Chapter 2

Managing relationships in networks

Chapter 4

Developing and implementing a relationship strategy

Chapter 6

INTRODUCTION

The 'network organisation' is a recent phenomenon that has been much analysed and commented on. These 'virtual' organisations are characterised by a confederation of specialist skills or capabilities provided by the network members. Such collaborative arrangements arguably satisfy customer needs at a profit more effectively than does a single firm that undertakes multiple value-creating activities. The growth of these network organisations has profound implications for relationship marketing and may potentially change the whole basis of competitive advantage.

From vertical to virtual: the rise of the network organisation

Over the years our thinking on how firms should organise themselves has changed dramatically. Almost since the time of the Industrial Revolution, it has been assumed that the entire value chain, from source of supply through to final sale, needed to be owned by the same company in order to keep effective control of the means of creating and delivering products. Traditional ideas of the theory of the firm[1,2] emphasised that ownership provided the managerial control that maximised efficiency. These ideas were modified by the advocates of transaction cost analysis,[3,4] and, more recently, by those who take a resource-based view of the firm.[5]

But today a different model is emerging, based on the idea of the firm as an element in a network that competes through the way it leverages the resources and capabilities of its individual members. Each member of the network specialises in that aspect of the value-creation process where it has the greatest differential advantage. This model of business activity sees the network, not the individual firm, as the value delivery system.

The early work of Michael Porter helped clarify our understanding of the firm as a 'value chain'. Nevertheless, his definition of the value chain was still a single firm concept. He wrote:[6]

[Competitive advantage] stems from the many discrete activities a firm performs in designing, producing, marketing, delivering and supporting its product. Each of these activities can contribute to a firm's relative cost position and create a basis for differentiation ... The value chain disaggregates a firm into its strategically relevant activities in order to understand the behaviour of costs and the existing and potential sources of differentiation. A firm gains competitive advantage by performing these strategically important activities more cheaply or better than its competitors.

The recognition that the supply chain as a whole, rather than the individual firm, creates and delivers value[7] has led to the idea of the value chain being extended into the concept of a value 'web' or 'constellation'.[8] Supply chains are, in effect, value webs.

In the past organisations were typically structured and managed to optimise their own operations with little regard to the way they interfaced with suppliers and customers. The business model was essentially 'transactional' – that is, products and services were bought and sold on an arm's-length basis and there was little enthusiasm for the concept of longer-term, mutually dependent relationships.

> Today's emerging competitive paradigm is a stark contrast to the conventional model.

Today's emerging competitive paradigm is in stark contrast to the conventional model. It suggests that sustainable advantage lies in managing the complex web of relationships that link highly-focused providers of specific elements of the final offer in a cost-effective, value-adding network.

The key to success in this new competitive framework is, arguably, the way in which the network of alliances and suppliers are welded together in partnership to achieve mutually beneficial goals. Thus, for example, Nokia and Ericsson compete not as independent businesses, but as two uniquely configured networks of alliances and partnerships.

The emergence of the value net

In 1991, IBM made the greatest financial loss in corporate history. For years IBM had been regarded as one of the world's most successful companies, and it was traumatised. Just a few years earlier, Peters and Waterman had featured it as a paragon of excellence in their book *In Search of Excellence* .[9] There were many reasons for IBM's fall from grace, but it was widely agreed that the company did not respond fast enough to a rapidly changing environment. In particular, it had always followed a business model in which it carried out most, if not all, of its value-creating and delivery activities in-house. In many respects it was a classic, vertically integrated business.

With the appointment of a new CEO, Louis Gerstner, a new philosophy began to emerge. In order to survive, the company would have to access technologies, knowledge and capabilities that lay not within the business but in other organisations and entities. Instead of trying to manage the entire value chain, from fundamental R & D through to making and installing hardware and software, IBM sought to recreate itself as the hub of a dynamic and highly agile value net.

In 1986 IBM spent only 28 per cent of its sales revenue on outside goods and services; today that figure is over 50 per cent. It used to build all its own printed circuit boards (PCBs) whereas today it makes only 10 per cent, and it makes just 15 per cent of its memory chips now compared with 85 per cent ten years ago.

But IBM was not just conforming with the general move towards outsourcing. It recognised that to compete in the fast-changing markets in which it was positioned it needed an agility that it could only acquire through creating networks. Networks are confederations of specialist organisations that exist for agreed periods of time to undertake specific tasks. The word 'confederation' describes these arrangements better than 'federation', which implies something more permanent, formal and, potentially, rigid. The Japanese concept of 'keiretsu' is a typical federation arrangement, while the group of companies that is collaborating with Mercedes to produce the 'Smart Car' is a confederation.

Originally, the Smart Car was a collaborative venture between Daimler Benz and SMH (the Swiss watch company mainly known for its range of Swatch watches). The Smart Car is assembled at a factory in Hambach, eastern France, from modules supplied by seven strategic partners, which operate their own facilities alongside the assembly line. So, for example, Magna manufactures and provides the 'Tridion' – the frame around which the rest of the vehicle is built – while Krupp-Hoesch makes the engine mounting, Bosch the front module and so on.

All the partners in this collaboration effectively share the pain as well as the gain. They are responsible for running their own part of the operation and paying their own workforce and they only get paid themselves once the cars are built.

Value nets or value webs[10] are emerging in response to increasingly volatile and turbulent markets. Because demand is much harder to forecast in these conditions, companies need to be more agile. Old-style, rigid organisations that create most value themselves or with long-established, long-term partners, are less able to respond to rapid change in market environments. The value net holds the key to agility. Agility has been defined[11] as 'The ability to respond with ease to unexpected, but anticipated, events'.

To be truly agile, networks need a number of distinguishing characteristics.

- They must be *market sensitive*, that is, they should be capable of reading and responding to 'real' demand. Most organisations are driven by forecasts rather than demand. In other words, because they have little 'feed-forward' from the marketplace by way of data on actual customer requirements, they are forced to make forecasts based on past sales or shipments and convert these forecasts into inventory. The breakthroughs of the past decade in the form of Internet-based information systems that capture data on demand direct from the point-of-sale or point-of-use are transforming the network's ability to hear the voice of the market and to respond directly to it.
- All members of an agile network must share the same *information*, so that they all 'sing from the same hymn sheet'. They must all be able to access demand data, see upstream and downstream capacity, production schedules and inventory, and share common forecasts.
- This information exchange is facilitated by *process alignment*, which means that the core business processes of network partners connect easily. Advanced computer software that provides a common platform for members of a network to share information and ensure seamless end-to-end process management is increasingly facilitating this 'connection'.

Value nets are more agile than individual companies because they comprise specialist entities, which are often relatively small and unbureaucratic, that exist only to perform specific activities. These specialist entities are joined together through shared objectives and an agreed strategy for exploiting a particular, often time-limited, opportunity. But while these relationships are, of necessity, very close, they are not necessarily long term. Agile networks need to be reconfigured as market conditions and competitive circumstances change.

A good example of an agile value web is the Swedish clothing brand GANT. At the centre of the web is Pyramid Sportswear AB, which employs fewer than ten people. Pyramid contracts with designers, identifies trends, uses contract manufacturers, develops the retailer network and creates the brand image through marketing communications.

Through its databases, Pyramid closely monitors sales, inventories and trends. Its network of closely co-ordinated partners means it can react quickly to changes in the market. The network itself changes as requirements change, and it will use different designers, freelance photographers, catalogue producers, contract manufacturers and so on, as appropriate. Figure 4.1 depicts the Pyramid virtual network.

The UK retailer Marks & Spencer typifies the conventional wisdom that long-term relationships are the way to compete – as indeed they may be in stable market conditions. Some of Marks & Spencer's suppliers had been with it for over fifty years. One company, Dewhirst, had supplied M & S since the retailer first set up over 100 years ago. While this type of relationship can work well it needs to be constantly refreshed and renewed or it will ossify. In a fast-changing and increasingly competitive marketplace M & S found its traditional paternalistic, even dictatorial, approach to managing its suppliers considerably restricted its agility.

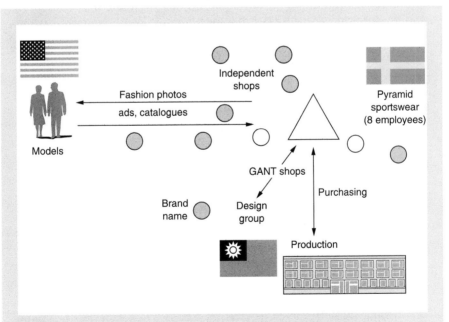

FIGURE 4.1 The Pyramid sportswear value web

Source[12]: *Virtual Organisations and Beyond*, Hedberg, B., Dahlgren, G., Hansson, J. and Olve, N., 1997. © John Wiley & Sons Limited. Reproduced with permission.

Ironically, despite its long history of supposed loyalty and mutual commitment from its suppliers, when Marks & Spencer finally started to change the structure of its supply base, it was sued by one of the major suppliers that it had discarded.

The shift to network competition

As we have suggested, the real competitive struggle is not between individual companies, but between their supply chains or networks. This view is sometimes challenged on the grounds that supply chains cannot truly compete since, because they frequently share common suppliers, for example, they are not unique configurations. But this view misses the point. What makes a supply chain or network unique is the way the relationships and interfaces in the chain or network are managed. In this sense a major source of differentiation comes from the quality of relationships that one business enjoys compared to its competitors.

> The real competitive struggle is not between individual companies, but between their supply chains or networks.

Companies need a new approach both to determining strategy and to managing relationships if they are to turn this radical idea into reality.

Clearly, when the business model is based on stand-alone competition, strategy is set by one organisation. But as the model changes to a collaborative network, it poses interesting challenges to the network partners in terms of how to create and implement inter-company strategic thinking. Every network needs a lead player or a champion for collaboration, and the more organisations outsource activities to others, the more they will need to understand the importance of relationship management.

Complex networks need to be managed tightly and actively if they are to function efficiently and effectively as competitive value webs. They need a 'network orchestrator' – or 'focal' firm – to drive and guide the development and delivery of customer value in the ultimate marketplace. The network orchestrator identifies strategic partners that can contribute to the value-creation and delivery process. It develops a platform, usually web-based, to enable the members of the network to exchange information openly. And it establishes common communication standards between network members and facilitates the capture and transfer of market information and ongoing demand data across the network.

Cisco Systems is one of the best examples of such a network orchestrator. Cisco is a world leader in providing data-networking equipment that enables communication to flow across the Internet. It is a highly focused and, in effect, virtual business. It has created a web of global partners to which it outsources most of its manufacturing. It bypasses traditional distribution centres by using specialist logistics service companies to perform 'merge in transit' operations. It captures most of its orders through the Internet and shares that information almost in real time with its network partners. Cisco also actively engages suppliers' suppliers in the network, recognising that second-tier suppliers affect its agility as much as first-tier suppliers do.

Managers from many of Cisco's key suppliers, such as Solectron, work within Cisco so that they can participate in daily production meetings and new product design programmes, for example.

But while Cisco is clearly in the driving seat in terms of orchestrating the network, it shares the gain and the pain. For example, Cisco shares cost savings with suppliers and even purchases component inventory on their behalf. This commitment to suppliers was dramatically illustrated in the second quarter of 2001 when Cisco announced a $2.2 billion write-down of inventory resulting from the worldwide collapse of demand for network infrastructure products. Cisco had purchased much of that inventory on behalf of its suppliers.

What makes networks work?

Networks involve *vertical* and *horizontal* relationships. Vertical relationships reflect the classic supply chain, that is

suppliers → manufacturers → distributors → consumers

Horizontal relationships might include competitors as well as specific services providers, so, for example, technology-sharing agreements or outsourced information systems management would be typical of this type of relationship.

It has long been recognised that networks are important vehicles for achieving competitive advantage. The work of the Industrial Marketing and Purchasing (IMP) research group (itself a network of interested academics and practitioners) has focused for several decades on this phenomenon.[13] The IMP work was originally based on examining, in some detail, the nature of successful relationships in a two-way exchange context, but it has since been augmented by others who have taken a wider network-based approach.[14]

The IMP researchers have established a significant reputation for their research on industrial markets. The IMP approach is worth noting as, unlike some of the better-known and more dominant models of buyer behaviour, it places equal emphasis on both buyer and seller characteristics. Conventional models, by contrast, tend to concentrate on the buyer's side of the transaction.

The general conclusions of this early work on networks were further reinforced by the research of Morgan and Hunt[15] who demonstrated the central role of commitment and trust in successful business relationships. The findings of their research were:

- A firm will trust its relationship partner when both partners share similar values, when communication in their relationship is healthy, and when their relationship history is not characterised by one partner maliciously taking advantage of the other.
- Relationship commitment arises not only from trust and its antecedents, but also from the direct effects of shared values and the belief that partners would be difficult to replace.
- More than half the differences in levels of co-operation from one relationship to the next can be explained by relationship commitment, trust and their antecedents.

These findings may seem obvious, but it is probably true that many business relationships are typified by a *lack* of trust and commitment, which is why so many corporate alliances fail.

Work by Rosbeth Moss Kanter[16] has further reinforced the need for a more open, collaborative approach to managing relationships if network alliances are to succeed. She suggested that successful business partnerships are founded upon the Eight Is:

Individual excellence: both parties have strengths and capabilities that they bring to the relationship.

Importance: both parties need to make the relationship work for strategic reasons.

Interdependence: both parties have a need for each other – they complement each other.

Investment: both parties should be prepared to commit financial or other resources to the relationship.

Information: both parties share information and have continuing and open communication.

Integration: there are many connections and linkages between the parties.

Institutionalisation: the relationship is formal and is company-wide, extending beyond the people who initiated it.

Integrity: both parties behave in ways that reinforce the mutual trust.

Partnerships: creating value through collaboration

The realisation that individual businesses no longer compete as standalone entities, but as collaborative networks, has been perhaps one of the most significant breakthroughs in management thinking in recent years. We are now entering the era of 'network competition' where the prizes will go to those organisations that can best structure, co-ordinate and manage relationships with their partners in a network committed to creating customer and consumer value through collaboration.

> We are now entering the era of 'network competition'.

Why partner?

In the past organisations tended to perform most of their activities in-house, in the belief, as we noted above, that owning the entire value chain would give them greater control and make them more efficient. Ford used to be a typical vertically integrated company. At one time Ford owned a power plant, a steel mill, a glass factory, a rubber factory and mahogany forests. Since then management thinking has gone through a 180° change as corporations focus on core competencies and outsource everything else. By definition, the more companies focus on those activities where they believe they have a differential advantage, the more they need to rely on others. As we have pointed out, as these external dependencies increase the nature of the relationship has to switch from arm's-length, transactional mode to a collaborative, partnership mode.

In Chapter 1 we referred to the four critical processes that underpin the business as:

- market understanding
- innovation management
- supply chain management
- customer relationship management

The business itself may lack the competencies and skills to master all these processes and will almost certainly need to rely on others to provide some, or all, of the key elements. But any company outsourcing anything runs the risk of losing control, and they need to manage outsourced activities even more closely than they would if they were in-house. The maxim must be: 'outsource the *execution* of a process but never the *control* of that process'.

You could even argue that we should talk about 'insourcing' instead of outsourcing. Outsourcing implies we are putting something *outside* the business (as in sub-contracting), whereas insourcing suggests we are bringing a strength we do not currently have *into* the business.

The realisation that the organisation no longer stands alone is prompting a new search for collaborative partnering. These partnerships may be with suppliers, distributors, retailers, specialist service providers, technology-sharing alliances and, increasingly, with competitors. Sometimes, the lines between suppliers, customers and competitors become increasingly blurred.

For example, Dell and IBM compete in the PC market but IBM also supplies Dell with components and has a technology-sharing agreement with the company. It has even been suggested that Dell might, before long, undertake certain assembly tasks for IBM!

This phenomenon of collaborating to compete has been called 'co-opetition'.[17] The principle that underpins co-opetition is that organisations may benefit from collaborating to 'grow the cake', but then compete over how to slice it. In many retail environments branded products' manufacturers compete with the retailers' own-label products. Yet the smart players in those markets have come to recognise the benefits of joint category planning in order to grow total demand within that category. In the UK, for example, Coca-Cola and Sainsbury (a retailer with its own-label cola) compete for share of the cola market but work together to grow the total sales of carbonated soft drinks through joint category management.

> The aim should be to maximise 'collaborative advantage'.

When competing as a network the aim should be to maximise 'collaborative advantage' rather than competitive advantage in its traditional, single-firm meaning. But in order to realise this collaborative advantage and to leverage the collective competitiveness and skills across the network, companies within the network need to share and harness knowledge (see Figure 4.2).

Creating collaborative advantage

How can collaboration help create stronger customer relationships? Perhaps one of the best current examples comes from the packaged goods industry where, as we noted above, manufacturers and retailers are pooling their knowledge of consumers and markets to create joint category plans. In many cases this activity has been widened to embrace the principles of collaborative planning, forecasting and replenishment (CPFR).

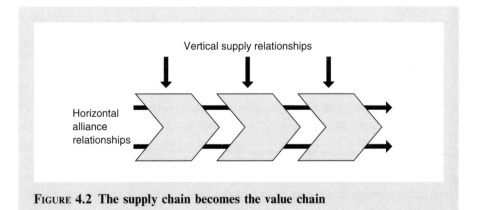

FIGURE 4.2 The supply chain becomes the value chain

CPFR is the umbrella term given to the wider collaboration between manufacturers and retailers. It springs from the efficient consumer response (ECR) initiative that yielded many benefits for supply chain partners. CPFR involves buyers and suppliers jointly developing strategies for products and product categories and executing those strategies through agreed forecasts and replenishment procedures.

As Fiddes[18] has pointed out, the CPFR model is based on five key principles: collaboration, shared forecasts, exploitation of supply chain core competencies, agreed performance metrics and an acceptance that benefits and risks will be shared. Early pilot studies have reported significant benefits to both supplier and customer as a result of this type of collaborative activity. For example, WarnerLambert and Wal-Mart developed a CPFR programme for the mouthwash Listerine which resulted in sales rising by $8.5 million in a single year, availability in-store rising from 87 per cent to 98 per cent and inventory falling by two weeks.

CPFR programmes involve a high level of information sharing between partners in order to create forecasts that all parties agree to, and then managing supply and demand to improve on-the-shelf availability. CPFR is an example of 'vertical' collaborative working leading to the delivery of greater customer and consumer value. 'Horizontal' collaborations between organisations marketing complementary products – such as Coca-Cola's long-standing global partnership with McDonald's – can also lead to stronger consumer appeal and greater value-added.

Innovation represents perhaps one of the most powerful opportunities to create competitive advantage through partnerships. Being able to enhance and accelerate innovation is critical to every organisation's success in today's markets. Innovation in both products and processes depends, at least in part, on the contribution of both horizontal and vertical partners. Vertical partnerships involve suppliers in the innovation process, and it is not uncommon today to see suppliers involved directly in new product development. The car industry – where ABS braking systems, improved engine management systems and advanced suspension systems owe as much to the suppliers as to the vehicle assemblers – is a good example. Equally, suppliers have significantly improved their customers' competitiveness through improving their process technology to enable higher quality components or critical materials to be made available at lower cost in just-in-time time windows.

At the same time, the increasing propensity of organisations to engage in horizontal relationships – often in the form of technology-sharing agreements with competitors – has resulted in hitherto impossible levels of profitable innovation. In telecommunications, for example, head-to-head competitors such as Nokia, Ericsson and Motorola have combined to agree standards and to help develop the next generation of mobile communications equipment and products.

Networks can dramatically reduce time-to-market by leveraging the capabilities of organisations that once operated as stand-alone entities, duplicating each other's efforts in terms of development time and costs.

Supply chain management (SCM) provides a further opportunity to achieve collaborative advantage through managing upstream and downstream relationships with suppliers and customers. SCM, by definition, is based on collaborative working across the network as a whole. The idea that organisations now compete as part of a wider network rather than as single entities calls for a number of new management practices, not least a change from 'silo' thinking to a much more 'collaborative' mode of working.

Collective strategy determination

If we accept the view that the supply chain, rather than the individual enterprise, competes as a value net, then it follows that a company must develop a strategy for the supply chain as a whole. But if the supply chain strategy is to be effective and efficiently implemented, then all the key players in the supply chain – suppliers, distributors and customers – need to be involved in developing it.

One idea that is worth exploring in the context of collective supply chain strategy determination is the idea of a 'supply chain council' or, as it has been described, an 'agile team'.[19] These teams cross organisational boundaries and comprise key players in the supply chain. The focal firm that forms the centre of a specific network normally assumes the role of team leader or 'supply chain captain'.

The fundamental principle of relationship management in an agile network or supply chain is that while there will always be a dominant player, there must be 'buy-in' from all the other key players. This 'stakeholder' concept of supply chain management is predicated on the idea that companies working together can grow the 'size of the cake'. Conventional supply chain relationships tend to focus more upon how the cake should be cut.

The value-added exchange of information

Underpinning successful supply chain relationships is the transparent and open flow of information throughout the network. Ideally information on customer requirements, inventory and replenishment schedules should be visible and available in real time to all members of the network. In the past, many organisations adhered to the philosophy that 'information is power', guarding information carefully and rarely sharing it. In today's agile networks the reverse is true; companies such as Cisco use extranets to relay customer orders to key suppliers as soon as they receive them, so suppliers see the order at the same time as Cisco. They are 'co-producers' manufacturing modules and elements which are then 'merged in transit' by a logistics service partner. Most products are never actually 'touched' by Cisco.

As Bowman has written,[20] from its inception Cisco

> viewed its supply chain as a 'fabric of relationships' rather than a line. The goal was to transcend the internal focus of enterprise resource planning (ERP) systems to embrace a networked supply chain of all trading partners. All 14 of its global manufacturing sites, along with two distributors, are linked via a single enterprise extranet ... The quest for a single enterprise has tied Cisco to its suppliers in unprecedented ways ... instead of responding to specific work orders, contract manufacturers turn out components according to a daily build plan, derived from a single long-term forecast shared throughout the supply chain.

In the retail industry, companies like Tesco are reaping the benefits of sharing sales information with suppliers through extranets. The Tesco Information Exchange (TIE) enables 'win-win' supply chain relationships. Tesco wins because it is reducing inventory while at the same time improving on-the-shelf availability. Suppliers win because they can plan and schedule production and distribution against real demand rather than forecast demand, reducing their need to carry safety stock.

Companies that fail to exploit the potential for collaboration in the supply chain incur significant and unnecessary penalties. For example, businesses that do not share information will have to carry additional inventory to buffer themselves against uncertainty. In turbulent markets this is very expensive. But even more serious for businesses that do not collaborate is that their agility is restricted because they can not see clearly from one end of the supply chain to the other. For example, if an upstream supplier can not see what is happening at the downstream end of the pipeline it will have to be forecast rather than demand driven. In today's turbulent markets, being able to see real demand is a vital component of competitive advantage.

The number of examples of collaborative working in the supply chain – even among competitors – is growing. For example, two direct competitors, Lever Fabergé and Colgate Palmolive, have shared the same distribution centre in the UK for a number of years and make combined deliveries to common customers. While these two companies compete head-to-head in the marketplace, they argue that they do not compete in the warehouse or on the truck, and therefore both benefit through collaboration. Another example is competing airlines that share inventories of high value spares, such as aero engines.

These types of collaboration are often facilitated by third party logistics service providers, which can provide a neutral platform.

Working in partnership

> Relationship marketing is, in effect, relationship *management*.

Relationship marketing is, in effect, relationship *management*. The process begins with the crucial strategic decision of whom to partner with. There are strategic stakeholders in each of the relevant multiple markets that surround the focal firm, and the focal firm must clearly articulate an agreed way of working and establish the role these stakeholders should play in the value-creating network.

In the key supplier and customer markets the old arm's-length, single point of contact model clearly has to be replaced with a much closer, open and multi-level relationship.

Key account management has emerged in recent years as a team-based way of managing major customers. The idea behind key account management is to focus on understanding the customers' business and markets in great detail in order to provide solutions to help them improve their profitability. These solutions are not just products, but might increasingly involve process alignment and improvement, consultancy and business development, for example.

In the supplier market, the equivalent of key account management is supplier development, whereby the customer seeks to develop mutually beneficial relationships with suppliers rather than the adversarial relationships of the past. This involves customers actively trying to find ways to work with suppliers both to reduce the total costs of ownership and further to differentiate their own offer through, for example, better quality, innovative design or unique technology.

Key account management and supplier development imply a much greater degree of openness and communication at multiple levels among partnering organisations. The new model challenges traditional organisational structures. For instance, the role of the conventional sales force and the old-style buyer will need to change radically if not actually disappear. But organisations will not want to adopt this type of relationship management for all their customers and suppliers.

A portfolio of relationships

Given the complexity of most business networks, which comprise hundreds, if not thousands of suppliers and customers, it is clearly not practical – nor is it necessary – to develop close relationships with all suppliers and customers. A more viable strategy is to create and manage a portfolio of relationships.

The idea behind the portfolio approach to supply chain relationships is that it is only possible to have close relationships with a limited number of suppliers. This has led many companies to reduce radically the numbers of suppliers they deal with. They can then implement the kind of supplier development programmes we discussed above, which aim to integrate strategic partners with the focal firm through sharing information and aligning processes. The initiating organisation often creates supplier development teams to work with its chosen suppliers to help create a 'seamless' or 'boundary-less' business. These teams are usually cross-functional and seek to maximise the potential value that lies in different parties working together in the supply chain or value web.

This very close, integrated way of working is only possible – and only necessary – with a small number of strategic suppliers. Strategic suppliers are those whose resources, skills and capabilities enable the focal firm to create superior value for its customers. A supplier could be strategic because it provides materials, products or services that are in limited supply, or because it can respond quickly in fast-changing markets, or because its product and process technology gives the focal firm an edge, and so on.

But other relationships will be more tactical or operational than strategic. Some products or services a company needs will be standard and readily available from a variety of sources at competitive prices. In such cases the company does not need and will not attempt to develop a strategic relationship with its suppliers.

One major British retailer has segmented its supplier base into four tiers. The tier structure, which can also be thought of as a 'career path' for suppliers, is depicted in Figure 4.3.

As the figure shows, potential new suppliers can only enter at the bottom of the hierarchy – that is, they start with the lowest supplier status. The company upgrades and downgrades suppliers based on a formal evaluation procedure involving several management levels in the organisation. Suppliers may be axed at any stage if their performance no longer meets the predefined performance standards. The four-tier classification system is central to the retailer's relationship management strategy and is communicated internally as well as to suppliers. Because the retailer plans to do more business with the higher-tier suppliers and invests more in these relationships, suppliers are motivated to achieve first-tier supplier status.

Sheth[21] has suggested that there will be four types of relationships in value webs depending on whether the relationship is 'ad hoc', 'ongoing', 'strategic' or 'operational'. Figure 4.4 depicts the alternatives.

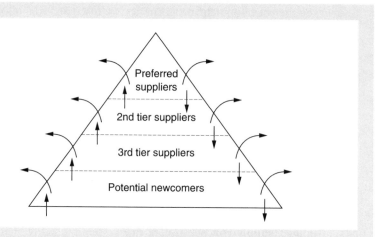

FIGURE 4.3 Supplier hierarchy

As the pace of change and market volatility increase, supply chain arrangements will need to become increasingly flexible, resulting in more 'ad hoc' than 'ongoing' relationships. The implication of this is that organisations will need to develop a 'pool' of partners with whom to have very close relationships, and then, for specific projects, draw from this pool to create a value web that will exist for the life of that project.

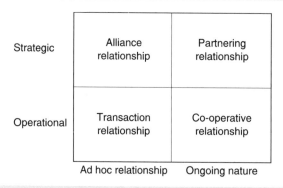

FIGURE 4.4 Relationship types

Source: Sheth, J.N. (1994), *Towards a Theory of Relationship Marketing*, Presentation at the Relationship Marketing Faculty Consortium, Center for Relationship Marketing, Emory University. Reproduced with permission.

But there are benefits to be gained through collaboration in all types of relationship. The consulting company Accenture, for example, reports a number of tangible benefits from collaborative, partnership-based relationships (see Figure 4.5). It is clear from this and other reported evidence that companies can win significant prizes if they can overcome the barriers to change.

Collaborative design	Collaborative forecasting and planning	Collaborative replenishment	Collaborative logistics optimisation
• Early concurrent involvement of suppliers • Improved workflow tracking and transparency • Improved product design cycle time • Shorter time-to-market • Reduced COGS • Reduced redesign and rework risks • Optimised time phasing of product life cycles • Provides a secure structure for maintaining intellectual property	• Increased forecast accuracy • Increased planning effectiveness, manufacturing efficiencies and productivity • Early identification of supply constraints, allowing for proactive issue resolution • Partners resolve exceptions through discussions and proposed plan revisions	• Trading partners share order scheduling and replenishment data • Reduced inventory and lead-times due to greater certainty of supply and visibility of delivery • Supply visibility facilitates improved production processes and reduction in inefficiencies • Intelligent alerts enable management by exception • Consolidation of supply base and subsequent leverage on input costs • Improved delivery performance	• Rapid establishment of advanced modelling capabilities for transport network optimisation • Provides forward capability during a new business/ network planning phase prior to rolling out the network • Lower transportation costs • Increased reliability of the distribution network and assured service levels

FIGURE 4.5 The benefits of partnership

Source: Accenture

Prerequisites for successful partnering

Based on the experience of organisations that have successfully made the transition from the old style of relationship management to the new, we can suggest three prerequisites for successful partnerships in value-creating networks:

The relationship must:

- be strategically important for both parties;
- be based on agreed strategic goals;
- enable the value-added exchange of information.

Strategic importance

If networks are to compete effectively then all parties need to demonstrate their commitment in terms of recognising the strategic importance of the arrangement. In other words, they must acknowledge that all parties are more likely to achieve their goals by being a member of the value web than they would on their own.

The collaboration between Honda and Rover, before Rover was sold to BMW, was a good example of how parties with different goals can achieve those goals more effectively through co-operating with other parties.

In 1979 the struggling BL (as Rover Group used to be called) formed an alliance with the Honda Motor Company. Globalisation of the motor industry had begun in earnest, and the two companies forged their alliance out of necessity. The partnership provided Honda with a way into the European market and BL with a technological lifeline. Under the original agreement the Japanese manufacturer would supply new engine technology in exchange for a 20 per cent stake in BL's core car manufacturing business. In addition, BL would produce a Honda car, badged as the Triumph Acclaim.

The agreement worked well and Honda and BL/Rover went on to produce several cars together, proceeding on a model-by-model basis. The collaboration resulted in separately badged vehicles based on shared common platforms, which allowed both companies to benefit from economies of scale in sourcing.

A transfer of process management know-how accompanied the transfer of product technology, with Rover gradually adopting the management philosophy and many of the working practices of its Japanese partner. Rover applied the Japanese-style management tools and techniques first to its internal relationships and then more widely as it set about building its own 'extended enterprise'. Over the years, the investment-starved Rover became increasingly dependent on licensed Honda technology and on the development expertise of its partners within the extended enterprise.

The alliance survived the Rover Group's return to the private sector and BAe's stewardship of the business, but came to an abrupt end after the sale of the Rover Group to BMW in 1994.

Managing network relationships*

As we have pointed out, every company maintains a variety of different relationships and may not want or be able to develop close ties with all parties. Companies need to invest a lot of time, money and resources in partnerships, and in so doing run both financial risks and strategic risks in the sense of making themselves more vulnerable to opportunistic behaviour. Therefore most companies maintain a portfolio of relationships, each with different characteristics.

Before developing a specific portfolio model, a company needs to be precise about its own corporate or business strategy and then define the role partnerships and, specifically, joint strategic activities play within this strategy. Xerox, for example, has been known for its quality-oriented strategy for many years. Developing close relationships with its suppliers and customers has been part of that strategy. More recently, however, the company decided to alter course slightly to put a heavier emphasis on costs. This has, allegedly, also had an impact on its choice of suppliers, as materials cost has crept back as an order-winning criterion, while quality is now seen as a given.

In supply chain contexts in particular, it is important to consider the structure of a potential relationship agreement. Companies will manage a bilateral structure quite differently from the way they would

* This section draws on material from Christopher, M. and Jüttner, U. (2000).[22]

manage a network comprising several parties. The more elements of the network the agreement spans, the more complex it will be. A primary concern for a company operating in a structure with several competitors is that the other parties will not engage in opportunistic behaviour. For example, a retailer receiving different category management plans from competing suppliers would need to balance the competing interests of those category managers rather than playing them off against each other.

It is also important to consider the impact of the relative power of different parties. Most companies will find themselves in a chain or network dominated by a so-called 'channel captain' or focus firm. It is generally impossible to dictate the terms of the relationship from a weaker position, but instead of remaining 'passive', companies can launch a 'willing follower' strategy. The ability of companies to be 'good at being led' is an important factor in achieving their corporate objectives.

Having defined their own strategy and position, companies should evaluate their existing relationships and future prospects. Many companies do not measure the value of their relationships at all, or, if they do, only on the basis of revenue and volume. In business-to-business contexts, though, the real value is related to other, more disguised criteria. While the need for a more comprehensive, standard measurement approach is now accepted, experience also shows that success criteria tend to be company and industry specific and, often, difficult to quantify. Among these criteria are the 'substitutability' of the buyer or seller, the indispensability of the goods bought or sold, the savings resulting from the partner's practices and the degree of common interest.[23]

In the case of substitutability, for instance, two customers with the same business volume may be completely different in terms of how easily a supplier can replace them. This is due to how indispensable the products bought or sold are: the more specific the product, the less likely the partner is to be substituted by another. The savings a company can make from having a long-term relationship with a partner also affect the value of the relationship. This is because so-called 'transaction costs' (effectively administration costs) decrease over time. Finally, the degree of common interest builds in a political dimension to the process of choosing strategic partners. There are a number of prospective business partners that, despite their high economic relationship value, should not be selected for partnership agreements because of, for example, their substantially different strategic objectives or corporate cultures.

Developing the right interface structure

The classic debate in the strategy literature is about whether a company's 'structure follows its strategy' or its 'strategy follows its structure'. This debate could continue in the context of relationship management. Experience shows that the quality of relationships – the degree of closeness between the parties, for example – is strongly influenced by the interface structure that has been set up to manage them day-to-day. Therefore, defining a balanced set of relationships for a company's chosen strategic partners and developing the right interface structure are mutually reinforcing.

Figure 4.6 illustrates four different typical interface structures.

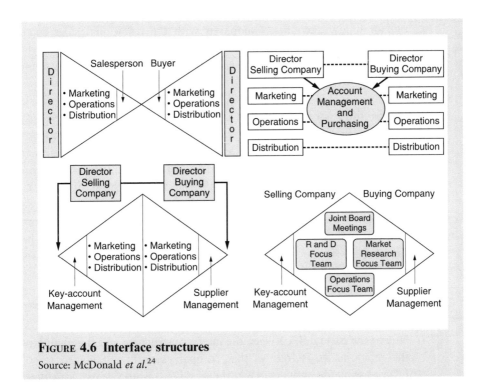

FIGURE 4.6 Interface structures
Source: McDonald et al.[24]

Moving from the top left to the bottom right the number of ties between the companies gradually increases and the relationship becomes multifaceted. The first structure (top left) shows an interface that is confined to a buyer–seller interaction. Other functions are not involved in the relationship. For such business relationships, the commercial deal is central and negotiations concentrate on price and margin. On the positive side, the interface structure can be set up with few resources and can therefore be used as a structural foundation for managing a large number of relationships. Likewise, switching barriers are low, which can be both an advantage and a disadvantage. On the downside, however, the structure limits value creation to mere product value, mainly because it does not enable the parties to get to know each other's business, a precondition for comprehensive value-generating processes.

The second structure (top right) is built around a closer collaboration between buying and selling. This closer collaboration is underlined by the change in titles from 'buyer' to 'purchasing' and from 'salesperson' to 'account management' for the boundary-spanning employees and departments. These people get back-up support from other functions on demand, but the functional people are not dedicated exclusively to one or a few accounts. Compared with the traditional sales force organisation described above, this second interface structure involves greater commitment of resources, which explains why strategic managers are involved.

In the third structure (bottom left), the relationship is organised between companies. Direct interactions between a range of functions emphasise collaboration across each partner's core business processes and create a stability that is independent of individual employee turnover. Managing a relationship on this basis requires substantial investment, and therefore decisions are linked directly to the company's overarching business strategy. The same applies to the fourth structure (bottom right), where company boundaries become blurred. The assignments of the focus teams further illustrate that the parties are not only jointly handling the day-to-day operational business but are co-operating on strategic issues like R & D, market research and market development.

Due to the close link between the interface structure and the quality of the relationship, it follows that companies with a balanced set of relationships do not manage them all from the same structural platform. The Case study illustrates how one company is currently addressing this issue.

Speedo

Speedo is a leading international maker of professional swimwear, based in the UK. Like many companies, Speedo has set up different, parallel structures for managing its diverse customer base.

Speedo currently has three distinct interface structures. It has a traditional sales organisation with a large and dispersed field sales force that deals with small independent sports stores. The sales force has traditionally been the pillar of the business and represented its main distribution channel. But the sports stores are low volume customers for Speedo, and, because they are spread all over the country they are best dealt with by individual salespeople. Because the company is concerned about brand erosion it places strong emphasis on an experienced, well-qualified sales force and employee retention.

A second customer segment, major high street retailers and sports multiples, accounts for a growing portion of the business. It represents about 50 per cent of Speedo's business today, and is forecast to rise to 80 per cent in the near future. Both the shifting balance and the concentration of business within this distribution channel, make the relationship with this group of customers very valuable, which justifies the time and money Speedo invests in maintaining the relationship. Dedicated account managers in both Speedo and its retail customers get back-up support from other functions in the company.

Finally, Speedo is developing even closer relationships with two potentially high growth customers. The relationship project and the corresponding interface structure are still being trialled, but both parties are extremely committed. One of the customers is Europe's biggest independent sports retailer with approximately 120 high street stores, additional in-store concessions and a number of superstores. For Speedo, the relationship is crucial: aside from the high economic relationship value, the customer shares its interests, stocking only leading brands and no own-label products. Speedo's operations director initiated the project and assigned an account development team to work exclusively on this one account. The team members were selected to match the retailer's supply management team and both teams' target is to improve the effectiveness and efficiency of the supply chain.

Source: Christopher, M. and Jüttner, U. (2000), 'Developing Strategic Partnerships in the Supply Chain: A Practitioner Perspective', *European Journal of Purchasing and Supply Management*, 6, 117–127.

SUMMARY

The effectiveness of a network or web is largely determined by the extent to which it acts in a co-ordinated, synchronised and unified way. This level of cohesion does not occur by accident, but stems from the way the focus firm manages relationships within the network. The proper role of supply chain management in the new Internet economy will be to manage relationships between partners that recognise that collectively they can achieve more than they ever could as stand-alone entities.

In this chapter, we have considered the particular challenges of managing relationships across networks of organisations. In Chapters 5 and 6 we go on to examine ways in which firms within such networks can create frameworks, structures and a culture to make these relationships happen.

References

1   Marshall, A. (1936), *Principles of Economics*, 8th edn, New York: Macmillan.
2   Stigler, G.J. (1941), *Production and Distribution Theories*, New York: Macmillan.
3   Coase, R. (1937), 'The Nature of the Firm', *Economica*, 4, 16, 386–405.
4   Williamson, D.E. (1979), 'Transaction Cost Economics: The Governance of Contractual Relations', *Journal of Law and Economics*, 22, 2, 223–261
5   Montgomery, C.M. (ed.) (1995), *Resource-Based and Evolutionary Theories of the Firm*, Dordrecht: Kluwer Academic Publishers.

6   Porter, M.E. (1980), *Competitive Advantage: Creating and Sustaining Superior Performance*, New York: Free Press.

7   Christopher, M. (1992), *Logistics and Supply Chain Management*, London: Pitman.

8   Normann, R. and Ramirez, R. (1993), 'From Value Chain to Value Constellation', *Harvard Business Review*, September-October, 65–77.

9   Peters, T.J. and Waterman, R.H. (1981), *In Search of Excellence*, New York: Harper and Row.

10   Boret, D. and Martha, J. (2000), *Value Nets: Breaking the Supply Chain to Unlock Hidden Profits*, New York: John Wiley.

11   Oleson, J.D. (1998), *Pathways to Agility*, New York: John Wiley.

12   Hedberg, B., Dahlgren, G., Hansson, J. and Olve, N. (1997), *Virtual Organisations and Beyond*, Chichester: John Wiley & Sons Limited.

13   Ford, D. (1990), IMP and the Interaction Approach, in Ford, D. (ed.), *Understanding Business Markets: Interactions, Relationships & Networks*, London: Routledge.

14   Gummesson, E. (1987), 'The New Marketing – Developing Long-Term Interactive Relationships', *Long-Term Planning*, **20**, 4, 10–20.

15   Morgan, R.M. and Hunt, S.D. (1994), 'The Commitment-Trust Theory of Relationship Marketing', *Journal of Marketing*, 58, July, 20–38.

16   Kanter, R.M. (1994), 'Collaborative Advantage: The Art of Alliances', *Harvard Business Review*, July–August, 96–108.

17   Nalebuff, B.J. and Brandenburger, A.M. (1996), *Co-opetition*, London: Harper Collins.

18   Fiddes, C. (1999), 'CPFR - delivering the vision of ECR', *Collaboration in the Supply Chain*, Financial Times Special Report, 10–12.

19   Mettes, G., Gundry, J., and Bradish, P. (1998), *Agile Networking*, New Jersey: Prentice Hall.

20   Bowman, R. J. (2000), 'At Cisco Systems, The Internet is Both Business and Business Model', *Global Logistics and Supply Chain Strategies*, 4, 4, 28–38.

21   Sheth, J.N. (1994), *Towards a Theory of Relationship Marketing*, Handout at the Relationship Marketing Faculty Consortium, Center for Relationship Marketing, Emory University.

22   Christopher, M. and Jüttner, U. (2000), 'Developing Strategic Partnerships in the Supply Chain: A Practitioner Perspective', *European Journal of Purchasing and Supply Management*, 6, 117–127.

23   Krapfel, R., Salmond, D. and Spekman, R. (1991), 'A Strategic Approach to Managing Buyer/Seller Relationships', *European Journal of Marketing*, **25**, 22–37.

24   McDonald, M., Millman, T. and Rogers, B. (1996), *Key Account Management – Learning from Supplier and Customer Perspectives*, Cranfield University School of Management Research Report.

Relationship marketing: integrating quality, customer service and marketing

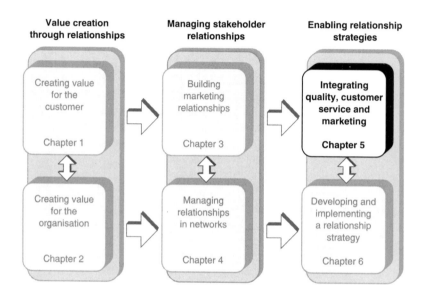

Value creation through relationships	Managing stakeholder relationships	Enabling relationship strategies
Creating value for the customer — Chapter 1	Building marketing relationships — Chapter 3	**Integrating quality, customer service and marketing — Chapter 5**
Creating value for the organisation — Chapter 2	Managing relationships in networks — Chapter 4	Developing and implementing a relationship strategy — Chapter 6

INTRODUCTION

Marketing is concerned with the exchange relationship between the organisation and its customers and, as we briefly discussed in Chapter 1, quality and customer service are key linkages in this relationship. The sub-title of the first edition of this book was *Bringing quality, customer service and marketing together*. But, ten years on – and with notable exceptions – many companies are still struggling to co-ordinate and control quality and service activities.

This chapter deals with the need for continuous collaboration in the firm and with marketing's role in aligning quality, customer service and marketing activity into a single market-oriented purpose. In other words, we argue that companies should adopt a relationship marketing approach towards aligning market intelligence into internal processes and the resources these processes need to function effectively.

Companies can no longer chart a path to the future based on marketing's traditional understanding of customers' needs, and on meeting those needs by controlling a limited range of critical activities that are marketing's direct responsibility. This traditional model assumed that if all key decision-makers within the firm played their part, this would lead to cross-functional co-ordination.

To be fair, cross-functional decisions are far from simple. Marketing operates in a complex multifaceted domain where it competes with legitimate demands from other areas of the business. Because marketing can not control everything, marketing resources tend to be allocated to those activities that it can control, while decisions may be taken in other areas of the business that affect marketing too. This makes it very difficult for the marketing department to translate its marketing strategy into effective action.

Paradoxically, many companies lost their deeply-shared knowledge of quality management techniques after ISO quality assurance became an entry requirement for business in the 1990s. Quality management is concerned with continuously improving quality, whereas quality assurance is essentially a quality audit that does not require continuous improvement. Everyone in the company needs to understand that customer service is the sum of all interactive contacts that create perceived customer value, or any improvements in relationship development will be compromised by the cost of lost customers.

Marketing's neglect of quality and customer service

Companies may usefully base some of their customer-acquisition strategies, such as allocating resources for buyer behaviour research, media communications, promotions, packaging and so on, on the traditional 4Ps of marketing – product, price, promotion and place – that we discussed in Chapter 1. But strategies for keeping customers involve delivering value that is largely outside the traditional scope of marketing resources decisions. This presents a critical intellectual and political challenge, because the quality of the external relationships a company forges largely depends on the quality of relationships within its internal environment.

The traditional marketing process of matching an organisation's external and internal environments and developing and protecting customer relationships largely neglects quality improvement and customer service activities. Moreover, as we outlined in Chapter 3, important exchange relationships extend beyond the customer domain to include other external constituents, including suppliers, new employees and sources of influence and referral, such as government agencies, loyal customers and so on. In other words, we need to recognise a complex pattern of dynamic relationships between the internal – or employee – market and a wider range of external markets.

In Chapter 1 we introduced the principle of aligning customer service, quality and marketing. If we accept that marketing has to extend its activities beyond the 4Ps orientation into the critical domains of customer service and quality management, the challenge becomes how to align these activities more closely with marketing (see Figure 5.1). This figure shows the integration between marketing, customer service and quality that companies must explore to achieve total customer satisfaction and long-term relationships. In the past organisations have treated these three areas as separate and unrelated.

FIGURE 5.1 Integrating quality, customer service and marketing

The role of customer service

At its simplest, customer service can be defined as:

> **The ongoing process of managing the buyer/seller interface to ensure continued customer satisfaction.**

Customer satisfaction is critical in maintaining relationships, which is why we emphasise it so strongly in this book.

Customer service is often seen as 'customer care', but this is a limited and partial perspective. As well as technical outcomes there are inter-active aspects to the service experience that contribute to customers' perceptions of the service quality and to their satisfaction. Many com-panies that have invested in 'service excellence' programmes have failed to see a real return on their investment because they did not make the necessary changes to the processes that affect the customer.

> Customer service is not a departmental responsibility.

Customer service is not a departmental responsibility. The ways in which service is delivered and maintained cut across functional boundaries and require a deep under-standing of what drives customer satisfaction.

Because customer requirements and characteristics differ, a company's service processes must be flexible enough to allow a degree of tailor-ing. They must also be interactive so that the business can respond quickly to changing customer requirements.

Marketers often ignore the 'part-time marketers', working at the boundaries, whose job is to provide service to customers.[1] These front-line service people need appropriate skills and reliable opera-tional back-up. This means companies need to align their internal processes with external customer requirements. They cannot just rely on good market information. Cursory investigations of firms' critical service processes usually reveal that many have no clear ownership patterns. In other words, a so-called 'end to end' process is often disrupted at departmental borders. A business may need a 'process alliance' manager to collaborate across functional borders and improve the process by redesigning it, managing it continuously as a complete cycle of activity. Without marketing input and pan-company collaboration in identifying the critical processes, customer service is unlikely to result in continued customer satisfaction.

The role of quality

Quality as a management concept is concerned with matching a company's offer to customers' requirements and expectations. Effective quality management requires quality thinking and know-how to be aligned across all departments. This quality approach needs to extend beyond the organisation to embrace the total relationship the firm has with its customers and suppliers on a continuous basis.

The traditional production concept of 'conformance to specifications' (sometimes referred to as 'internal quality') has been superseded by concepts of quality defined by customers – or 'customer perceived quality'. But because the manufacturing and operations functions have largely led the advances in quality management thinking and practice, the emphasis is on systems and processes, performance reliability and continuous improvement.

The gurus of quality – Deming,[2] Imai,[3] Juran[4] and Oakland[5] – certainly came from production and operations disciplines. But without collaborative marketing involvement, quality will never achieve its goals and will fall short of customer defined requirements.

Best practice in quality management has moved from relying on final inspection of products to assessing whether critical internal processes are well controlled and capable of matching customers' requirements and expectations. In manufacturing industries, for example, the emphasis has changed from inspecting production outputs to monitoring the variation in routine work activities and making adjustments in real time while goods are still being processed. This new approach allows companies to reduce drastically the variation in output quality and to eliminate waste, leading to more reliable products for customers. Also, by examining just how the various processes link together, firms can reduce cycle time (a factor that is often overlooked in service industries) by improving their overall responsiveness to customer requirements, which again cuts out waste.

Quality management has spread across all industries as a reasoned and disciplined approach to continuously improving work processes, and across all functions within companies as a way of meeting customer requirements at 'least cost'. But quality assurance (ISO accreditation) alone does not guarantee that customers receive quality. Quality may take a variety of forms, depending on individual customers' perceptions and depending on the time. It is clearly marketing's responsibility to monitor and interpret customers' perceptions of quality, but the marketing discipline has tended to sweep the concept of company-wide collaboration in quality management under the carpet.

The problem is that while the overarching goal of quality management is to meet customer requirements consistently, this is only tenuously linked to customer expectations and the changing dynamics of value exchange. As Gummesson has pointed out, quality has helped to integrate production and marketing orientations.[6] But marketing practitioners and academics have been largely reluctant to recognise the quality movement's achievements in helping to implement marketing concepts. In many organisations, marketers still see quality as primarily the responsibility of manufacturing or engineering, and in such firms marketing managers are neither involved in quality, nor provide it with rigorous market research.

Where effort is duplicated and misaligned, marketing management is seen as saying one thing while apparently doing another. Staff may well read such 'mixed messages' as evidence that the organisation has no central guiding strategies, when this may be far from the truth. Organisational defensive routines thrive in such conditions and may seriously block communications.

Bringing marketing, customer service and quality together

Organisations can no longer confine quality management, customer service and marketing inputs to creating and delivering customer value, to discrete departments such as marketing, manufacturing, logistics or complaint handling. Clearly, the customer's experience is the result of cross-functional processes. For example, customers often regard call centre operations as creating 'distance' rather than 'intimacy' because of their call-waiting messages and their prescriptive range of solutions to a multi-dimensional range of customer service issues and complaints. Companies need to view marketing, customer service and quality inputs as the customer sees them – as part of a seamless offering. This does not mean that we need a marketing 'takeover' to put things right – indeed, that might create just another singularly sub-optimal solution. But it does mean that pan-company collaboration and dialogue is essential, so that the organisation can consider and integrate the inputs from different specialist functions. This is the only way to improve customer service and quality, and it represents an opportunity to develop internal (employee) relationships within the organisation.

Customer service plays a critical connecting role in the pre-sale, sale and post-sale interactive phases of value exchanges. If the 'sale' is seen as the outcome of the interaction, customer service is the relationship development part. Businesses that shift the marketing emphasis towards relationships may find that, in the course of customer service interactions, there emerge opportunities for working together with customers to 'co-create' value. In other words, the supplier and the customer can create unique value, either through mutually improved benefits or reduced costs.

Traditionally, the literature on customer service is only concerned with the interaction between suppliers and their customers. But customer service plays a role in all the relationship markets we talked about in Chapter 3. Members of alliance/supply markets, referral markets, internal markets, recruitment markets and influence markets all represent opportunities for the business to interactively co-create value. We shall return to the potential for co-creating value in Chapter 6.

Relationship marketing involves creating bonds with members in different markets through exchanging value, where the quality of what is exchanged and the service that delivers it conform to – or even exceed – what has been promised. Quality is both the act of differentiating the offering and the way the receiver evaluates it. Quality is the receiver's perception of the offering's uniqueness and value. It is also the means by which the firm sustains its position over time among competing offerings. This notion of total quality, achieved through service, reliability and continuous improvement, reconciles marketing promises and perceived performance. Traditionally, marketing has focused on customer acquisition. Retaining customers involves delivering value through fulfilling promises. Efforts within the firm to integrate quality, customer service and marketing competencies should aim to keep valuable customers as well as win them.

Delivering customer value

The concept of interaction is essential in relationship marketing in the sense that value is created and shared through interaction. Interaction starts with any action that generates a response. This may sound simple, but it provides the basis from which to examine the value delivery process that brings quality, customer service and marketing together.

Services marketers are familiar with guiding, influencing and designing the context and nature of regular customer interactions to achieve superior quality control and enhance value for the customer. For example, interaction is the basis for the so-called 'moments of truth' between customers and suppliers, for the role of customers as co-producers of services, for the role of a firm's customer service people, and, most importantly, for the way all these connect with the firm's internal support systems.[7]

In services industries customer value is created, delivered and consumed simultaneously, provided it is backed up with adequate internal service support. As a consequence, in service companies the value-creation process partly parallels the value delivery process. In manufacturing and distribution, on the other hand, one follows the other, end to end. Of course, the delivery process may be a composite of many processes, as in the case of multiple distribution channels.

Every firm is potentially a service firm

Every firm is potentially a 'service' firm. Many manufacturers now consider service to be the dominant part of their competitive advantage. Every company, through a mix of functional utility, service, support of various kinds, information and advice, and ongoing 'services', can now design and manage its own unique set of solutions to meet customer requirements. Dell Computer, for example, assembles the computer in 'quick response' soon after the customer orders it. This kind of service capability is reshaping the market for computers.

> Every firm is potentially a 'service' firm.

To take the shift to a service emphasis one step further, consider the emerging 'service experience' industry. We can understand Disneyland in traditional terms, but interactive TV may open up unexpected service-driven pathways. Also, as the Internet continues to develop it will certainly open up new and more interactive ways of keeping in contact with customers. Businesses therefore need to take a flexible approach to potential new marketing opportunities.

The traditional image of 'service' is that it is 'performed' by individuals. But this is a limiting perspective. Do bank automatic telling machines deliver a product or a service? In the world of fast foods, is the 'McDonald's experience' a product or a service? And does it matter? All classifications are partially flawed because what is meant by 'service' depends on time, tangibility and tasks. For example, production is a time-based work activity that builds up an accumulation of value that we traditionally call a 'product'. These values are either consumed more or less immediately, or, if not, amortised by the customer over the lifetime of the product. Where the customer amortises the value, what they get or hope to get from the product is 'service-ability'. Service in this sense occurs after the point of sale. So rigid distinctions drawn between 'products' and 'services' are somewhat arbitrary.

But we can bypass these distinctions by orientating relationship marketing around the customer, because then our prime concern is the ongoing relationship in which products and services are fused.

The customer value chain and the customer activity cycle

The *customer value chain*[8] is an intellectual framework for thinking through what a customer actually does with a product or service. In other words, the supplier's offering is the input into the customer value chain, while the links in the chain represent customers' activity patterns. These links control or modify the way the customer uses the supplier's output. Putting this into a services context, a bank account may serve a variety of functions. It might be a device to pay bills, an investment for a 'rainy day' or a day-to-day savings account, according to how particular customers manage their money and what their priorities are. Marketing needs to identify what the customer is *trying to do* with the firm's service offering before it reaches any conclusions about how to improve it.[9] It would be even better for the firm to match its offer with customers' goals and aspirations, which would mean determining what the customer is *trying to achieve*.

The sustainable value a supplier can create for a customer reflects how closely it can align its own value chain with the customer's value chain. The way a firm interacts with its customers and suppliers and how it co-ordinates the value delivery activities *within* its own value chain are critical (see Figure 5.2).

A company could use the 'customer activity cycle' framework proposed by Vandermerwe to make its customer's value chain more explicit.[10] The customer activity cycle divides customers' activities into three over-lapping phases: pre-purchase, purchase and post-purchase. Companies can then use the framework to identify the sequential activities of the customer – providing they have a profound understanding of the nature of customers and the differences between customer segments.

Managers should then try to understand, through research and observation, each critical activity point in the cycle and map these in a circular process diagram. Customer activity cycles can be designed for either a company or an individual, so they are appropriate in both b2b and b2c markets. Companies' objective in doing this analysis should be to understand the activity cycle of key existing and potential customer segments so that they can identify points in that cycle where there is most opportunity to create additional value for the customer or reduce their costs.

Managers should challenge internal organisational activities that do not add value or reduce costs for customers. In other words, internal customers and internal suppliers create and deliver value, as do external customers and suppliers. Making these internal links and ties more transparent makes it easier to review and manage them. This is the

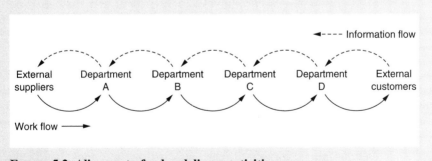

FIGURE 5.2 **Alignment of value delivery activities**

starting point for exercising some customer-oriented design control over the value delivery sequence.

Cross-functional work flows

If organisations do not manage work flows and processes laterally across their own value chain, costs will mount and quality will fall all along the various strands of the chain, from each internal supplier to the next internal customer, through to the end customer. When one department's output does not match another department's input needs, there will be an internal quality gap.

Internal quality problems tend to arise between departments rather than within them. Businesses that over-manage and over-control various job roles within functions find, paradoxically, that they reduce the potential value-adding effect of exchanges between divisions. In other words, optimising parts of the chain, without regard for the whole chain of effects, results in sub-optimising the whole value delivery sequence. As such, companies will find themselves saddled with the extra cost of all these mismatched internal activities, including the cost of delays and 'fire fighting', on top of the cost of achieving value for external customers (see Figure 5.3).

> Quality problems tend to arise between departments rather than within them.

Managers need to be alert to these critical cross-functional organisational linkages and attempt (collaboratively) to remove any blockages, if they are to reduce the cost of achieving customer perceived value. One way of addressing these issues is to look at the internal variables of *job design* (who does what), *environmental setting* (where it is done), and *process flow* (how it is done), as well as dealing with any *people* issues. We go on to discuss how companies can improve these four key variables towards the end of this chapter.

De Bono[11] has used the phrase 'designing a way forward from a field of parallel possibilities' to describe an approach to seeking solutions to problems that require new thinking. Businesses could apply this idea to recognising any barriers to cross-functional work flow that relate to the four variables mentioned above, understanding that there is no one solution nor ideal pattern, but many. In this way they could control delivery costs but not at the expense of customer value.

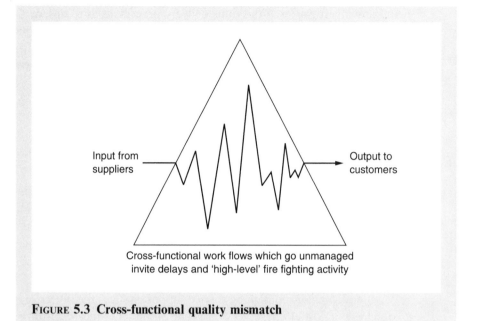

FIGURE 5.3 Cross-functional quality mismatch

Redesigning internal processes, even with the help of excellent market information about customer wants and expectations, continues to challenge many companies. It is easy to lose the customer 'voice' and make a final offering that falls short of customer requirements.

How do you begin to redesign internal processes? Every work activity is part of a process and every process links to other processes through a series of inputs and outputs. One possible starting point is to take an area that market research or customer complaints has identified as a critical customer concern, and then trace a sequence of connected activities 'upstream' back to their original sources of input. Some of these processes may appear to be totally unco-ordinated and uncontrolled, or appear to be outside the control of the firm, or to belong to a particular department or division within it. That is all the more reason to include them in any examination.

The rationale for this kind of investigation is that all work activities eventually connect 'downstream' through the value chain to the end customer. It is important to determine whether these activities are adding value to the customer, or merely adding cost to the company, and any investigation of the value delivery process needs to differentiate between the two. Companies should begin by using a technique called 'flow-charting' or 'blueprinting'. They might also use another diagnostic tool – the so-called 'fishbone', also called an 'Ishikawa diagram' after its Japanese inventor Dr Kaoru Ishikawa – to explore opportunities to improve quality. We will describe these quality management tools later in this chapter.

Redesigning service support systems

Logistics are normally associated with the movement of physical materials and products. But logistics are equally important value-delivering mechanisms in a service context. For example, they are crucial to the way support systems for financial services, call centres, Internet interfaces or hotel checkout procedures are designed.

When designing or redesigning service support systems the objective is to achieve a cost-effective yet consistent output that meets customer requirements. But organisations will only achieve that objective by looking in detail at each stage of the value delivery process, and at the interfaces between those stages.

Organisations whose service support systems are haphazard and poorly managed are likely to experience a high level of service failures. One reason for this loss of quality is that no one person in the chain is responsible for its overall performance – indeed managers are rarely aware of the total chain of cause and effect. Also, in loosely co-ordinated support systems, output tends to be very inconsistent. For the benefit of the mathematically inclined, if a service support system has ten stages and if a failure or mistake occurs at each stage on one in a hundred occasions, then 11 per cent of the final output will be affected [that is, $1 - (1 - 0.01)^{10}$]. Also, a business may find that errors in, say, the order-entry stage, which may appear insignificant, can trigger errors in the accounts department or other areas. A major challenge for most companies is to overcome the fragmented nature of their service support systems in order to ensure a consistent quality output.

It is no coincidence that the companies most frequently cited as service leaders – McDonald's, Disney and Dell Computer, for example – pay careful attention to the way they design and manage their delivery systems and have installed integrated processes and procedures to ensure consistent outputs.

Flow-charting the service support system

An organisation could start the process of designing and improving its service support system by diagnostically analysing it with quality tools and then modelling it to improve operating performance – in much the same way that manufacturing systems can be diagnostically analysed and modelled.

A flow chart provides the basic starting point. A flow chart essentially analyses the systems of any end-to-end work process and maps out the linked activities. Shostack[12] first introduced the technique into the marketing literature and called it 'service blueprinting'. But we will use the more generic term 'flow-charting', as it seems better to describe what is involved. The essential steps are as follows:

- First, record all the links and steps in the process sequence so that you can clearly and objectively see the end-to-end connections.
- Next, identify the 'fail points' – that is, any areas that seem likely to fail or are unreliable. At first this is a matter of intuition and judgement, but you often discover data to support your hunches – once you know where to look for it.
- Then set 'execution standards' or target values for service performance at critical points in the process. These execution standards need to allow for some performance tolerances. Higher standards and target values usually imply higher service costs, but the whole point of the flow-charting exercise is both to improve service quality and to reduce costs.
- Finally, identify where and when in the process tangible evidence of the service becomes available or is offered to the customer. These are the 'encounter points' in the process – that is, the points where customers and suppliers interact. We examine these encounter points in more detail later in the chapter.

Building up a flow chart requires a basic tool kit that uses a set of symbols for describing key steps in any work process (see Figure 5.4). The flow chart is a picture of the interaction between people, materials, equipment, information, methods and environment within a particular process that connects to some customer encounter point.

Activity	Description
 ☐	*Inspection* A checking function
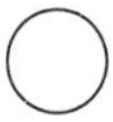 ◯	*Operation* Indicates the main steps in a process. It involves the addition of information to a paper or a handling operation, such as stapling, folding, sorting, collating, assembling, filing and so on
 ◗	*Delay* This symbol means that there is a time delay in the process
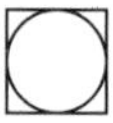 ⬡	*Combined activity* When two activities are performed at the same time, or at the same work station
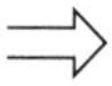 ⟹	*Travel* Travelling occurs when something is moved from one place to another
 ▽	*Storage/filing* This symbol is used when a form of document is filed or stored for a period of time

A flow chart is a diagram which shows a series of events that occur in a process from beginning to end, made up of symbols that help to identify what type of action occurs at each step in the process. The table defines each symbol used to draw a flow chart.

FIGURE 5.4 **Flow-charting symbols**

Mapping out these interactions reveals areas in any of the process linkages where time and resources are being wasted. Once the links are committed to paper in this way it often becomes obvious how various activities can be simplified, and the supplier and customer's time and resources saved.

An example (see Figures 5.5 and 5.6) shows the 'before' and 'after' flow-charting of a process for giving cash advances on credit cards at a

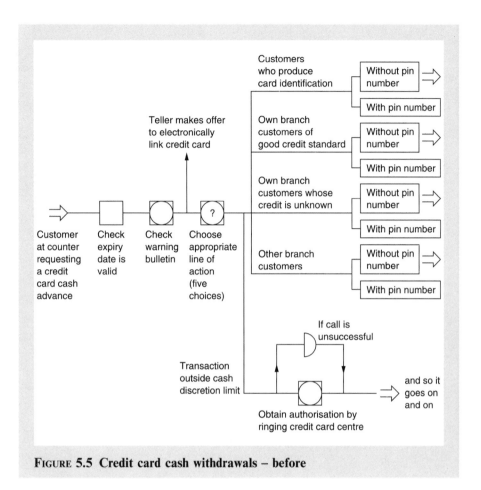

FIGURE **5.5 Credit card cash withdrawals – before**

retail bank. In the 'before' example, bank tellers had to choose one of five procedures according to the type of card and the amount of cash they were allowed to hand out in any one transaction. Cash advances outside the teller's discretion needed to be authorised over the telephone by the credit card service centre. Flow-charting this process showed immediately just how complex it was and why tellers had such difficulty in 'carrying out laid-down procedures'. The procedures were inherently prone to mistakes. More important, the bank had to pay a service fee for the authorisation call to the credit card centre. Furthermore, delays for authorisation were common, which increased the call time, reduced the teller's ability to deal with the transaction efficiently and caused queues to build up in the bank.

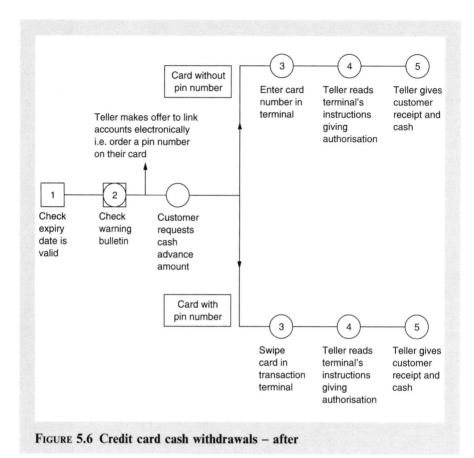

FIGURE 5.6 **Credit card cash withdrawals – after**

Once the company had signalled the problem of connecting with the credit card centre to its data processing department, the solution proved to be quite simple. A short programme rewrite enabled the tellers' electronic terminals to be connected online to the credit card customer database. The teller could then obtain authorisation at their workstation without incurring costly phone calls or delays. The department won approval to make the changes quickly because the flow chart highlighted the problem and the solution far more vividly than a departmental report would have done. The bank saved almost £1 million in call costs in the first year – not to mention the time savings and flow-on efficiencies.

The details of this case vignette may seem unreal. Surely the need for an electronic link was obvious? But the need was not obvious because the service support sequence crossed over many departmental borders, and so people within those individual departments thought their own procedures were logical. Clearly, the whole sequence was less effective than the sum of the parts. Only when the company charted cross-functional work flow for the first time did it make the broader connection between the customers' waiting time, the tellers' wasted time and the hidden costs 'upstream'.

Flow-charting can be even more effective if it includes time data. This data might show, for example, how long each stage in a process takes, how long a customer has to wait (dead time), how long they spend participating (active time) or how long they spend 'non-participating' (unused capacity). Research and development teams and manufacturing management have used flow design and control methods for years. But these tools often lack market intelligence on customers' experience at the service encounter point, and this is where marketing's input is critical.

Service quality diagnostics – the fishbone diagram

The impact of quality management in manufacturing industry is well documented. But, as we argued earlier in this chapter, the concept of quality goes far beyond the product itself to embrace the entire relationship between the organisation and its suppliers and customers. Many of the concepts and techniques of quality management that work in the factory can also dramatically improve the quality of the service delivery system.

Diagnosing a firm's critical service issues is best done by the people involved in the work processes being reviewed. So a first step might be to organise a series of task forces that cut across departmental lines and include people involved in the 'lines of flow' reflected in the service flow charts.

The fishbone diagram is another diagnostic tool that companies can use to improve service delivery systems. The fishbone is a way of structuring a particular work process by representing all the probable cause-and-effect relationships in a simple but non-linear diagram. The 'effect' is really the problem in the process being studied and is represented by the forward end of the central backbone of the 'fish'. The various fish bones are used as a way of structuring thoughts about the causes of the problem and each main 'bone' represents a particular category of probable causes.

Once people realise the diagnostic potential of the fishbone diagram they begin looking at the causal elements in greater detail and finding probable subsidiary factors that need to be investigated. These are written in as 'tiny bones' connected to main causal elements. The example given in Figure 5.7 shows how a fishbone diagram can be used to diagnose the cause of flight departure delays at an airport.

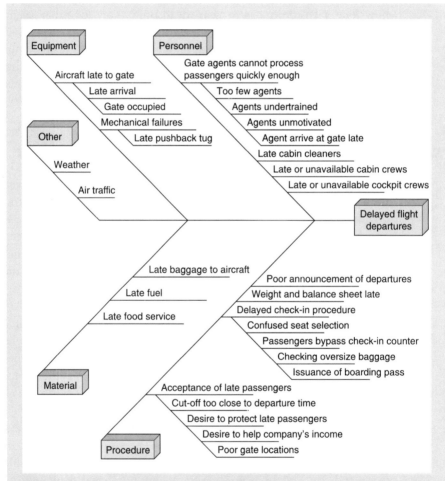

FIGURE 5.7 Causes of flight departure delays

Source: Reprinted by permission of Elsevier Science from 'New Tools for Achieving Service Quality', by Wyckoff, D., *The Cornell Hotel and Restaurant Administration Quarterly*, November, 78–91, Copyright 1984 by Cornell University.[13]

Once a firm has mapped out a particular problem in this way (and we emphasise again that this is an intuitive and creative approach), it can investigate any particular factor that seems promising.

The next stage involves shifting the emphasis from analysing problems to generating solutions. This time, the company enters the most likely solution at the head of the fishbone as the 'effect' being studied. Then the 'what if' dialogue begins again until the 'bones' of the diagram become a set of categorised factors which potentially represent part of the solution. But the cause-and-effect relationships identified on the fishbone diagram are only hypothetical, and companies should conduct follow-up research to back up their hunches. There are as many uses for the fishbone in marketing applications as there are on the factory floor.

The relationship marketing benefit of using such quality management tools is their collaborative approach to improving service support systems and the wider range of value delivery sequences. It is through using common methods like these, adapted to suit specific organisational needs, that employees learn to speak a common language and cross-functional quality barriers start to fall away.

Service quality management

We will now set out some conceptual approaches and practical guidelines that companies can adopt to monitor and manage their quality performance. As we indicated earlier in the chapter, one challenge peculiar to service offerings is that service tends to be produced and consumed at the same time and place – that is, within the service interaction. As in theatre,[14] each service performance unfolds as it goes along. There will be a common script, various actors and behind-the-scenes people. The audience (like customers) must play their role otherwise there will be no theatre, and they will sometimes be called upon to participate directly, to become part of the act and its outcomes.

> Service tends to be produced and consumed at the same time and place.

Grönroos has developed a service quality model[7] where interactive real-time service encounters between buyers and sellers generate for customers what he calls 'functional' (or process) quality – that is, the quality of their interactive experience with the supplier. What remains after an interaction sequence is what Grönroos terms 'technical' (or outcome) quality. This model highlights the importance of service quality in relationship marketing. The aim is to sustain relationships with valuable customers, not only by delivering on promises made during the sale, but by focusing on the quality of the customer's interactive experience with the supplier before and after the sale.

Mapping 'moments of truth'

The 'encounters' between buyers and suppliers are sometimes described as 'critical incidents' or 'moments of truth'.[15] Moments of truth, of course, might turn out to be potential 'fail points' for the supplier if things go wrong. But identifying and managing the encounter points is critical if businesses are going to achieve consistent service quality.

Each encounter point is an opportunity for the service provider to demonstrate the quality of its service – be that good or bad. It is also an opportunity to listen to what the customer is trying to do and gauge what is needed. Some airlines have successfully used this approach. Confident in the quality of their service, some have even sought to increase the number of moments of truth in any service interaction in the belief that this would enhance the customers' overall perception of their service quality. But simply increasing the number of encounter points is a futile exercise. If those extra service interactions do not offer the customer perceived value, they are a waste of time and resources. The sparse but competitive in-flight service offered by low-cost airlines such as easyJet and Southwest Airlines suggests that, while customer requirements come first, there are value segments of customers who will require and respond to different offerings.

Using the customer activity cycle framework that we referred to earlier in this chapter, companies need to identify the most common points of contact between themselves and their customers during the pre-sale, sale, and post-sale cycles of service. They can then use these to explore opportunities to improve the customer experience.

Mapping out the encounter points or 'moments of truth' within the various episodes of a typical customer interaction cycle may reveal defects in the way the sequence is organised and which of the encounter points are critical, and why.

A suitable mapping framework (with encounter points to be filled in) is shown in Figure 5.8. Mapping out the cycles of service for key customers or value segments represents an opportunity to align effort between suppliers and their customers.[16] The 'right' way is the way that best reflects what customers are trying to do with the firm's offer and how they value it.

In this sense it is the customer who sets the quality standard for performance – though we would normally refer to it as 'meeting customer expectations'. So how customer expectations are dealt with becomes an important issue. That might seem obvious, but in relationship marketing any gaps between what is promised – either implicitly or explicitly – and what is delivered will undermine customers' trust in the supplier, and this in turn affects the quality of the relationship and its future.

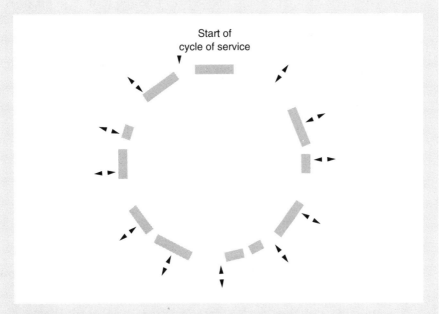

FIGURE 5.8 Mapping 'moments of truth' in the cycle of service

Monitoring and measuring service quality

We recommend that companies adopt a step-by-step customer feedback and monitoring system so that they can improve and adapt their value delivery process and service support systems in a customer-oriented fashion.

Customer satisfaction is a popular measure of service quality, but it is normally so broad that it is useless for anything other than decorative executive wall charts. This kind of measure will, at best, show how you are doing, but not why. Controversies abound as to the best measures of customer satisfaction and service quality,[17] so we propose a pathway that will allow firms to avoid most of the problems most of the time.

To us, monitoring service quality means doing regular customer service tracking studies and identifying both emerging and critical service issues. This should be supported by staff attitude surveys (or employee 'climate monitors' as they are sometimes called), 'risk point' feedback systems and routine reviews of internal service quality performance standards. A broad range of monitors and measures like this will capture what customers value and in what context. For example, the package of service quality research monitors highlighted in Figure 5.9 would suit a branch-based service provider or a franchise operation.

Measuring is one thing but doing something about the results is another. Seldom can one person or department within an organisation uniquely 'fix' a particular service problem. Using interdepartmental review teams is the best way to deal with chronic problems. This means that each periodic cycle of research should prompt a review of the internal processes involved and any cross-functional bottlenecks that may be causing poor or variable performance.

Brief details of various kinds of service quality monitors follow:

1. Customer service tracking studies

Service measurement techniques must stay close to the customer's reality, and reflect their needs, wants, expectations and goals as closely as possible. The first task is to develop a list of service attributes or critical

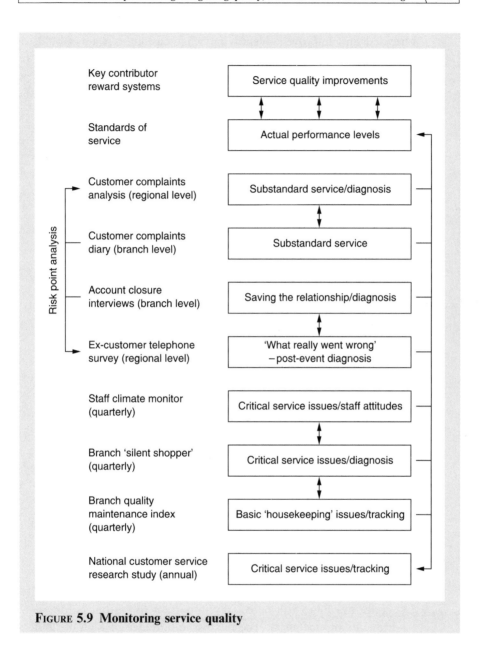

FIGURE 5.9 Monitoring service quality

service issues. Customers know what they like but they might not always express it. Also, what is critically important may change over time. As a consequence, any list of service attributes should be regarded as provisional, a working hypothesis. It can always be revised and improved. Identifying what customers want should, of course, be done through dialogue with them. This dialogue can be informal or formal. The way a company might identify and review service attributes using qualitative research methods is set out in the box below.

Identifying the critical service issues

The first step in research of this type is to identify the influences on customers' buying decisions, or, in the case of consumer markets, the common decision-making patterns within a particular value segment of consumers.

Once it has identified these basics, a company can initiate a small-scale qualitative research programme based on personal interviews with a representative sample of customers. The purpose of these interviews is to elicit, in the customers' language, first, how important they rate service compared with other value elements such as price and product quality, and second, how important they rate individual components of customer service, and why. As a result, the company will be able to identify a number of specific customer service attributes, as we outlined in Chapter 2.

The company can then use this kind of qualitative data to develop internal quality benchmarks for internal standard setting, or they can use quantitative work (customer surveys) to measure the importance to the customer of various attributes as well as actual service performance. The key point here is that the attributes being measured in survey work must be relevant to customers, which means that they must be periodically checked and restated, again through qualitative research. Not all service attributes will be equally important to customers, or segments of customers. The relative importance of each attribute is likely to change over time, and sometimes quite suddenly should customers reorder their priorities. But companies should negotiate service standards individually with key customers, as generalised standards may not adequately reflect their requirements.

Wherever possible, depending on the size and scope of market opportunities, companies should routinely monitor the performance of their service attributes and measure them quantitatively using a survey questionnaire. Because customer requirements are a moving target, the company will need to conduct periodic surveys – hence the term 'tracking studies'. We outlined a methodology for identifying the relative importance to customers of particular service attributes, and for monitoring the firm's performance on those attributes, in Chapter 2. An organisation can use exactly the same methods for customer service tracking studies, extending the survey, if that is practicable, to include the customers of one or more key competitors.

Many companies fail to recognise that frequently there are substantial differences between the importance that different customers accord to different service performance attributes. Consequently, they miss opportunities to identify segment needs and develop the kind of service segmentation strategies that we discussed in Chapter 2.

Companies often gain the most important insights from customers during dialogue at the qualitative research stage. Moreover, qualitative research enables firms to develop their own specific set of service attributes, customised by their own customers. No proprietary list of service quality attributes can be more relevant than a list of service attributes based on the specific requirements of a firm's own customers.

2. Service environment/branch quality maintenance index

Companies often take for granted the ambience and practical utility of the interface with customers – the store or branch environment, for instance. But this is an area where careful design and 'good housekeeping' is essential. A company should measure the specifics of its own service environment against a checklist of items, such as adequacy of outside parking, convenience of entry points, adequacy of lighting, functional layout, general cleanliness and so on. Some service providers conceptualise their interior 'service-scape' into a number of 'service activity zones' where the ambience or facilities differ from one service zone to the other. The physical service environment needs to be routinely assessed to establish whether it can support the firm's service objectives and whether it is being maintained in good order. The same audit principles apply equally to Internet based service-scapes, where the computer screen is a window to the service provider's virtual book-shop (as in the case of amazon.com), computer warehouse (dell.com) or whatever the case may be.

3. Silent shopper

The 'silent shopper' is a survey monitor that attempts to replicate the shopping experiences of the typical customer. Skilled market researchers act as surrogate customers and sample and report on their shopping experience. When they are also genuine customers of the firm, that makes their admittedly subjective reports more authentic. The purpose of this monitor is to diagnose what it feels like to be a customer and what service improvements the business might be overlooking.

4. Staff climate monitor

Measuring employees' views of customer service and defects can be revealing, especially when there is a gap between their perceptions and customer perceptions of service quality. Companies can conduct an internal 'climate' study as a counterpoint to external customer service research. As well as canvassing staff views on customer service, the survey could also assess the impact of the firm's service philosophy on things like staff motivation, while at the same time discovering areas of more general concern.

5. 'Risk point' analysis

The firm can put in place various forms of analysis to monitor 'risk points' and 'fail points' in the way customer service is delivered. These analyses might include account closure follow-up, customer complaint analysis, customer exit interviews and so on, as we suggest in Figure 5.9.

Many organisations handle very carefully customers who complain, but some go even further, monitoring the key categories of complaints statistically and diagnosing the causes in order to take corrective action.

The 'Pareto Law', which we referred to in Chapter 2, can be helpful here. We usually find that around 80 per cent of complaints refer to a common 20 per cent of issues. Similarly 80 per cent of malfunctions or failures are due to 20 per cent of root causes. By monitoring systems and processes continuously companies can ensure they identify and manage these critical points.

6. Review of service standards

'Production-oriented' companies tend to set up internal service standards without the benefit of market research and market intelligence. This short cut is best avoided because it presumes that managers know what customers want, which is unlikely – unless they have asked them.

When a company obtains service performance feedback from a range of sources, as mentioned above, then it can use customer issues, such as 'next day delivery', to establish internal service standards that relate to key internal processes, like 'order cycle time'. Every time it reviews the external service performance data, it can, if necessary, recalibrate internal quality targets (or metrics) in the light of actual market performance. It may also need to redefine service standards to take account of any new customer service issues.

Service quality gaps

Service quality is a function of customer perceptions and the firm's resources and activities. It is normally defined as the match between what customers expect and what they experience (or perceived performance).[18] Any mismatch between these two is a 'quality gap'. In effect, quality is whatever the customer says it is. So far as service quality is concerned 'perceptions are reality'. But past experiences and actual needs, word-of-mouth information, advertising and promotion all mediate the acceptability of the offering by influencing customer expectations.

> So far as service quality is concerned 'perceptions are reality'.

There are two problem areas in service quality. First, you have to interpret 'expectations' as customers' desired level of service, not what they expect will happen. Otherwise, the implication would be that when consumers expect bad service and receive it they would be happy with that, which is clearly absurd. Some companies, however, seem to operate this way. But it provides an unstable foundation on which to build relationships. Second, despite a certain level of desire, customers may be willing to accept less, as an 'adequate' level of service, either under all circumstances or at particular times, within a 'zone of tolerance' that lies between what they desire and what is adequate.[19]

The zone-of-tolerance concept leads to some necessary introspection about just how stable apparently loyal and committed relationships actually are. Because of past investments customers have made in the relationship – in terms of time, resource and so on – they may be willing to put up with minor and sometimes major irritations. The zone of tolerance acts as a buffer and all is well over time – except that their dissatisfaction may go unnoticed and unreported. What is more, customers can reach a threshold where their dissatisfactions outweigh the past investment they have made in the relationship. In such cases, the outcome of the next service episode becomes critical and any minor negative incidents can propel the customer outside the zone of tolerance – and the supplier unexpectedly loses a customer.

Any quality gap is a mix of facts and judgements, so each party is always ignorant to some extent of the other's changing intentions and expectations. In business-to-business contexts, expectations are best 'negotiated' between the parties involved through interaction, dialogue and agreement. Under these circumstances, service quality is measured in terms of the extent to which the customer perceives the supplier's performance meets or exceeds what have been agreed as appropriate levels of service. We will discuss the potential of dialogue in deepening value creation between partners in Chapter 6.

Service quality research by Parasuraman and his colleagues[20] has led to the development of a 'gap model' that shows five kinds of 'quality gaps' or potential breaks in the relationship linkages that lead to quality shortfalls. A popular service quality measurement instrument known as SERVQUAL was developed from the gap model. Parasuraman *et al.* have suggested that a number of basic service quality dimensions can be generalised across markets as a standard form of measurement. These are reliability, responsiveness, assurance, empathy and tangibles.

Though SERVQUAL's value as an all-purpose measure has been criticised in recent years,[21] the original gap model (see Figure 5.10) is

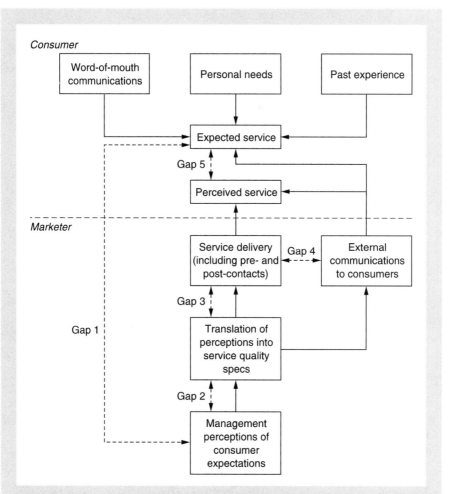

FIGURE 5.10 Conceptual model of service quality
Source: Reprinted with permission from *Journal of Marketing* published by the American Marketing Association, Parasuraman, A., Zeithaml V. A. and Berry L. L., 'A Conceptual Model of Service Quality and its Implications for Future Research', 1985, Fall, **49**, 41–50.

insightful and remains a practical framework to use in service quality management.

The service gaps are as follows:

- Gap 1 is not knowing what customers expect
- Gap 2 is not selecting the right service designs and standards

■ Gap 3 is not delivering up-to-service standards
■ Gap 4 is not matching performance to promises.

These four gaps lead to a fifth gap which is an aggregate of gaps 1–4.

■ Gap 5 is the gap between customer expectations and customer perceived performance.

In other words, gaps 1–4 are service gaps that account for gap 5.

A simple metric for gap 5 would be:

$$\text{Service quality} = \frac{\text{Perceived performance}}{\text{Desired expectation}} \times 100$$

Using this formula, anything less than 100 per cent is deemed to be less than ideal service. Therefore the service quality challenge is simple – to bring perceived performance and customer expectations into line.

Figure 5.11 represents a situation where expectations and perceived performance do not coincide. The organisation can respond in two possible ways, neither of which excludes the other.

The first response is to explore why perceived performance is low. For example, actual performance could be low across a range of critical

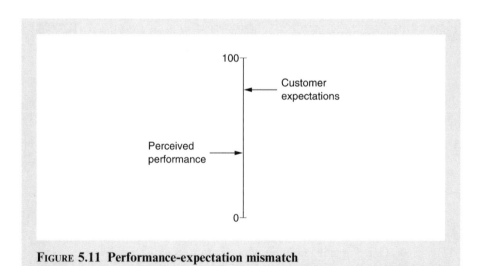

FIGURE 5.11 **Performance-expectation mismatch**

issues. Alternatively, customers' perceptions may have been influenced by negative experiences or unreliability in one particular aspect of performance. For instance, they may have had difficulty in getting satisfactory responses to telephone queries, even though the product is always delivered on time. Either way, there is work to be done within the firm in terms of gaps 1–4.

The second response is to explore whether the firm has properly understood customer expectations. In other words, have customers built expectations that are out of line with the firm's ability to perform? Advertising may create expectations that the firm finds hard to deliver on, for example. Likewise, in order to close a sale, salespeople sometimes make promises regarding delivery that a company is just not able to keep. Alternatively, some customers may just expect a higher level of service than the company has planned to deliver. In that case, the firm might be trying to satisfy too many segments of consumer interest with one solution. Service levels should be 'negotiated' or agreed in advance whenever possible to reduce the scope for misunderstandings later. Again, there is work to be done within the firm in terms of gaps 1–4.

> Service levels should be 'negotiated' or agreed in advance.

Management stands little chance of working systematically to close gaps 1–4 if it does not understand customer perceived quality determinants and routinely measure them as part of a range of monitoring systems, as we discussed earlier. This task should be guided by the service needs of different value segments that it should already have identified, as we discussed in Chapter 2.

Benchmarking

Companies should also assess perceptions of service performance against some appropriate industry benchmark. That benchmark could be the market performance of key competitors or the internal capability, in any given area, of non-competitors. Indeed, it is unwise to measure your performance only against competitors, as this can lead to the kind of complacency expressed in the statement 'we are no worse than anyone else'. Benchmarking should attempt to provide a relative measure of best practice that is relevant to the marketplace in which a firm competes. A checklist of key areas for benchmarking is shown in Figure 5.12.

You can create benchmarks for practically any part of your operation. This list of potential benchmarking categories can help measure your operations against your competitor's

Advertising
Expenditure
Themes

Sales
Terms
Sales force

• size
• structure
• training/experience
• compensation
• number of cells
• turnover rates

Sales literature
Proposals

• style
• structure
• pricing

Accountability
Cross-selling

R&D
Patents
Staff
R&D $/sales
Government contracts

Customers/products
Sales/customer
Breadth of product line
Product quality
Average customer size

Distribution
Channels used
Middlemen

Marketing
Product/brand strategy
Market share
Pricing

Financials/costs
Profitability
Overhead
Return on assets
Return on equity
Net worth
Margins
Cash flow
Debt
Borrowing capacity

Plant/facility
• size
• capacity
• utilisation
• equipment costs

Capital investments
Integration level
Quality control
Fixed and variable costs

Organisation
Structure
Values
General goals
Expected growth
Decision-making level
Controls

Strategic plans
Short term
Long term
Core business/expansion or stability
Acquisitions

FIGURE **5.12 Benchmarking checklist**
Source: Based on Strategic Intelligence Checklist, Fuld & Co. Inc., Cambridge, Ma.

The Japanese term *dantotsu*, which means the attempt to become the 'best of the best', aptly summarises the idea of benchmarking. Benchmarking involves continuously assessing the company's products, services and practices against the standards of companies that are identified as industry leaders, and it results in continuous improvement in products and processes.

Camp[22] has identified a number of benefits a company derives from benchmarking. These include:

- The 'best practice' from any industry can be creatively adapted and incorporated into the activities and processes of the firm.
- Benchmarking can provide stimulation and motivation to the professionals whose creativity is required to perform and implement benchmark findings.
- Benchmarking breaks down ingrained reluctance to change. It has been found that people are more receptive to new ideas and their creative adoption when those ideas did not necessarily originate from their own industry.
- Benchmarking may also identify a technological breakthrough that would not have been recognised, and thus not applied, in a company's own industry for some time to come.

One of the earliest firms to formulate benchmarking as a market-sensing process was Xerox Corporation. It first started benchmarking in its manufacturing activity and, following successes there, top management directed that all cost centres and business units should benchmark their activities. Employees were deeply involved in the benchmarking process.

But over the past twenty years benchmarking has expanded from purely focusing on competitors to embracing a wider but selective focus on top-performing companies regardless of their industry sector. Non-competitive benchmarking is now recognised as a good way of leveraging improvements to any internal aspect of a company's operations. It involves outperforming rather than matching the efforts of the benchmarked company. Clearly, gaining information on non-competitors and their internal systems and processes is going to be easier than it would from competitors, especially as benchmarking partnerships can generate two-way exchanges of knowledge.

The value chain concept that we discussed earlier can be especially useful in benchmarking studies. Businesses can identify areas for improvement by systematically comparing processes within each element of their value chain with those of competitors. Such systematic comparisons can highlight areas where they can secure gains. For example, a firm might discover that competitors are subcontracting activities to third parties more cheaply than they could do them themselves.

Managing service variability

Companies have to manage variability in the way service is delivered, as it certainly will not correct itself. Very often no one really knows why a routine procedure was established the way it was, why jobs are organised the way they are, or why the physical work environment was designed the way it was. Nor does it occur to people that things could be done another way. They simply assume, for example, that if a quality problem were easy to fix, it would have been fixed already. But companies often find that what, at first, seems impossible to change can actually be changed, once the assumptions about the nature and purpose of the underlying cross-functional process are made visible.

> Companies have to manage variability in the way service is delivered.

The quality 'gap model', already discussed (see Figure 5.10), provides a useful starting point for reviewing the service system overall and attending to quality gaps. This is also the way to begin investigating any unwarranted service variability. But critical quality issues tend to be interrelated and modifying sections of a service system without identifying the 'root causes' of problems runs the risk of unknowingly creating bottlenecks elsewhere. One useful approach is to consider any service system as having four structural levels, as represented in Figure 5.13. Using this diagnostic model as a guide, businesses can consider whether to remove constraints in the service environment (servicescape), process flow (sequential activity links), job design (who does what), or in employee training (skills and empowerment).

This kind of analysis opens up service design and redesign possibilities. Again, because each structural level is part of the total value delivery where all parts are interrelated, these possibilities should not

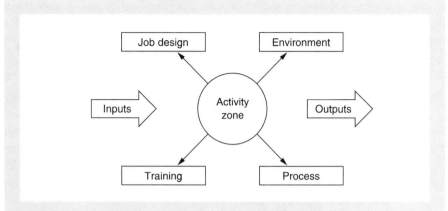

FIGURE 5.13 Diagnostic model: find the structural constraints

be seen as mutually exclusive but as threads that may be woven in different ways into the total design fabric.

1. Environmental setting

The environment, or service-scape, in which the customer 'faces' the service provider is critical to the perceived quality of service. The 'situational' variables are often overlooked. The physical aspect is obviously a major component of environmental design but there are emotional and psychological features as well.[23]

In other words, the environment affects customers' behaviour by influencing the meaning they draw from a particular setting. This includes issues of orientation, learning where we are, where we are going, how things work and what behaviour is expected from us as a customer or as a service provider.

Each and every service encounter may be said to prescribe and to be prescribed in a 'service interaction zone'. In any service organisation there will be a number of different service interaction zones and service access 'channels' through which customers will see service differently. Defining the key service interaction zones can give suppliers a contextual framework for analysing customer perceived service quality, and that, in turn, can lead to radical redesign of these zones. The ideal service environment setting will prepare the customer by giving visual, procedural and psychological cues that both define and support their expectations of service quality.

2. *Job design*

A service company earns its reputation for good service by consistently delivering what customers expect of it. Over time, jobs often develop haphazardly with little regard for customer concerns. In extreme cases jobs can become arbitrary groupings of activities that machines can not do, and this leads to role conflict or ambiguity. People tend to take job designs for granted, and assume that poor performance in the job must be the worker's fault.

But badly-designed jobs often conceal defects in the environment and the design of processes. Indeed, a badly-designed job performed well can disrupt the work performance of the next internal customer 'downstream' who has to put up with inadequate inputs. Managers often forget that they need to keep in mind cross-functional linkages between internal customers and internal suppliers when they are designing jobs. Staff are motivated to perform well if they have good working conditions and a sense of their own worth in an organisation. Companies can create this environment by designing jobs where tasks are clear, where there is some autonomy and variety and where cross-functional linkages are transparent.

3. *Processes*

Service design or redesign includes changing the way a firm sequences its external (interactive) processes and manages its internal (service support) processes. We discussed this at length earlier in this chapter. Poor process design prevents workers from giving their best, increases waste and increases the time it takes to complete a service process cycle. One way to proceed is as follows:

■ Select a critical customer service issue that needs attention.
■ Identify the external (interactive) and internal (service support) processes that might connect to the particular customer service issue. An Ishikawa diagram (fishbone technique) may help here. One problem is that the language of the customer (complaints about waiting time in queues, for example) does not indicate

which particular processes are involved. You may also need to address cross-functional issues.

- Record the steps in the external (interactive) process next, that is, the time cycle of service as experienced by a typical customer.
- Identify which steps in the cycle contribute to customer value and which do not. This is best handled by a team-based diagnostic review, using whatever service quality data is available.
- Identify which internal service support processes critically connect with the external (interactive) sequence already identified above. Record all the steps, end to end, for any internal (service support) process that seems to impact critically on the particular external (interactive) process under review. Use flow-charting techniques for this.
- Identify which steps in the process contribute value and eliminate or modify the rest. You can also use the fishbone technique here as a brainstorming aid in generating some possible solutions to process problems. Changes might be made to job design and environmental setting, as well as the process under review. In other words, a process problem can end up having a job design solution. Alternatively, the service interaction zones might need to be modified. The test is always: which possible changes contribute most to customer value at least cost? People still do not fully appreciate that substantial improvements in service quality can result in substantial cost savings.

4. Training

We pointed out in Chapter 2 the key role employees play in delivering customer value. Clearly, appropriate training is critical. Staff find the job they do and the training they receive motivating when they have a goal that clearly relates to producing customer value. They respond to opportunities to test their personal limits and, in so doing, contribute to the customer relationship and the organisation's success.

The sequence of events is different in services marketing from product marketing. A service is typically 'sold' before it is produced or consumed. Unlike manufacturing systems, the operations processes cannot be isolated from customers and staff as both these groups may contribute to the service performance. The interactions of customers and staff transform the service production and delivery system from static to dynamic. This presents both problems and opportunities for marketers. For example, employees may have to be given considerable latitude if service performance is to improve.

Some organisations are tempted to focus too closely on training in their plan for improving service quality. Training is vital but our own work in this area suggests that there is a 'recursive' (that is, backwards and forwards) relationship between the environmental setting for service, the design of jobs, the people (who are involved in the operational processes) and the processes (which involve people). Each structural element is embedded in the other and each is part of the key to effectively designing or redesigning the service.

Having said all this, you will never entirely eliminate variability in service performance. The firm's goal should be to reduce unwarranted variations in quality so long as the value being added exceeds the total cost of achieving the objective. Indeed, one eminent Japanese statistician, Genichi Taguchi, has said that there is an incremental economic 'loss' for each deviation from customer 'target requirements', and that this has a flow-on effect to society as a whole, in the form of environmental degradation and waste of human potential.

Empowerment and collaboration

It is all too easy to attribute the quality of service, or lack of it, to the strengths or weaknesses of front-line service staff. But service 'performance' is the sum of the internal processes and activities for which staff are the agents and in which customers are the co-participants. In addition, giving front-line staff a degree of performance latitude, rather than controlling them by rules, may improve the value delivered. The fact that all customers are different adds weight to the case for empowerment. It seems obvious enough to give staff discretion, within guidelines, to match customer needs with what is on offer. But the idea of empowerment is often illusory, or else forced on staff in such unreasonable ways that it demotivates them.[24] Losing employee commitment means losing value-creating potential.

Certainly front-line service staff must perform well and need to be educated in customer service skills. This is a separate and important marketing function. But trying to improve 'front-line' service performance by improving staff customer-service training will add cost, not value, unless the design of work activities, the environment in which service is delivered, and the processes involved are all targeted for improvements as part of a continuous diagnostic review.

Internal suppliers and internal customers need to collaborate to build relationships in external markets. Any marketing activity within internal markets that involves the collaboration of internal customers and suppliers can be considered as internal marketing – an issue we raised in Chapter 3.

For us, internal marketing involves creating an organisational climate where employees can contribute significantly to improvements in cross-functional quality and service. As such internal customers and suppliers feel motivated to challenge continuously the activities that need to be changed. But this level of internal marketing requires a strategy for developing relationships between staff across internal organisational boundaries, in order to exploit fully the combined knowledge of people in different departments.[25] We will return to this issue in Chapter 6 in more depth.

SUMMARY

Surviving in volatile markets depends on managers understanding that getting and keeping customers requires continuous improvement and innovation. Firms have to choose whether to drive workers harder at their assigned tasks or invite them to participate in generating new ways of improving performance. The first way treats people as 'prisoners' of the process and the second invites people to be agents of the process – an entirely different challenge and one to which their experience within the process makes them ideally suited.

Poorly-designed processes lead to poor outcomes. Invariably, we find that the process is the villain not the worker. So companies need to review the policies, premises, procedures, machines and job structures which support – or hinder – the quality of employees' work. Processes can not be entirely standardised, of course, but at least firms can discover the 'fail points' by flow-charting the relationship between various work activities and use this knowledge to reduce the variability of key processes.

Managerial knowledge – the sum of their accumulated experience – is seldom broad or deep enough to sustain an ongoing diagnostic review of work processes in changing markets. Generating and sharing knowledge within organisations and participating in improvement up, down and across organisations is what is required to start the wheel of quality improvement turning.

In the next and final chapter we extend and embed these ideas in a broad framework for developing and implementing a relationship strategy for the business. Companies need to find ways of linking strategies across multiple markets to create value for all their stakeholders. This is the vital last step in the value-creation and delivery sequence.

References

1   Gummesson, E. (1991), 'Marketing Revisited: The Crucial Role of the Part Time Marketer', *European Journal of Marketing*, **25**, 2.

2   Deming, W.E. (1982), *Out of the Crisis*, Cambridge, MA: Massachusetts Institute of Technology.

3   Imai, M. (1986), *Kaizen: The Key to Japan's Competitive Success*, New York: Random House.

4   Juran, J.M. (1989), *Juran on Leadership for Quality*, New York: Free Press.

5   Oakland, J.S. (2000), *Total Quality Management*, 2nd edn, Oxford: Butterworth-Heinemann.

6   Gummesson E. (1988), 'Service Quality and Product Quality Combined', *Review of Business*, **9**, 3.

7   Grönroos, C. (2000), *Service Management and Marketing: A Customer Relationship Management Approach*, 2nd edn, Chichester: Wiley.

8   Porter, M.E. (1985), *Competitive Advantage: Creating and Sustaining Performance*, New York: Free Press, p. 130.

9   Ballantyne, D, Christopher, M. and Payne, A. (1995), 'Improving the Quality of Services Marketing: Service (Re) design is the Critical Link', *Journal of Marketing Management*, **11**, 1–3, 9–10.

10 Vandermerwe, S. (1993), *From Tin Solders to Russian Dolls*, Oxford: Butterworth-Heinemann.

11 De Bono, E. (1994), *Parallel Thinking*, London: Viking/Penguin Books.

12 Shostack, G.L. (1985), Planning the Service Encounter, in *The Service Encounter*, Czepiel, J.A. (ed.) Lexington, MA: Lexington Books.

13 Derived from Wyckoff, D. (1984), 'New Tools for Achieving Service Quality', *The Cornell Hotel and Restaurant Administration Quarterly*, November, 78–91.

14   The theatre metaphor of service can also be understood as *dramaturgy*. See Grove, S. J., Fisk, R.P. and Bitner, M.J. (1992), 'Dramatizing the Service Experience: A Managerial Approach', *Advances in Service Marketing and Management*, 1.

15   There is a sematic confusion in terms in use for service interaction. In a *Nordic School* perspective from Liljjander, V. and Strandvik, T. (1995), 'The Nature of Customer Relationships in Services', in Bowen, D., Brown, S.W. and Swartz, T.A. (eds), *Advances in Services Marketing and Management*, Greenwich CT: JAI Press, the interaction process is characterised as a sequence of *episodes*, which contain *acts*. These can also be understood as *moments of truth* or *critical incidents*.

16   Other mapping processes for the 'cycle of service' are described by Albrecht, K. (1990), *Service Within*, Homewood IL: Dow Jones-Irwin, and also as 'customer activity cycles' in Vandermerwe, S. (1993), *op. cit.*

17   For a good critique of customer satisfaction and service quality measurement logics, see Oliver, R.L. (1997), *Satisfaction: A Behavioral Perspective on the Consumer*, New York: McGraw-Hill.

18   Grönroos, C. (1984), *Strategic Management and Marketing in the Service Sector*, Bromley: Chartwell-Bratt, 38–40.

19   Zeithaml, V.A., Berry, L. L. and Parasuraman, A. (1993), 'The Nature and Determinants of Customer Expectations of Service', *Journal of the Academy of Marketing Science*, 21, 1, 1–12.

20   Parasuraman, A., Zeithaml, V.A. and Berry L.L. (1985), 'A Conceptual Model of Service Quality and its Implications for Future Research', *Journal of Marketing*, 49, Fall, 41–50.

21   See for example, Oliver, R.L. (1997), *op. cit.*

22   Camp R. E. (1989), *Benchmarking: The Search for Industry Best Practices that lead to Superior Performance*, New York: ASQC Quality Press.

23   Bitner, M.J. (1990), 'Evaluating Service Encounters: The Effects of Physical Surroundings and Employee Responses', *Journal of Marketing*, 54, 69–82.

24   Argyris, C. (1998), 'Empowerment: The Emperors' New Clothes', *Harvard Business Review*, May–June, 98–105.

25   Ballantyne, D. (2000), 'Internal Relationship Marketing: A Strategy for Knowledge Renewal', *International Journal of Bank Marketing*, 18, 6, 274–86.

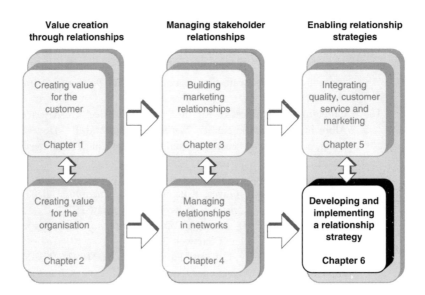

Value creation through relationships — Managing stakeholder relationships — Enabling relationship strategies

Creating value for the customer — Chapter 1

Building marketing relationships — Chapter 3

Integrating quality, customer service and marketing — Chapter 5

Creating value for the organisation — Chapter 2

Managing relationships in networks — Chapter 4

Developing and implementing a relationship strategy — Chapter 6

INTRODUCTION

Throughout this book, we have emphasised the central role that delivering and creating value play in business success. In this final chapter we look at how to develop and implement a relationship strategy based on this approach to value. In addressing the subject we examine a number of issues. First, we discuss how relationships with multiple stakeholders create value, and describe two models – the relationship value management framework and the service profit chain – that can help a business understand just how relationships in key market domains contribute towards value. Second, we discuss how a business should go about choosing appropriate relationship marketing strategies for different types of customer. Third, we examine how to do detailed planning within the six markets. And fourth, we explore in detail how a firm can use the relationship management chain, introduced in Chapter 1, as a framework for developing and implementing a relationship marketing strategy.

> A pan-company cross-functional approach ... requires most organisations to make a considerable investment in organisational change.

We then turn our attention to the critical role of organisational change and implementation issues. We advocate a pan-company cross-functional approach to relationship marketing, but this requires most organisations to make a considerable investment in organisational change. We explore five paradoxes of change management and then address the way businesses can generate knowledge through dialogue. Finally, we make some observations on the future of relationship marketing.

Relationships as a source of value

Creating value, and, more specifically, customer value, is increasingly seen as the next source of competitive advantage. There are several reasons for emphasising value in the broader context of relationship marketing. First, value has traditionally been concerned with 'the value customers create for a firm' rather than the 'value the firm creates for the customer' – and even then there has been too much focus on a narrow transactional perspective.[1] Second, value in marketing has mainly focused on the transaction or exchange and has not taken sufficient account of the value of ongoing relationships after the sale. Third, until recently, the role of value in the context of the multiple stakeholder view of relationship marketing has been largely ignored.

Recent developments in value research

Academic research into value has started to reflect more explicitly the role other stakeholders play in the value process.

Practitioners and academics have grown increasingly interested in shareholder value. However, we believe that a lot of what has been written about shareholder value to date emphasises maximising shareholder value, while largely ignoring the issue of customer value. Management's main goal is generally agreed to be to increase shareholder value. But maximising shareholder value may come at the expense of other stakeholders, leaving in its wake diminished job security, higher unemployment, poorer products and services and, ultimately, reduced shareholder value. As an example, in the short term a business could enhance shareholder value by reducing customer value through, for instance, cutting customer service budgets.

Firms need to consider customer value and shareholder value together. Placing too much emphasis on either one of them at the expense of the other could have an adverse long-term impact. Some organisations might deliver high customer value with poor shareholder value, for instance, while others might maximise shareholder value while reducing customer value. What is more, firms also need to take into account the role employees and internal processes play in creating value.

Companies can no longer view value as deriving from an individual transaction. Creating value involves acknowledging the ongoing interactions over time between a company and its customers. Value is created over time and is subject to changes and external influences such as other stakeholders.

A framework for relationship value management

A framework for relationship value management is shown in Figure 6.1.[2] This framework represents a strategic approach to managing an organisation in order to maximise value to customers and the organisation through the integrated management of relevant stakeholders. There are two main elements to the framework: the central value process and the surrounding stakeholder interaction processes. The aim of the central value process is to determine a value proposition for the organisation, and involves four sequential value-based activities: *value determination*, *value creation*, *value delivery* and *value assessment*.

The framework also illustrates linkages between the value process and specific stakeholders. All stakeholders in the six markets model potentially play a role. These stakeholders are represented in the three circular stakeholder groupings: customers, employees and external stakeholders. Shareholders are a particularly important group of stakeholders in public companies.

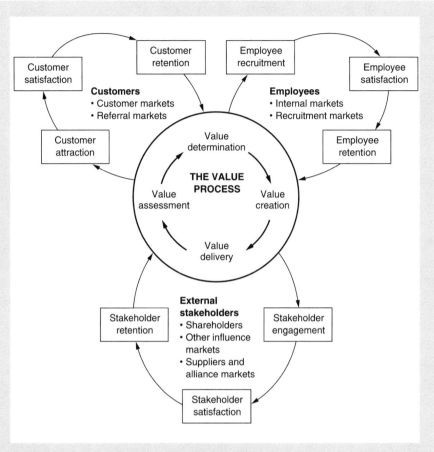

FIGURE 6.1 A framework for relationship value management
Source: Payne and Holt[2]

Each of the six market domains is represented within the three circular groups. These are: customer markets and referral markets (within the customer group); internal markets and recruitment markets (within the employee group); and influence markets – including shareholders – and supplier and alliance markets (within the external stakeholder group). Each of the three major stakeholder groups represents opportunities to create and deliver value.

In each of the three stakeholder groups represented in Figure 6.1 there are a number of key value activities that are illustrated as three circular sub-processes. Within the customer group these key activities are customer attraction, customer satisfaction and customer retention. Within the employee group the key activities are employee recruitment, employee satisfaction and employee retention. The external stakeholder activities involve stakeholder engagement (engaging the right stakeholders, such as investors and suppliers), stakeholder satisfaction and stakeholder retention (retaining them by ensuring that their needs are satisfied). Most organisations place much of their emphasis on shareholders within the external stakeholder group, but they must also manage other stakeholders. For example, influence markets might be particularly important for the not-for-profit sector. But supplier and alliance markets must be managed too to ensure they are also part of the whole value process.

The four activities of the central value process have their roots in the value literature we discussed earlier in this book. In particular, the value process builds on the McKinsey value delivery sequence described in Chapter 1. We consider that there are subtle but important distinctions between the McKinsey approach and the four-step process represented in our framework. First, the value delivery sequence places more emphasis on the value to the company than the value to the customer. Second, we argue that value determination, as shown in our framework, involves a much more rigorous understanding of both what the customer values and the customer's lifetime value to the firm than the McKinsey value delivery sequence allows for. Third, there is no value assessment activity within the value delivery sequence but we consider this to be a critical step in providing measurement and feedback on customer-perceived value. The value process in our own framework emphasises the broader perspective of relationship value as it relates to employees and other external stakeholders as well as to customers.

Value determination is equally important for employees and external stakeholders. For external stakeholders, such as shareholders, value determination involves identifying factors such as what will make them invest, what will make them continue to invest and what returns they expect. Understanding what value determination means for shareholders is especially important – not least in cases where companies struggle to keep shareholders.

The *value creation* activity involves developing and aligning the company's products and services – including its processes and employees –

to meet the requirements it identified at the value determination stage. To determine what value creating activities it should undertake, the organisation will probably need to assess the customer's value to the firm (see Chapter 2). This involves understanding which customers are profitable and/or have a significant lifetime value. The firm could then target bespoke value offerings at these groups. But this strategy should aim to retain existing customers as well as attract new ones. Companies also need to consider the role of employees and external stakeholders in creating value. Value creation for employees needs to be viewed from two perspectives – the value employees create for the organisation, and the value the organisation creates for employees.

For the *value delivery* activity, the value chain literature also provides a framework for considering the connection between the organisation and the customer. In particular, considering the interaction between the organisation's value chain and the customer's value chain helps inform decisions about the value delivery process, as we outlined in Chapter 5.

Chapter 5 also highlighted a number of tools and models such as customer satisfaction surveys and service quality monitors that companies can use to help them in the *value assessment* process.

But firms must assess the value of their employees as well as their customers. Employees tend to perceive behaviour-based evaluation as a reliable indicator of the value they deliver.[3] Assessing the value of employees is closely linked to employee retention. Long-standing employees are more likely than relative newcomers to know their jobs and the goals of the organisation and thus be more productive.

Firms must also assess their own value to external stakeholders and external stakeholders' value to them. Academic literature places a lot of attention on shareholders in this context, which, given their high profile and significant influence on an organisation's activities, is understandable. But as we have already mentioned, the shareholder value literature focuses on methods for assessing the value the organisation delivers to shareholders and places relatively little emphasis on the value shareholders deliver to the organisation.

But other external stakeholders are important too. For example, the interaction between a company and its suppliers may be critical. The

IMP research that we discussed in Chapter 4 is particularly relevant here in terms of an organisation's relationship with its suppliers and other key alliance partners.

A company can feed back the results from its value assessment – which should also involve assessing the value of the customer to the firm *after* the value delivery activity – into the initial stage in order to reassess value determination. Thus the value process is dynamic and iterative.

The services marketing literature suggests that three key stakeholders are closely linked. Research on what is now known as the 'service profit chain model' focuses on the relationship between employee satisfaction, customer loyalty and profitability and shareholder value.

From customer value to stakeholder value

> Employees, customers and shareholders are particularly important in creating value.

Employees, customers and shareholders are particularly important in creating value. Figure 6.2 shows the 'employee-customer-profit chain' or 'linkage model', which is a form of the service profit chain developed by researchers at the Harvard Business School.[4] This diagram depicts the sequential roles employees and customers play in creating shareholder value.

Reichheld, author of *The Loyalty Effect*, argues that the three key stakeholders – employees, customers and shareholders – are the 'forces of loyalty'.[5] So while other stakeholders can play a major role, these three are central to achieving success. This reflects the practice of many leading service organisations. For example, Bill Marriott Jr, chairman of Marriott Hotels, is a strong exponent of the need for the business to satisfy the three key groups of customers, employees and shareholders. Many service experts believe that employee satisfaction should be ranked first among these, because employee satisfaction impacts customer and ultimately shareholder satisfaction.

The logic in this diagram argues that improving leadership and management behaviour positively affects employee attitudes and satisfaction. The more satisfied and motivated an employee, the longer they are likely to stay with an organisation and the better they will do their job. This positively affects customer satisfaction, so customers will stay

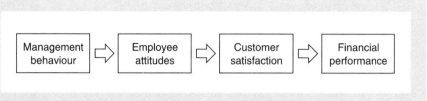

FIGURE 6.2 **The linkage or service profit chain model**

longer and generate higher sales for the company. The result is strong profitability and increasing shareholder value.

But it is not clear, for any given organisation, how much one variable needs to improve to achieve a given level of improvement in another variable. For example, if employee attitudes and satisfaction increase by a measurable amount, what impact will this have on customer satisfaction and resulting profitability?

Sears, Roebuck & Company, the leading US department store, is an outstanding exemplar of the use of metrics within the service profit chain. Sears, one of the great turnaround success stories of the 1990s, underwent a radical transformation.[6] Much of its success was attributed to rigorous measurement systems that tracked employee attitudes and their impact on customer satisfaction and profitability. Critically, management is aligned around the metrics and there is widespread understanding throughout Sears of how their model works.

CASE STUDY   **Sears and the development of value metrics**

In 1992 Sears, Roebuck & Company reported massive losses of $3.9 billion on sales of $52.3 billion. When Arthur Martinez was appointed as CEO he streamlined the business, closing 113 stores and terminating the 101-year-old Sears catalogue, a household institution in the United States. He also changed the service strategy, focusing on women who were the most important buying decision-makers. As a result, in 1993 Sears reported a net income of $752 million – a dramatic reversal in the fortunes of such a mature company.

Martinez set up task forces to define world class status in each of five categories – customers, employees, financial performance, innovation and values – and to identify obstacles and define metrics for measuring progress. The task forces spent months listening to customers and employees, observing best practice in other organisations and establishing measures against objectives. Gradually it became apparent that the company needed a model to show direct causation from employee attitudes, through customer satisfaction to profits. Sears needed to know how management action, such as investment in sales force training, would directly translate into improved customer satisfaction, retention and higher revenues. It needed a measurement system around the employee-customer-profit model.

Sears defined a set of measures based on its objectives, which were to make Sears 'a compelling place to work, to shop at and to invest in'. It identified relationships between changes in key metrics using advanced statistical techniques.

The results were impressive. It identified direct links between employee measures, customer measures and revenues, and these enabled it to establish total profit indicators for the company. It discovered that employee attitudes towards the job and company were critical to employee loyalty and behaviour towards customers, while customer impressions directly affected customer retention and recommendations. After further refinement, the model is now used to predict revenue growth: a 5 unit increase in employee attitude drives a 1.3 unit increase in customer impression, a 0.5 unit increase in revenue growth and a quantifiable increase in store profitability.

Sears had to change the behaviour of its senior managers and encourage them to take responsibility for the company's culture and understand how this affected revenues before it could successfully implement the service profit chain model. In addition, it had to align employee rewards to the model for financial and non-financial measures. The results have been impressive: employee satisfaction at Sears has risen by 4 per cent, customer satisfaction has risen by almost 4 per cent, and more than $200 million additional revenues have been achieved through this value-creation process. A further benefit has been the streamlining of IT from eighteen separate legacy databases to a single, integrated system.

These relationships were modelled by CFI, a leading US consulting firm specialising in econometric modelling. Sears' confidence in the CFI data was such that it computed, depending on the type of managerial role, between 30 per cent and 70 per cent of executive compensation from these measures. In terms of shareholder value, the total return to investors between September 1992 and April 1997 was 298 per cent – again a remarkable improvement for such a mature business.

Not every organisation will be able to be as sophisticated as Sears, Roebuck, but all business leaders should aspire to improve their companies' performance through developing appropriate metrics to measure value.

Choice of relationship strategy

A company will probably need different types of relationship strategy for different types of customer. Factors affecting the choice of relationship strategy might include an uncertain and volatile marketing environment,[7] the degree of commoditisation and hence price sensitivity of the market and the size of transaction costs. In particular the firm's overarching business strategy will influence the kind of relationships it chooses. In this 'contingency' approach to relationship marketing strategy companies will find the three 'generic' business strategies identified by Treacy and Wiersema[8] very useful:

- operational excellence
- product leadership
- customer intimacy

Treacy and Wiersema called these three routes to success 'value disciplines'. Based on their research they suggested that marketplace success was usually built on 'what kind of value proposition the companies pursued – best total cost, best product, or best total solution'. They continued:[8]

by operational excellence, we mean providing customers with reliable products or services at competitive prices, delivered with minimal difficulty or inconvenience. By product leadership, we mean providing products that continually redefine the state of the art. And by customer intimacy, we mean selling the customer a total solution not just a product or service.

While these three 'disciplines' or 'generic' strategies are not mutually exclusive, companies tend to have different strengths – or weaknesses – in each of the three. Therefore we believe that companies need to support each of these three generic strategies with an appropriate relational strategy in each of the six key market domains.

There is a connection between Treacy and Wiersema's three value disciplines and the six markets model that we discussed in Chapter 3. In order to become a leader through one or other of these generic strategies a company will need to vary the emphasis it places on each of the six markets in the overall marketing strategy of the business.

So, for example, organisations seeking to follow the discipline of 'operational excellence' will need an internal culture that is based on efficiency. In other words, the focus of the internal marketing effort should be on continuous improvement, multi-skilling and activities such as quality circles that lead to greater internal efficiency. The organisation should also place significant emphasis on the supplier market domain since materials and supplies account for a major proportion of many organisations' total cost. By working more closely with suppliers the organisation will identify many opportunities to reduce cost and improve quality. Likewise, the firm will also need to manage closely the interface with downstream intermediaries such as distributors and retailers. Using electronic data interchange (EDI) and other forms of electronic commerce, for example, firms can often significantly enhance the responsiveness and cost-effectiveness of the supply chain.

Those firms seeking to base their strategic focus on 'product leadership' will need to construct a six-market strategy that places different weight on each domain. For example, they might choose to invest in creating an internal culture that encourages innovation, risk-taking and entrepreneurship. As such they will want to recruit people who can contribute to the innovation process, people with skills and experience that indicate their creativity or in-depth knowledge of technologies or markets. Microsoft, an acknowledged world leader in its field, has declared its sole recruitment criterion to be 'intelligence'.

Businesses seeking product leadership will also need to focus on their relationship with suppliers. In many industries today suppliers drive a significant proportion of innovation. Bringing suppliers into the product development process can often lead to breakthroughs in design and functionality. Most of the innovative features that we now take for granted in motor cars, for example, originated with the suppliers.

Companies seeking product leadership will also benefit from developing alliances with other organisations to gain access to their specific skills, knowledge bases and market understanding.

Companies choosing to pursue a strategy of 'customer intimacy', meanwhile, will need to put their emphasis on developing ever closer, more customised – even personalised – relationships with customers. As such the 'internal' market is critically important to them. Many studies now confirm the impact of employee motivation and commitment on customer satisfaction. Developing customer intimacy also depends on identifying those customers or segments who are more likely to seek this type of relationship. Certain types of products and services and certain buying occasions are more likely to lend themselves to this kind of strategy than others. So customer-intimate companies tend to focus on building relationships with existing customers with the greatest potential for growth and profitability.

> Many studies now confirm the impact of employee motivation and commitment on customer satisfaction.

Planning for the six markets

Relationship marketing, as we see it, does not lend itself to a highly prescriptive approach to developing marketing plans. There is no 'proper' way of developing marketing strategy; companies need to make choices, avoiding both overly prescriptive models and non-actionable descriptive formulations. Mintzberg has pointed out that the strategic planning literature has confused decision-making with strategy-making by assuming that strategy making must involve selecting a single course of action at one point in time.[9]

It is now widely acknowledged that making marketing decisions based on the '4Ps' of product, price, promotion and place can be too restrictive. In essence, the 4Ps is an organising principle for decisions about the way *financial* resources are allocated. As we pointed out in Chapter 5, in practice the range of resource decisions is limited by the scope of the marketing budget, which is the province of the marketing function. This encourages an overemphasis on those kinds of decisions that concern discrete marketing services activities like advertising and research, which can be funded without the collaboration and commitment of people outside the marketing function. Therefore it is often difficult for marketing to actually implement marketing strategies.

To focus and integrate strategies for each of the six markets into a cohesive whole is a challenging task (see Figure 6.3). Marketing has long sought to structure plans around market-based objectives, whatever the organisational climate for change may be. But in the era of

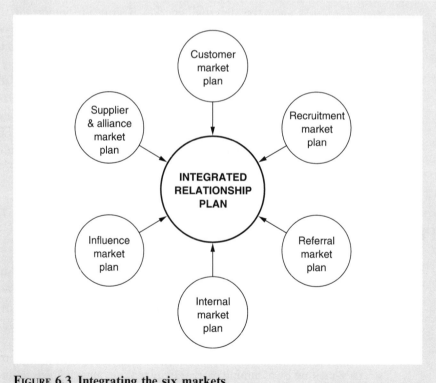

FIGURE 6.3 **Integrating the six markets**

relationship marketing, organisations need to take more interest in the prevailing employee 'climate', and we will return to this point later. Certainly there needs to be a more collaborative approach to planning in order that firms can align activities that traditionally fall within marketing's domain and those that fall outside it. The objective of the periodic planning exercise is to ensure there is a cohesive and pan-company approach to determining and implementing a market-oriented strategy.

Some markets may not always need detailed plans, although organisations may find it useful to develop them. However, firms should develop some form of relationship marketing objectives for each of the market domains, together with value propositions that support these objectives. Otherwise, strategies will not be aligned and organisations will not change.

In Chapter 3 we examined in depth the concept of building relationships with market domains using the 'six markets model'. We suggested that while all businesses should aim to build a strong position in each of these markets, the emphasis they place on each market should reflect their chosen underlying generic strategy. A six markets strategy can be conveniently summarised in the relationship marketing network diagram, which shows the company's present and desired emphasis for each of the six markets. Each market domain can be divided into a series of further sub-groups or segments. Figure 6.4 illustrates this idea with the example of the referral market for an accounting firm.

A firm can augment the information it draws from the relationship marketing network diagram by looking at the affect of positive or negative performance in each of the six market domains on success or failure in the final customer market. Firms may find it useful to summarise the key aspects of such analysis along the lines of the Euro Disney example we provide below. Euro Disney opened in 1992 and struggled for several years to build a significant customer base. Figure 6.5 highlights a number of failings across the company's six markets that may have contributed to its difficulties.

Once a business has identified critical issues within its six market domains it needs to put key metrics in place to monitor performance in each of those markets. Figure 6.6 illustrates some of the potential metrics that could be used within each market domain.

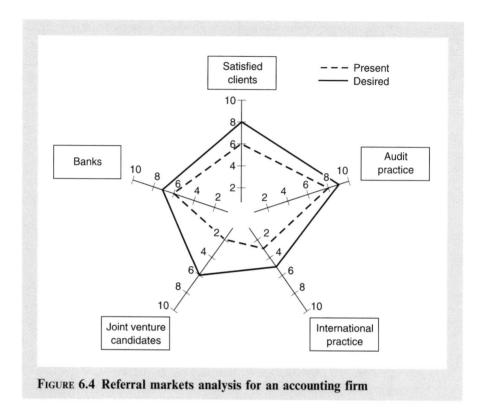

FIGURE **6.4 Referral markets analysis for an accounting firm**

The relationship management chain

Transactional marketing is often more product focused than customer focused. Companies have tended to see the customer as someone to whom an offer is made, that offer having been predicated by the organisation's own capabilities and competencies. But while companies clearly have to focus their offer around their own skills and strengths, true relationship strategies begin not with the concept of a bundle of features or even a brand, but with a clear understanding of what constitutes value in the eyes of the customer.

> Transactional marketing is often more product-focused than customer-focused.

The goal of relationship marketing is to create and deliver superior customer value on a continuing basis. To help companies develop an

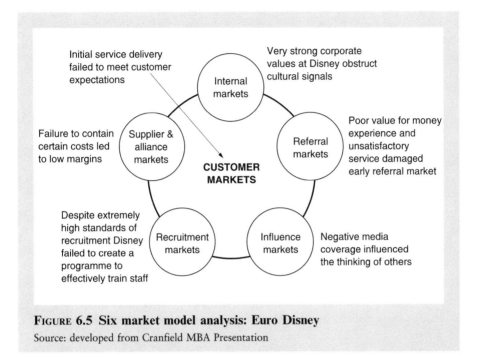

Initial service delivery failed to meet customer expectations

Very strong corporate values at Disney obstruct cultural signals

Failure to contain certain costs led to low margins

Poor value for money experience and unsatisfactory service damaged early referral market

Despite extremely high standards of recruitment Disney failed to create a programme to effectively train staff

Negative media coverage influenced the thinking of others

Internal markets

Supplier & alliance markets

Referral markets

CUSTOMER MARKETS

Recruitment markets

Influence markets

FIGURE 6.5 Six market model analysis: Euro Disney
Source: developed from Cranfield MBA Presentation

integrated approach to achieving this goal we propose a planning template known as the relationship management chain, shown in Figure 6.7.

The relationship management chain seeks to operationalise the six markets model by getting everyone to focus on creating customer value. There are four distinct – but linked – elements in the chain:

1 Defining the value proposition.
2 Identifying appropriate customer value segments.
3 Designing value delivery systems.
4 Managing and maintaining delivered satisfaction.

Defining the value proposition

Every customer has a different idea of what represents value, and what is valuable to one customer may be less valuable to another. At its most fundamental, value represents customers' perceptions of the benefits they believe they will receive from owning or consuming a

MARKET DOMAIN	CONCEPTUAL TOOLS/ FRAMEWORKS	ILLUSTRATIVE METRICS
1. CUSTOMER MARKET (inc. consumers and intermediaries)	• Customer retention economics • Customer satisfaction studies	• Customer retention • Share of wallet
2. SUPPLIER/ALLIANCE MARKET	• Supply chain management efficiency	• Improved quality • Cost reduction • Time to market
3. RECRUITMENT MARKET	• Personality inventories Capability inventories	• Offers/acceptances ratio • Adaptation/innovation continuum
4. INFLUENCE MARKET	• Familiarity/favourability matrix	• Shareholder churn • Publicity impact
5. REFERRAL MARKET	• The referral balance sheet	• Share of sales/profits derived from referral sources
6. INTERNAL MARKET	• Climate surveys • Employee satisfaction surveys	• Employee retention • Employee motivation • Employee satisfaction

FIGURE 6.6 **Potential metrics for use within the six market domains**

product or service relative to the total costs of owning it. Customer value is best defined as 'the impact the supplier's offer has on the customers' own value chain'. If the offer enhances performance, increases perceived benefits or reduces the customer's costs, then customers will see it as clearly adding value to them.

So the starting point of any relationship marketing programme should be to define and specify the precise nature of the value to be delivered, market segment by market segment – or even customer by customer. This is the 'value proposition' or, to express it more simply: 'how do we intend to create value for our customers?'

Identifying appropriate customer value segments

Customers' different perceptions and requirements of value give marketers a powerful means of segmenting their markets. In-depth customer research will help reveal the salient dimensions of value, and techniques such as 'trade-off analysis' can identify groups of customers

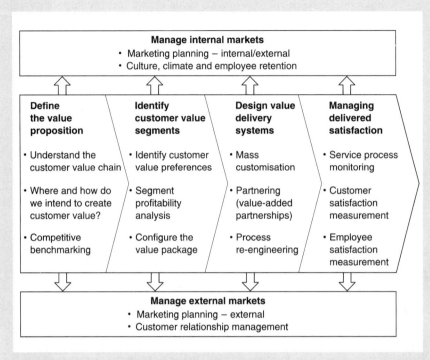

Manage internal markets
- Marketing planning – internal/external
- Culture, climate and employee retention

Define the value proposition	Identify customer value segments	Design value delivery systems	Managing delivered satisfaction
• Understand the customer value chain	• Identify customer value preferences	• Mass customisation	• Service process monitoring
• Where and how do we intend to create customer value?	• Segment profitability analysis	• Partnering (value-added partnerships)	• Customer satisfaction measurement
• Competitive benchmarking	• Configure the value package	• Process re-engineering	• Employee satisfaction measurement

Manage external markets
- Marketing planning – external
- Customer relationship management

FIGURE 6.7 The relationship management chain

who share common value preferences. In other words, companies can segment markets on the basis of groups of customers who share common value preferences. The resulting segments might well cut across the more traditional bases for segmentation such as demographic or socio-economic variables, but marketing strategies based on customer value preferences are more likely to succeed.

Designing value delivery systems

The means by which a company 'delivers' value to customers is in itself a key element of the relationship. When we talk of delivery systems we do not mean just the physical delivery of products or the way services are presented, but also the marketing channels a company uses, the flexibility of its response, the way it links buyer and supplier logistics and information systems, and so on. In other words, we view the design of the value delivery system as a critical way of forging stronger linkages between the customer's value chain and the supplier's value chain. Increasing fragmentation of many industries' markets has led customers to demand greater variety in products or services, which means suppliers need to make their delivery systems more flexible – in other words, to tailor products and services to the precise needs of individual customers or segments.

To build such flexibility into their delivery systems companies will frequently have to radically review the conventional wisdom on manufacturing and distribution. For example, they may need to focus on reducing batch quantities in production and distribution and move to a just-in-time delivery environment that involves delaying the final configuration of the finished product.

Managing and maintaining delivered satisfaction

Because the quality and strength of customer relationships is so critical to the survival and profitability of any business, companies must regularly monitor the processes that deliver satisfaction, as well as the customers' perceptions of performance. In the same way in which the quality of physical products depends on how well companies control the process that manufactures them, so too the quality of customer service depends on how well companies control the way it is delivered.

> Companies must regularly monitor the processes that deliver satisfaction.

In Chapter 5 we stressed how important it is to align quality, customer service and marketing. But most companies manage these key ingredients of relationship marketing as discrete activities, with insufficient overlap. The example in Figure 6.8 depicts a manufacturing company that puts too much emphasis on quality and has an isolated and impoverished marketing function.

Firms should monitor their service process continuously, ensuring that they identify all potential 'fail points' and, if they can not make these fail-safe, carefully control them. As we pointed out in Chapter 5, the way a company manages its 'moments of truth' with customers dictates whether customers are satisfied or disappointed with any element of service.

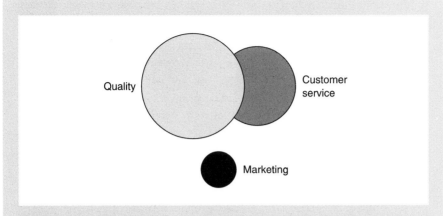

FIGURE 6.8 An imbalance between quality, customer service and marketing

Employee satisfaction studies and customer satisfaction studies should form an integral part of the way companies manage their service delivery. Many companies already conduct such studies but only on an ad hoc basis. Paradoxically, companies that monitor brand awareness or attitudes and usage every month often pay much less attention to vital performance indicators such as employee and customer satisfaction.

Implementation and organisational issues

Because relationship marketing is a pan-company concept, companies will often need to change substantially in order to implement it. Conventional organisations are 'vertical' – that is, designed around functions. But market-facing companies must be 'horizontal' – that is, focused on processes. As we have already observed, process management requires cross-functional working and a major transition from the classic 'silo' mentality to a 'customer-centric' view of the world.

The role of marketing in the firm, under the new paradigm of relationship marketing, is more challenging than ever before. Now marketing has to take responsibility for initiating specific plans for each of the six markets. Once the organisation as a whole has decided how it wants to compete and what value propositions it wants to deliver, marketing has to identify and link the key process strategies together to achieve corporate goals.

Such a pan-company plan might appear eminently attractive, but in most cases it will not be achieved without significant organisational and cultural change. For instance, working across functions using multi-disciplinary teams will have to become the norm.

The types of skills and breadth of knowledge required to make this philosophy succeed are quite different from those inherent in the traditional functional management model. Continuous management development in areas such as cross-functional process management and leadership skills, for example, will be critical. The McKinsey 'Seven S' model shown in Figure 6.9 shows the many dimensions of organisational change that are involved in moving to a process-oriented relationship marketing strategy.

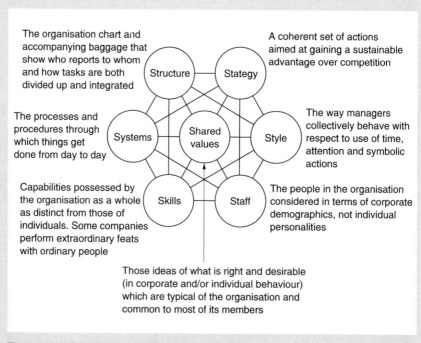

FIGURE 6.9 McKinsey & Co 'Seven S' framework
Source: Waterman, Peters and Phillips[10]

The traditional view of organisation is that strategy is the starting point for implementing change and that the type of organisational structure required will be clear from this strategy. Likewise, the types of systems needed to carry out the strategy will follow logically from the strategy and structure. The 'Seven S' model, by contrast, suggests that companies need to consider four additional elements – style, staff, skills and shared values. While the average and poorer-performing companies tend to place most emphasis on strategy, structure and systems, the top performing companies place emphasis on all seven elements in the McKinsey framework.

The starting point in the Seven S framework is shared values. These should reflect the positive key aspects of the organisation's culture. In a sense, the shared values are the 'glue' that holds the organisation together. The Seven S model suggests that organisations become effective and implement change successfully by carefully orchestrating the seven elements. McKinsey & Co use the metaphor of a compass to describe how each of these elements should be lined up, like compass needles pointing in the same direction, so that they support each other. The Seven S framework was originally developed as a way of thinking broadly about the problem of effective organisation, but it has also proved to be an excellent tool to judge how easy it would be to implement a new strategy. Strategy implementation is not only a matter of getting the strategy and structure right, but also involves all the other elements in the Seven S model. If the needles of the compasses are aligned the company is purposefully organised to carry out the task. If the needles are not aligned, then the company needs to look at each of the elements to see if it can alter it or realign it to integrate the organisation round a common task or purpose. As such the Seven S framework is an excellent way to check the strategic fit between the different elements in an organisation.

Let us consider the strategic change a company will need to make if it wants to shift from a transactional orientation to a relationship orientation. Figure 6.10 provides a summary of the key changes the company will need to make the transition.

The changes involved in making the transition to relationship marketing management are clearly profound. There are a number of potential obstacles to this transition, not least the entrenched interest in preserving the status quo.

	From	To
Strategy	Market to major customer segments	Add value to individual customer relationships through tailored interactions
Shared values	Serve customers well	Service customers differently; serve best customers really well
Structure	Product orientation with focus on current period economics	Customer-segment orientation with focus on lifetime customer value
Skills	Analytical orientation with focus on current period economics	Ability to gather, analyse and interpret data and design systems to exploit a large, constantly evolving customer information base; ability to react at individual customer (or at least micro-segment) level
Staff	Marketing analysis managed statistically; information technology acts as support, but not as an active partner	Integration of marketing creativity with systems competencies to create capability that is both ideas driven and analytically intense
Systems	Detailed, segmented, but relatively static decision support tools	Extensive, dynamic and flexible marketing support tools, programme management and execution systems, and operating links to support front-line actions
Style	Marketing plan orientation with emphasis on programmes for major segments delivered within standard period; mass media focus	Analytical approach and experimental attitude with emphasis on continuous learning (do, test, measure, fix) and value of data
Leading measures of success	• Marketing share • Current period profits	• Share of most attractive customers (based on lifetime profit potential) • Continuous learning/tailored marketing • Large impact on a small set of customers

FIGURE 6.10 **Changing the organisation**
Source: Child *et al.*[11]

Organisational change

So now we are left with an inescapable conclusion. Somebody has to start the wheel turning. Managing change is strategic. Getting support from senior management as a sponsor of change is critical. What is really at stake is an 'organisational transition' to collaborative management that will help align the major company-wide processes of innovation, demand/supply chain and customer relationship management.

Committing to a precise goal at an early stage could be misguided, given that the move to relationship marketing management is a qualitative goal. Having said that, a company will need to take a number of definite steps, each of which will involve doing things differently – a process of 'learning by doing' in effect. A company needs to plan these steps, set up and complete individual projects to achieve them and put in place motivational and organisational structures.

James Quinn introduced the concept of 'logical incrementalism' to corporate strategic planning in the late 1970s. Following Quinn,[12] we recognise that companies can achieve goals in each of the six markets through many means, and that they may be politically unwise to proscribe unilaterally a particular set of means too early in the process. Incremental changes generate new knowledge and applying that knowledge leads to new incremental change processes. Logical incrementalism is not 'muddling through' but a way of staying open to new information and reaching for sources of information up and down the organisation.

People and process

In relationship marketing there is a recursive (that is, backwards and forwards) relationship between people (who are involved in work processes) and processes (which involve people). Each is the key to the effectiveness of the other. But to leverage this relationship companies need to invite people to support and participate in improving the way processes are designed and organised. As such, the people-process relationship within the organisation becomes the internal driving force for change. But achieving change through people-process drivers poses a potential challenge to marketing managers' influence and authority.

As any manager knows, doing things differently is unlikely to be applauded unless the project succeeds – and sometimes not even then. So we would recommend that the CEO endorses any change plan by getting actively involved. If this endorsement is not forthcoming, then marketing might limit the programme to a 'pilot'. It is easier to launch a pilot project when faced with organisational or cultural resistance to change than it is to 'hit the wall' head on. Without top-level support, marketing innovators can only stretch the cultural 'elastic' so far, and it is counter-productive and politically misguided to attempt to challenge and overturn the company's system of beliefs and assumptions. There are other ways for marketing to achieve its ends.

One solution might be to suggest a pilot programme to another department or division where collaboration between it and marketing seems likely to succeed. For example, marketing might collaborate with logistics to improve supply relationships, or with human resources to foster talent. Although this approach lacks the legitimacy of a company-wide proposal, the power base is shared between two or more organisational units. Not only does such an approach protect marketing against becoming isolated within the company through its pursuit of counter-cultural activities, it also provides different perspectives on a project and further opportunities to co-operate and collaborate.

Many company-wide changes are triggered by a crisis, whether real or imaginary. When marketing can take the lead or support

> Many company-wide changes are triggered by a crisis, whether real or imaginary.

another department's initiative, its market orientation and strategic vision often lend meaning and purpose to what might appear to be unconventional organisational thinking. An outbreak of excellence in one department or in a group of collaborating departments sends powerful signals through the organisation about new ways and means of achieving better results. But organisational change requires both social skills and technical skills – or, in other words, both people and processes.

Resistance points in any organisation-wide change process

Implementing relationship marketing across the six markets involves a radical shift, over time, in the way people work with each other and the responsibility they take for that work. We have identified four phases of organisational commitment to change that represent a collaborative change process to realign work activity across functional borders within the internal market (see Figure 6.11).

The process starts with those people who are already committed and therefore most active. They derive their legitimacy and support from the senior executive in charge of the change process. As we have already mentioned, if this person is not the CEO, then the ambitions

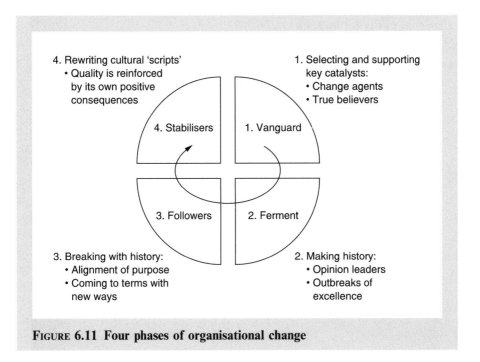

4. Rewriting cultural 'scripts'
• Quality is reinforced
  by its own positive
  consequences

1. Selecting and supporting
   key catalysts:
   • Change agents
   • True believers

4. Stabilisers   1. Vanguard

3. Followers   2. Ferment

3. Breaking with history:
• Alignment of purpose
• Coming to terms with
  new ways

2. Making history:
   • Opinion leaders
   • Outbreaks of
     excellence

FIGURE 6.11 Four phases of organisational change

and scale of the change process should be confined within the corporate culture, at least for the pilot phase.

This vanguard group should be identified early as change agents for the whole process. After all, there is a political component to change and those people most committed to the process – including managers – will need to be supported and trained in persuasion and influencing skills.

The vanguard's job is to create a 'ferment' – or stimulate the involvement of those people who intuitively understand the marketing message and are sufficiently influential to help spread it. These are opinion leaders certainly, but they might come from any level in the organisation and be quite different from those people we normally associate with leading opinion. Moving around the circle clockwise, 'followers' of course follow, and 'stabilisers' often provide very necessary analytical skills that help institutionalise proposed changes. There is no fixed point at which you could say 'critical mass' has been achieved and the organisation has changed. This is partly because innovation and improvement are continuous activities.

Project teams as internal networks

The key to managing organisation-wide change is to create structural supports or 'safety nets' that allow staff to move from what they know, based on past experience, to what is unknowable – the future.

We recommend that small teams should work on internal market issues. The role of leader for a small team of, say, three to five people, can easily be shared between members of the team, according to the talents of the individuals and the changing maintenance needs of the team. This avoids the common problem of finding great numbers of 'suitable' leaders. The issue then is not so much how to train leaders, but how to create a climate for change where people can grow into leaders quickly, with as much mature insight as possible. Internal facilitators might oversee a number of small teams, and their role will connect more to overall strategic objectives than to the specific tasks of particular teams.

Small teams established in the internal market to solve problems or improve quality tend to operate as networks that cross functional and hierarchical lines. Because they exist outside the organisational system as well as within it, while they have no special freedoms in terms of decision-making authority they do have freedom in the way they generate ideas and knowledge. It is this pluralistic relationship, outside and within the organisation, which provides most opportunity to challenge the way things are done. In practice, using teams in this way does not visibly 'change the culture' overnight, but empowers pre-existing sub-cultures within the organisation. Freeing up these network channels contributes to creating a climate for change and innovation.

Five paradoxes of change management

Most of what needs to be done in terms of managing change is hidden from sight. It is easy – but wrong – to interpret the visible part as the only thing that needs addressing. This is the big paradox of change management. Below we set out five common traps that companies should steer clear of when implementing change.

Paradox one

 We will cascade our commitment down to the troops. That should fix it.

Employees may reject marketing messages unless they are communicated logically and coherently in a way that equates with their own past experience. As with advertising, internal marketing communications work best when they 'preach to the converted'. Messages that try to persuade people to change their minds are often doomed to failure; they work best when they reinforce how people already feel and think. Two-way messages are better, while dialogue – a process of joint reasoning – works best of all.

People do not so much resist change, they resist being changed, especially when they can not grasp the reasons for the change. Internal marketing communications that try to change people's minds can work as signals of strategic intent. People are willing to suspend disbelief while they wait for some demonstrable action that confirms the truth of the message. Their attitude is 'you've told me but show me'.

This is particularly so at middle-management level. Middle managers need to know that there is substance behind the organisation's 'commitment' before they can effectively cascade the message down. Middle management will want to know what effect the change programme will have on their roles and responsibilities. Unless top management demonstrate commitment, middle management may well go through the motions and then make sure that nothing happens.

> Communication has to be backed up with evidence – both real and symbolic – of change.

Senior management often fail to recognise what an ambiguous effect their apparently direct and clear communications can have, particularly where they seem at odds with established decision-making processes and organisational power bases. Communication has to be backed up with evidence – both real and symbolic – of change, or it will be seen as empty rhetoric.

Paradox two

 We must invest in more training.

The most common mistake is to jump directly into intensive training. In marketing terms the questions that should be asked (and often are not) are:

- Who is my target audience?
- What are their expectations?
- What knowledge do they need now?
- What skills do they need now?
- How can we monitor the learning process?

The investment in training is wasted if too much training is provided for too many people too soon. It is a matter of scale. On the other hand, training in skills is necessary so that people can adjust to changing work contexts. This kind of learning has been called 'single loop learning', especially where the intention is to keep organisational performance stable within organisational norms. But where more fundamental and widespread training is required – in new organisational processes, for example – training becomes strategic because the change that triggers it challenges the patterns of operations and the assumptions that previously defined effective performance. This second kind of learning is called 'double loop learning'.[13]

What is needed is effectively a process that allows line managers and specialists to get information from all over the company in order to solve problems without the constraints of the usual departmental blocks. The knowledge gathered in this way needs to be codified over time, and retained in the organisation. Knowledge management technology and data capture is a step in the right direction. But if the organisation cannot teach itself to learn – which is the intention of 'double loop learning' – it will find itself pouring money into a bottomless pit. Companies would be well advised to invest in learning how people might best learn in their organisation, and then develop the training based on their findings.

Paradox three

 We intend to build a strong culture as a priority.

Corporate cultures are shaped and sustained by deeply-held values and beliefs just as the cultures of nations are. But to change the culture of a particular company successfully demands great subtlety. You can, for example, change the cosmetics such as logo, signage, mission statements, 'corporate wardrobe' and the design of the stationery without changing the culture at all. Changing a company's superficial identity may signal a change of direction, but it will have no significant or lasting cultural impact.

Yet corporate cultures do change. To change its culture successfully a business needs to back up its intentions with actions. Culture change starts with a company's vision of what it wants to be – or, as we prefer to say, its strategic intent. But you cannot talk a culture into changing. The company needs to confirm its strategic intent with a series of coherent actions such as doing things in new ways, communicating the effects and using some events symbolically to shine light on the meaning of those new ways.[14]

The leaders of organisations have a major impact on corporate culture because they alter the way companies initiate and respond to opportunities and threats. Just as brand values must be congruent with brand image, corporate values must be congruent with corporate aspirations. A company needs the kind of culture that suits its purpose, competencies and market opportunities.

Paradox four

 We want to get everybody involved.

Getting everybody involved sounds fine in theory, but in practice it comes down to the question of time-scale. Many companies give the impression of wanting to get change over and done with. But staff tend to be so focused on solving day-to-day problems that they end up shutting out messages that signal opportunities and possibilities all around them.

Starting small can be a very good idea. It allows the company to build commitment based on action programmes and broadcasting the results across the organisation. These actions signal to others that the commitment has integrity. More and more people become involved in each recurring cycle of activity. We described the employee 'buy-in' phases of vanguard, ferment, followers and stabilisers earlier in this chapter. It is futile to try to involve everyone at once if the company cannot support them with committed people and training.

Paradox five

 Our bottom line tells us when we are succeeding.

There is no single way of measuring the score, and a company will find a range of external and internal feedback mechanisms that enable a 'fix' on performance more useful. We outlined one example of a suite of performance feedback mechanisms in Chapter 5.

Financial accounts rarely reveal much about the activities that costs are based around. Investing in quality improvement, for example, can actually reduce the cost of quality by cutting out waste and cutting down process time without reducing the value delivered to the customer.

The final score in terms of shareholder value is traditionally profits or surplus expressed in numbers and set in a historical cost-accounting framework. This is an important convention, but it is only one dimension. We are now in the era of the Balanced Scorecard,[15] which recognises the importance of non-financial performance indicators alongside the more traditional financial measures. Relationship-oriented metrics should be key elements in this new multi-dimensional concept of performance measurement. For example, measures such as customer retention, customer satisfaction, perfect order achievement, complaints, customer referrals and 'share of wallet' must stand alongside the more traditional performance measures such as achievement against budget. Where possible these measures should be process based, such as 'time-to-market', 'time-to-serve' and 'cost-to-serve'. Equally they should be widely communicated and, ideally, incorporated into incentive schemes such as quarterly bonuses and employee recognition awards.

Generating knowledge through dialogue

We have referred several times to the value delivery sequence of 'choose the value', 'provide the value' and 'communicate the value'. When developing effective relationship marketing strategies companies need to ensure that they use the third element to 'close the loop'. But communication has to become more of a two-way process or dialogue within a relationship.

Directing effective and efficient communications at external markets is a fundamental marketing responsibility. But, despite the potential afforded by direct marketing, the Internet and customer relationship management (CRM) systems, this communication is too often one-way. Relationship marketing also recognises that developing relationships in the six markets can provide a solid platform for generating new knowledge about business conditions, opportunities and constraints. Companies gain this new knowledge through purposefully interacting with their stakeholders – as well as formal market research.

Marketers face the even more immediate challenge of ensuring that the firm can deliver on the explicit or implicit promises that are embedded in marketing messages. If the firm cannot meet customers' expectations, it will lose their custom, which is a form of lost value.

When satisfied customers become voluntary advocates for their favourite products, services and suppliers, they make 'word-of-mouth' recommendations, as we discussed in Chapter 3, specifically in relation to the referral market. But word-of-mouth can be negative too, and do untold damage to a firm's reputation and future prospects as the 'word' gets around. But word-of-mouth occurs outside marketers' realm of direct control.

By focusing on integrating outgoing marketing communications, marketers are curtailing the long-term potential to develop value exchanges with customers. Instead, they should be listening to customers and learning what they consider to be valuable, so shifting the marketing communication strategy from one-way messaging to two-way communication, with the emphasis on interaction and the potential for dialogue. This in turn supports the development of ongoing value exchanges between the various parties.

The nature of dialogue

The words we use to communicate, no matter how carefully we choose them, rarely explain our experiences adequately. But the notion of dialogue implies that we should continue to grapple with the problems inherent in everyday language, to persist and go deeper in communicating and listening to get to the bottom of any misunderstanding we may have with another party. Dialogue aims to reconcile what seems contrary, making meaning possible between people. One way of expressing this idea is to say that dialogue is about reasoning together to build shared meanings.[16]

Not all actions initiated by either a supplier, a customer or an employee necessarily lead to two-way communications, and certainly not all two-way communications justify the depth of listening and learning associated with dialogue. Nevertheless, dialogue is valuable because of its spontaneity and creative potential, both within the internal market and in any other market where there is an opportunity to work through problems or opportunities together.

A view of the marketing communication process as a whole is shown in Figure 6.12 with some key parallel processes made visible between the firm and its customers. According to Grönroos[17] these multiple processes set up the conditions for a relationship-based dialogue.

First, the episodes in the interaction process are shown. Second, a planned communication process may initiate the interaction process. Thus one-way (planned) communication and two-way (interactive) communication connect at some point. Grönroos argues that when both planned and interactive processes work in parallel, the customer relationship is likely to be further enhanced.

> A successful relationship requires that two or more parties learn from each other.

A successful relationship requires that two or more parties learn from each other in order to sustain or improve value exchanges between them. This involves a deepening dialogue based on an understanding of mutual needs, values and habits.

Ongoing dialogue supports the learning relationship and the learning relationship supports the dialogue and this may lead to a common knowledge base developing. If all parties can trust each other (or at least suspend distrust) in this dialogue of reasoning together, then relationship bonds will grow stronger. This may lead to new business opportunities and more creative solutions to problems than would otherwise have been found.

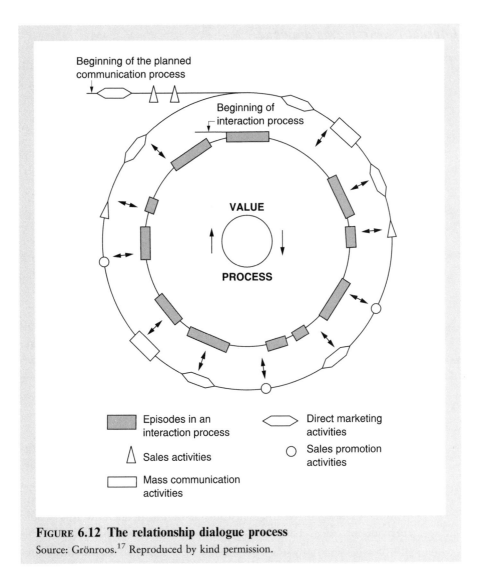

FIGURE 6.12 The relationship dialogue process
Source: Grönroos.[17] Reproduced by kind permission.

Of course, at some point the relationship may be broken or terminated if needs change, if there are better offers elsewhere, or if the customer and supplier's experience of each other falls short of their expectations. The relationship will become stressed if the needs of both customer and supplier are not met. When all goes well, despite occasional defects, the relationship is likely to be maintained, which creates the right environment for continuing dialogue.

Internal marketing as dialogue

We have already discussed some of the prerequisites for, and pitfalls of, successful organisational change. But we think internal marketing can contribute to organisational change too, specifically through creating and circulating knowledge in the firm.

More than twenty years after Berry[18] first advocated treating employees as 'internal customers' there is renewed interest about what internal marketing means.

Berry believed that internal marketing starts by viewing jobs as if they were 'internal products' offered to employees. The logic is that organisations need employees who are satisfied with their jobs (as products) in order to have satisfied customers. The internal marketing task is to improve the job 'products' using marketing thinking to gain new insights and deliver new benefits to employees. Grönroos,[19] writing around the same time, emphasised making staff at all levels more motivated and customer conscious through better two-way communications and by co-ordinating tasks between front-line and support staff. His approach to internal marketing focused on enhancing the work employees did in order to meet the needs of external customers more capably.

Later, Berry and Parasuraman[20] cautioned that a company's performance is adversely affected when its various parts act 'without cohesion or a unified spirit', thus constraining front-line customer contact employees. They emphasised the value of treating staff the way you would want them to treat customers, in the belief that this would provide an ideal climate for changing marketing behaviour. This approach has merit, but it runs the risk of being overgeneralised into a 'happy staff equals happy customers' logic.

These formative concepts have endured, but there is still no general agreement on whether internal marketing should have a singular or multiple intent, nor is there a common conceptual framework. You could argue that Berry's 'internal customer' concept was flawed because it did not emphasise the critical link between internal customers and internal suppliers in creating value for the external market. This cross-functional perspective has, in many ways, been a sub-theme of this book.

There are, arguably, three major perspectives on internal marketing, and their associated knowledge exchanges operate in different ways.

Internal customer approach

This means one-way communication to employees, supported by marketing intelligence. This is the most common form of internal marketing and is suitable for circulating simple policy statements, procedural explanations, new product information and so on. This internal customer approach uses 'top-down' communication to build a climate for changing marketing behaviour. However, all but the simplest of enforced organisational changes run the risk of attracting the suspicion, resistance and hostility of employees and decision-makers alike.

Internal customer and supplier approach

This means two-way communication between internal customers and internal suppliers, supported by market intelligence. This approach requires working with non-marketers to access and re-interpret the rich experience of staff and their 'on-the-job' knowledge and experience. However, internal marketing of this kind may also bring with it some surprises and conflicts of interest. This is because long-cherished assumptions embedded in the policies and procedures being studied may need to be challenged in order to find new and better ways of creating customer value.

Networked approach

This also means two-way communication between internal customers and suppliers, supported by market intelligence. However, this approach taps into the know-how of a broader range of employees. This approach is ongoing, based on collaboration and relationship development through networks of voluntary participants. It is acted out through dialogue and its purpose is to renew organisational knowledge continuously. We believe this approach is needed during economic periods of rapidly changing market requirements, or when internal responses to external market requirements are a tangle of complex of issues.

The future of relationship marketing

As we approach the end of this book, we will pause to reflect on the future of relationship marketing. This ostensibly new discipline has taken off over the past ten years or so with enormous vigour, and yet marketing has always been embedded in relationships. Have relationships been staring us in the face and have we been too preoccupied to see them? Theodore Levitt certainly thought so when he said that the purpose of business is to create and keep a customer. Len Berry thought so too. He said that relationship marketing is not a new but more a 'new-old' idea in the sense that creating value and loyalty in business dealings is as old as merchant trade itself. What is new is the examination of *how* this might be achieved.

Why the growing interest in the relationship marketing concept, and why now? First, in our global deregulated open markets, there are no certain prescriptions for success based on our past experience in relatively stable markets. Supply chain management, the deployment of new technology, service quality management and product development cycles remain, of course, ongoing concerns. But there will always be turbulence and risk in open markets. Second, establishing more open relationships with key customers, suppliers and other stakeholders is a strategy for minimising risk, by staying open to opportunities within more trusting, collaborative relationships. But open market conditions create more complexity *within* organisational boundaries too. Mainstream marketing's toolbox is not up to this internal challenge, and what is needed are new and more diversified internal marketing skills.

Looking to the future, we expect the idea of value exchange as the foundation stone of relationship marketing to be developed further still. There are a number of perspectives on value in this relationship context:

1 Value is created as an offering and delivered through recurrent transactions within a managed relationship.
2 Value is created through mutually interactive processes and shared through negotiated agreement within the life of a relationship.
3 Value is created and shared by interactions that emerge from within networks of relationships.

The first of these is closest to mainstream marketing management, but is a more enlightened form in the sense that it involves both meeting customer requirements and a longer-term management view. The second perspective is based on interaction and seen as a social process with economic outcomes, where value is created and shared collaboratively between the parties involved. The third is a strategic perspective where the firm is seen to be embedded in a network – a 'supra-organisation' that is nonetheless real in the sense that the firm's position within it determines what value emerges. In this perspective the firm creates value jointly with customers and other stakeholders, transcending normal organisational boundaries.

These value perspectives, in order, might be called:

1 Managed value
2 Interactive value
3 Emergent value

Aligned to these three value perspectives are three major knowledge-generating pathways that can be applied within firms. They are:

1 Hierarchical knowledge
2 Cross-functional knowledge
3 Network knowledge

In the first case, expert knowledge is exchanged and legitimised through formal hierarchical channels. In the second, knowledge is generated and exchanged between internal customers and internal suppliers, along the value chain, end to end. In the third case, knowledge is generated by internal networks – that is, spontaneous communities of employees who collaborate in project teams or diagnostic problem-solving groups. No single knowledge-generating pathway can be successful on its own, but if any one pathway is inoperative, it will limit the effectiveness of the value perspective to which it is most closely aligned.

Combining value perspectives with their dominant knowledge-generating pathways, we get the following propositions:

1 Given hierarchical knowledge, value can best be created as an offering and delivered through recurrent transactions within a managed relationship.

2 Given cross-functional knowledge, value can best be created through mutually interactive processes and shared through negotiated agreement within the life of a relationship.

3 Given networked knowledge, value can be created and shared by interactions that emerge from within networks of relationships.

The relationship marketing approach that we advocate in this book emphasises that collaboration is as important as competition, and that keeping valuable customers is as important as getting them in the first place. The first of these tenets requires a managerial shift in perspective from the singularity of the economic transaction to the fuzzier boundaries of socio-economic exchange. The second tenet requires a reframing of marketing time horizons to include not just the immediacy of the transaction but the long-term implications of the relationship.

Much of what we call progress occurs through people changing their views to recognise a new pattern of ideas and to see things differently. Establishing and supporting a cross-functional process or network orientation for knowledge management challenges the control structure or silo mentality, as we have emphasised. In the work we do, we see more companies adopting the interactive and emergent value perspectives, with the role of managed value diminishing.

This value-based approach to relationship marketing recognises the need for planning and organising, but more in the sense of recurrent phases of reflection and action. While organisations will probably continue to need a hierarchical control function, rigid hierarchical control is less effective in getting things done than leadership and the willing commitment of employees to organisational goals that will extend the life time value of the customer. Some academics and practitioners might say this is marketing as it should be, or as it used to be, in which case relationship marketing is getting back to some Arcadian ideal. This seems unlikely – although it really depends upon the starting point you choose to build a historical perspective.

In this book, we have advocated exchanges of mutual value within a 'six markets' network of relationships. Using the 'six markets' framework for strategy-making, an action taken in one domain, say the customer market, can affect the supplier market and probably the internal (employee) market, with perhaps wider environmental impacts that require careful management and planning. This approach is not just a way to think about delivering value but about the value-creating possibilities of working within relationships. The six markets model encourages a *systemic* approach to planning.

But a bigger paradigm shift, in the sense of its implications for the future, is the idea that businesses from one end of a supply chain to the other are embedded in loose-knit stakeholder networks that are so subtle they might be better described as 'value constellations' of related interests.[21] This world-view opens up the possibility that it is networks that compete, not firms. This is not just a shift in language but a shift in ideas about how value is created and an acknowledgment of new organisational forms.

> Increasingly value will be created jointly between a firm and its customers and other stakeholders.

We think that increasingly value will be created jointly between a firm and its customers and other stakeholders, through a cross-functional approach to marketing and management. But there is also a 'view from the edge'.

The view from the edge

Is relationship marketing a new paradigm for marketing? Though the 'paradigm' word is overused, we think the 'paradigm challenge' comes when we recognise the character of the new scientific world-view underpinning recent network thinking. That is, you can view marketing as a systemic, holistic, and, above all, a dynamically complex activity.

Increasingly we are seeing business situations as being constructed of *dynamic* complexity rather than the less challenging *detailed* complexity. The Internet is one of the more striking examples, demonstrating as it does that relationships can be social or technical, or both. So conventional business assumptions no longer apply. Peter Senge,[22] for example, has popularised the idea that conventional forecasting, planning and analytical methods will not be agile enough to capture dynamic complexity, except in the very short term. In other words, business actions and reactions are no longer linear, mono-causal or exactly traceable back to their cause. Indeed, they never really were. Thinking has shifted to consider the whole rather than parts and to recognise new patterns of relationships, especially in a broader contextual framework, in order to begin again to understand the nature of those relationships and the organisational boundaries that they bridge.

This new challenging world-view connects with the new science of complexity in which interaction is characterised as a near chaotic state.[23] Because feedback from each interaction leads to more than one possible response, there will be a variety of consequences and the effects of these are amplified over time. Likewise, the effects of small changes to any plan may also be amplified, and fed back into dialogue, so that the consequences of any action become less certain.

Any one market interaction can affect any other interaction, so any relationship between a firm and the customer – even a single customer – will 'interfere' with other relationships. Surely this is a challenge to traditional marketing, as we know it?

Relationship marketing is both an optimistic agenda for the future and a defence against mental straitjackets and marketing myopia. Whenever boundaries are breached or shifted, marketing relationships help the organisation respond to the new challenge by acting as conduits to generate and circulate value.

SUMMARY AND CONCLUSION

Developing and implementing a relationship marketing strategy around six key market domains is a main theme of this book. The fundamental idea that underpins strategy setting in a six markets context is that marketing can no longer be seen as the responsibility of a single departmental function. Relationship marketing challenges organisations *internally* to support cross-functional change management and *externally* to support a shift to long-term relationships with a broader range of stakeholders, among which the customer is of central but not exclusive importance.

Though customers are central to relationship marketing, the term itself does not necessarily imply that the firm should seek intense interactive relationships with all its customers. Nor, indeed, do customers necessarily need or want that sort of relationship. Companies can foster a number of different relationships with their customers. However, all customers do want the company to meet their needs and to deliver on the promises it makes them. If the organisation is to meet or exceed customers' requirements, it needs to become customer facing.

To be truly customer facing it has to move from 'vertical' to 'horizontal' management structures and deal with the power shift that entails. Dealing with organisational change and associated cultural aspects is critical for successful relationship marketing. A corporate culture that recognises that delivering stakeholder value is the primary purpose of the business underpins any successful relationship market strategy. Performance measurement, culture change and behaviour are all closely intertwined. The success or failure of a relationship marketing strategy will be largely determined by how well companies manage these critical issues.

Ideas are still evolving around the convergence and integration of value concepts and relationship marketing into what we term 'relationship value management'. But this area will become increasingly important. More work needs to be done in the whole area of measurement and developing metrics around the value process. Some measurement systems such as customer satisfaction and service quality already exist, but what is required is a comprehensive integrated set of measures across the whole value process. We believe this to be one of the most important areas for future research.

Relationship marketing has been one of the key developments of modern marketing science and has generated enormous research interest. This emphasis on relationships, as opposed to transaction-based exchanges, is likely to continue to redefine the marketing domain. It should lead to a new general theory of marketing, as its fundamental axioms explain marketing practice better than other theories.[24]

References

1   Grönroos, C. (2000), Relationship Marketing: The Nordic School Perspective' in Sheth, J.N. and Parvatiyar, A. (eds), *Handbook of Relationship Marketing*, Thousand Oaks, CA: Sage, 95–118.

2   Payne, A.F.T. and Holt, S, (2001). 'Diagnosing Customer Value Creation in Relationship Marketing', *British Journal of Management*, **12**, 2, 159–82.

3   Anderson, E. and Oliver, R (1987), 'Perspectives on Behaviour-Based Versus Outcome-Based Salesforce Control Systems', *Journal of Marketing*, **51**, October, 76–88.

4   Heskett, J.L., Jones, T.O., Loveman, G.W., Sasser, E.W. Jr and Schlesinger, L.A. (1994), 'Putting the Service-Profit Chain to Work', *Harvard Business Review*, March-April, 164–74.

5   Reichheld, F. F. (1996), *The Loyalty Effect*, Boston, MA: Harvard Business School Press.

6   Rucci, A. J., Kirn, S.P. and Quinn, R.T. (1998), 'The Employee-Customer-Profit Chain at Sears', *Harvard Business Review*, January–February, 83–97.

7   Cravens, D.W., Piercy, N.F. and Shipp, S.H. (1996), New Organisational Forms for Competing in Highly Dynamic Environments: The Network Paradigm, *British Journal of Management*, 7, 203–18.

8   Treacy, M. and Wiersema, F. (1995), *The Discipline of Market Leaders*, London: HarperCollins.

9   Mintzberg, H. (1994), *The Rise and Fall of Strategic Planning*, Hertfordshire: Prentice Hall.

10 Waterman, R.H., Peters, T.J. and Phillips, J.R. (1980), 'Structure is Not Organisation', *Business Horizons*, June, 14–16.

11 Child, P., Dennis, R.S., Gokey, T.C., McGuire, T., Sherman, M. and Singer, M. (1995), 'Can Marketing Regain the Personal Touch?', *McKinsey Quarterly*, No. 3, 112–125.

12 Quinn J. B. (1989), 'Strategic Change: Logical Incrementalism', *Sloan Management Review*, Summer, 55.

13 Argyris, C. and Schon, D. (1978), *Organizational Learning: A Theory of Action Perspective*, Reading, MA: Addison Wesley.

14 Schein, E. H. (1985), *Organizational Culture and Leadership*, San Francisco: Jossey Bass.

15 Kaplan, R.S. and Norton, D.P. (1993). 'Putting the Balanced Scorecard to Work', *Harvard Business Review*, September–October, 134–47.

16 Schein, E. H. (1994), 'The Process of Dialogue: Creating Effective Communication', *The Systems Thinker*, **5**, 5, 1–4.

17 Grönroos, C. (2000), *Service Management and Marketing: A Customer Relationship Management Approach*, 2nd edn, Chichester: Wiley, p. 280.

18 Berry, L.L. (1981), 'The Employee as Customer', *Journal of Retail Banking*, 3, March, 25–8.

19   Grönroos, C. (1981), Internal Marketing – An Integral Part of Marketing Theory, in Donnelly, J.H. and George, W.R. (eds), *Marketing of Services*. Chicago, IL: American Marketing Association, 236–8.

20   Berry, L. L. and Parasuraman, A. (1991), *Marketing Services: Competing through Quality*, New York: The Free Press, p.152.

21   Value constellations is a term used by Normann, R. and Ramirez, R. (1993). 'From Value Chain to Value Constellation: Designing Interactive Strategy', *Harvard Business Review*, July–August, 65–77.

22   Senge, P. (1990), *The Fifth Discipline*, New York: Doubleday, 71–2.

23   Stacey, R. (1996), *Complexity and Creativity in Organisations*, San Francisco: Berrett-Koehler.

24   See: Sheth J.N., Gardner, D.M. and Garrett, D.E. (1988), *Marketing Theory: Evolution and Evaluation*, New York: John Wiley; and Sheth, J. N. and Parvatiyar, A. (2000), 'The Evolution of Relationship Marketing' In: Sheth, J.N. and Parvatiyar, A. (eds), *Handbook of Relationship Marketing*, Thousand Oaks, CA: Sage, 119–45.

Index

Marketing titles from Butterworth-Heinemann

Student List

Creating Powerful Brands (second edition), Leslie de Chernatony and
  Malcolm McDonald
Direct Marketing in Practice, Brian Thomas and Matthew Housden
eMarketing eXcellence, PR Smith and Dave Chaffey
Fashion Marketing, Margaret Bruce and Tony Hines
Innovation in Marketing, Peter Doyle and Susan Bridgewater
Integrated Marketing Communications, Tony Yeshin
Internal Marketing, Pervaiz Ahmed and Mohammed Rafiq
International Marketing (third edition), Stanley J. Paliwoda and
  Michael J. Thomas
Key Customers, Malcolm McDonald, Beth Rogers and Diana Woodburn
Marketing Briefs, Sally Dibb and Lyndon Simkin
Marketing in Travel and Tourism (third edition), Victor T. C. Middleton with
  Jackie R. Clarke
Marketing Plans (fifth edition), Malcolm McDonald
Marketing: the One Semester Introduction, Geoff Lancaster and
  Paul Reynolds
Market-Led Strategic Change (third edition), Nigel Piercy
The New Marketing, Malcolm McDonald and Hugh Wilson
Relationship Marketing, Martin Christopher, Adrian Payne and
  David Ballantyne
Relationship Marketing for Competitive Advantage, Adrian Payne,
  Martin Christopher, Moira Clark and Helen Peck
Relationship Marketing: Strategy & Implementation, Helen Peck,
  Adrian Payne, Martin Christopher and Moira Clark
Strategic Marketing Management (second edition), Richard M. S. Wilson and
  Colin Gilligan
Strategic Marketing: Planning and Control (second edition),
  Graeme Drummond and John Ensor
Successful Marketing Communications, Cathy Ace
Tales from the Market Place, Nigel Piercy
The CIM Handbook of Export Marketing, Chris Noonan
The Fundamentals of Advertising (second edition), John Wilmshurst and
  Adrian Mackay
Total Relationship Marketing (second edition), Evert Gummesson

Forthcoming

Marketing Logistics (second edition), Martin Christopher and Helen Peck
Marketing Research for Managers (third edition), Sunny Crouch and
  Matthew Housden
Marketing Strategy (third edition), Paul Fifield
Political Marketing, Phil Harris and Dominic Wring

The Fundamentals and Practice of Marketing (fourth edition),
  John Wilmshurst and Adrian Mackay
The Marketing Book (fifth edition), Michael J. Baker (ed.)

Professional list

Cause Related Marketing, Sue Adkins
Creating Value, Shiv S. Mathur and Alfred Kenyon
Cybermarketing (second edition), Pauline Bickerton and Matthew Bickerton
Cyberstrategy, Pauline Bickerton, Matthew Bickerton and
  Kate Simpson-Holley
Direct Marketing in Practice, Brian Thomas and Matthew Housden
e-Business, J. A. Matthewson
Effective Promotional Practice for eBusiness, Cathy Ace
Excellence in Advertising (second edition), Leslie Butterfield
Fashion Marketing, Margaret Bruce and Tony Hines
Financial Services and the Multimedia Revolution, Paul Lucas,
  Rachel Kinniburgh and Donna Terp
From Brand Vision to Brand Evaluation, Leslie de Chernatony
Go-to-Market Strategy, Lawrence Friedman
Internal Marketing, Pervaiz Ahmed and Mohammed Rafiq
Marketing Made Simple, Geoff Lancaster and Paul Reynolds
Marketing Professional Services, Michael Roe
Marketing Strategy (second edition), Paul Fifield
Market-Led Strategic Change (third edition), Nigel Piercy
The New Marketing, Malcolm McDonald and Hugh Wilson
The Channel Advantage, Lawrence Friedman and Tim Furey
The CIM Handbook of Export Marketing, Chris Noonan
The Committed Enterprise, Hugh Davidson
The Fundamentals of Corporate Communications, Richard Dolphin
The Marketing Plan in Colour, Malcolm McDonald and Peter Morris

Forthcoming

Essential Law for Marketers, Ardi Kolah
Marketing Logistics (second edition), Martin Christopher and Helen Peck
Marketing Research for Managers (third edition), Sunny Crouch and
  Matthew Housden
Marketing Strategy (third edition), Paul Fifield
Political Marketing, Phil Harris and Dominic Wring

For more information on all these titles, as well as the ability to buy
online, please visit **www.bh.com/marketing**